READING DIAGNOSIS
for
TEACHERS

Rebecca Barr

University of Chicago
and
National College of Education

Marilyn Sadow

Chicago State University

Longman

New York & London

To Bob and Leo

372.4076
B27r
146315
apr. 1989

Reading Diagnosis for Teachers

Longman Inc., 95 Church Street, White Plains, N.Y. 10601
Associated companies, branches, and representatives
throughout the world.

Developmental Editor: Lane Akers
Editorial Supervisor: Carolyn Golojuch
Interior Designer: Nina Tallarico
Production Supervisor: Karen Lumley
Composition: Progressive Typographers
Printing and Binding: Alpine Press

Library of Congress Cataloging in Publication Data

Barr, Rebecca.
  Reading diagnosis for teachers.

  Bibliography: p.
  Includes indexes.
  1. Reading — Ability testing.   I. Sadow, Marilyn W.,
1925–   .   II. Title.
LB1050.46.B37 1985   372.4'076   84-17193
ISBN 0-582-28527-5

Manufactured in the United States of America
Printing: 9 8 7 6 5 4 3 2 1   Year: 93 92 91 90 89 88 87 86 85

Contents

Preface v

Acknowledgments xi

1   Model for Reading Diagnosis   1

2   The Development of Print Translation Strategies   13

3   Diagnosing Print Translation Strategies   41

4   Vocabulary Knowledge   69

5   Comprehension: Its Nature and Assessment 111

6   Reading Comprehension: Diagnosis and Instruction 143

7   Diagnosis Based on an Instructional Passage 175

8   Diagnosis with a Series of Passages 199

9   Diagnosis with Standardized IRIs 219

Appendix A   Dolch Basic Sight Vocabulary 243

Appendix B   Blachowicz Informal Phonics Survey 245

Appendix C   Complete Records of Performance on
              an IRI: James 249

References 273

Index 285

Preface

In almost every classroom, one or several students find their schoolwork difficult because of reading problems. And teachers spend much of their reflective time considering how these students may be helped. Typically, two types of solution are attempted. Some teachers try to incorporate disabled readers into the ongoing program of their class by adjusting their instructional support in such a way that reading assignments can be understood by the poorer readers. For example, discussion of important concepts contained in a passage and guidance in decoding difficult words may decrease the problems typically encountered. Alternatively, and sometimes concurrently, special work that more directly meets the needs of disabled readers may be provided by either the classroom teacher or a special reading teacher in or outside the school.

The degree to which teachers are successful in solving reading problems depends on three types of expertise: knowledge about reading problems and their correction, ability to assess class conditions, and familiarity with resources in the school and the neighborhood that can provide supplemental reading support. Knowledge about reading diagnosis and correction supplies the framework for determining whether, in fact, a student suffers from a reading problem, the nature of his or her problem, and what may be done about it. Optimal courses of action can be determined on the basis of knowledge about a student's reading difficulty, but the course actually followed will depend on the resources available to teachers. Teachers face the dual responsibility of meeting the needs of a collection of students and managing the instruction of individuals; if a particular individual requires an inordinate amount of attention, the learning of the class as a whole will suffer. Therefore, courses of action chosen to help students with reading problems involve bending optimal solutions to fit the realities of teacher responsibilities and to take into account alternative possibilities for individual help. The provision of individual instruction outside the class, however, does not relieve the teacher of the need to devise ways of incorporating disabled readers into class activities. Accordingly, we take the position that as teachers are frequently responsible for students with reading problems, they must know about reading diagnosis and correction. They must be able to judge when students need special reading help that they are unable to provide given their other responsibilities, and they must know how to adjust their ongoing instruction to help students cope with assigned readings.

BASIC CONSIDERATIONS

Several major influences have shaped our thinking about what should be included in a text dealing with the development of diagnostic knowledge and skill. First, we have been guided by our belief that skill can only be acquired through guided practice. Thus, we have provided training procedures for the development of basic observational skills and a sequence of tasks of increasing complexity that involve practice of previously acquired skills.

Second, we believe that an understanding of reading disability and its diagnosis can be achieved only through consideration of a variety of cases exemplifying different sorts of problems. Accordingly, most chapters in the book include several cases, which are the focus of study and instructional planning. In total, the book presents nearly twenty cases — a useful basis from which to derive some understanding of the various forms of reading disability.

Third, we believe that diagnosis for classroom teachers and reading specialists working in school settings should differ in several important respects from the diagnostic procedures developed for reading clinics. Classroom conditions make it difficult for a reading specialist or teacher to undertake certain diagnostic procedures. For example, both extensive work with individual students and the use of testlike tasks are often impractical. Perhaps more important, useful alternative procedures are available. We emphasize the basic differences between the conditions or constraints under which reading clinicians and classroom teachers work because we believe these differences have profound implications for *how* the procedures of reading diagnosis, which were developed originally in the clinical setting, should be modified for use in the classroom.

A clinician typically sees a student for a limited period of time for the specific purpose of evaluating his or her reading skill and identifying appropriate instruction. The evaluation is based on a variety of standardized and informal tests of aptitude and achievement. In order to judge whether a reading problem exists, the clinician compares the reading achievement of the student with his or her expected level of achievement, the latter based (usually) on measures of verbal and nonverbal ability, with years of schooling and/or age sometimes taken into account. The clinician then identifies specific areas of reading difficulty by analyzing the student's performance on standardized and informal measures of reading and language skills. Instructional recommendations are generally based on the clinician's tutorial experience with students experiencing similar reading difficulties.

However, it is difficult for a teacher to incorporate these procedures into his or her repertoire of skills. One reason is that formal testing represents a departure from the typical instructional activities and is difficult to undertake on an individual basis along with the responsibilities of managing a class. But more to the point, whereas standardized tests are essential for the clinician because they provide a normative frame of reference, they are much less important for the classroom teacher who has the performances of other children in the class available as a normative standard.

Further, standardized tests are unnecessary because teachers have access to a wealth of evidence about the reading and language development of their students on a daily basis. They listen to children read orally, note their answers to comprehension questions, and observe how they think and talk about a variety of topics. Nevertheless, teachers' observations tend to be haphazard, partly because they are constantly faced with the job of managing the class as well as instructing students — but partly because they have had little training in how to observe and interpret students' responses. Most teachers have not been taught to design informal "probe" questions or oral reading tasks in order to clarify the nature of a student's misunderstanding. Typically, teachers are trained to diagnose reading difficulties by interpreting scores and reading behaviors on standardized and informal reading tests. They must then generalize from the results of these tests back to the student's performance on classroom materials. We believe that a more sensible approach is to help teachers acquire the observational and interpretive skills that will enable them to use the wealth of evidence that is available on an ongoing basis in the classroom.

Teachers usually see their students over an entire school year. By contrast, a clinician usually sees a student for a limited number of diagnostic sessions. Accordingly, the clinician is under considerable time pressure to make an accurate diagnosis and does so by the administration of multiple tests. Because teachers work with students for an extended period, "working hypotheses" rather than diagnostic conclusions would seem to be a better goal for classroom diagnosis. That is, teachers have the opportunity to revise and modify their understanding of their students' reading skills on the basis of successive observations interlaced with instructional intervention. This time advantage needs to be capitalized on in developing an effective diagnostic strategy.

Teachers possess information about their students' current instructional program and response to it, and they are in a position to evaluate their physical and social well-being. Thus teachers can set goals and expectations that are consistent with the classroom program. The aim of the teacher is to help students who encounter some reading difficulty to acquire the skills necessary to reenter the mainstream of class instruction. By contrast, in the clinical setting, the student's verbal and sometimes nonverbal abilities constitute the main basis for establishing an expected level of reading. As a result, some very able and relatively good readers are identified as disabled readers simply because there is a discrepancy between their reading and their (high) verbal development. Similarly, students with low verbal ability and commensurately low reading skill may be viewed as having no reading problem even though they are unable to cope with the reading materials used by the class.

We recommend that the expected reading level of students — and whether or not they are considered to have reading problems — be established in terms of the levels of materials used by the class or by a subgroup thereof. We believe that this recommendation reflects the reality of instructional alternatives in classrooms and the objectives teachers are expected to help their classes achieve. We are not arguing that it is wrong to use aptitude or verbal ability as a standard against which to evaluate reading achievement but, rather, that such measurements are simply less useful in the classroom setting than in the clinic.

In sum, given the differences between clinical and classroom settings, we believe that classroom diagnosis and instructional planning should be based on students' performance with classroom instructional materials, that the existence of a reading problem should be determined on the basis of a discrepancy between a student's reading level and that needed in order for him or her to learn from class materials; that both diagnosis and instruction should be modified on an ongoing basis; and that instructional plans should be formed with the conditions of the classroom and school in mind.

GOALS

The goal of the book is to help reading and classroom teachers acquire the knowledge and skill that is necessary for reading diagnosis and instructional planning. What must be learned falls into three main categories. First, teachers must acquire a systematic framework for diagnosis — one that identifies the major decisions that have to be made as well as the evidence that is needed in order to make them. Second, teachers must develop observational skills in the areas of listening to children read and answer questions. Finally, they must learn how to translate diagnostic findings into a plan for instructional support that is realistic in view of both the student's needs and the school's resources.

ORGANIZATION AND CONTENT

The book is organized into three main sections. The first part, Chapter 1, presents a framework or model for diagnosis, and this model is used as the organizing perspective in subsequent chapters. The model focuses on three components of reading: print translation, word meaning, and reading comprehension.

In the second part, each of these components is fully elaborated. Chapters 2 and 3 develop a theoretical perspective on the acquisition of print translation skills. They describe how oral reading responses and reading rate may be used as evidence of proficiency in these skills and provide training in listening to and interpreting oral reading evidence. Also provided are instructional strategies for helping students refine their skill in recognizing and identifying words. Chapter 4 discusses knowledge of word meaning and its role in comprehension, and then shows how this knowledge may be assessed and the results interpreted. Chapters 5 and 6 provide an overview of the nature of comprehension, introduce procedures for developing comprehension questions that pertain to the text as a whole, and describe the interpretation of comprehension performance as well as useful instructional procedures for enhancing comprehension.

In the third section of the book, knowledge and skills acquired in the preceding chapters are combined in comprehensive diagnosis of different types of reading disability. Although necessarily systematic and compressed, the case study presentations are intended to develop diagnostic, observational, and interpretive skills that the teacher can then use in a more flexible fashion during classroom or tutorial instruction. Chapter 7 presents cases in which the diagnostic material consists of a single textbook selection. Chapter 8 demonstrates how the acquired skills can be used with a series of graded passages to obtain greater understanding of students' difficulties. And finally, Chapter 9 shows how diagnostic strategies can be used with standardized informal reading inventories to delineate in comprehensive fashion the reading problems that students encounter.

COMPARISON WITH OTHER
READING DIAGNOSTIC TEXTS

Several characteristics distinguish this book from other books on reading diagnosis. As mentioned, this book presents and discusses many case studies of students with reading problems. Each case study is presented so as to require active teacher participation in some aspect of observation, analysis, and interpretation. Because reading diagnosis is a complex process, we have broken it into component skills for ease of study and practice; at the same time, we have retained the integrity of each case. As a result, teachers become aware of how component processes fit within the whole. In the final chapters, teachers must deal with all phases of the diagnostic process.

Each time a case is considered, the diagnostic model developed in the first chaper is used as an organizing framework. Our interest is not only in the development of observational and analytic skills, but in enabling teachers to make comparisons across areas of a student's reading and language functioning in order to identify strengths and weaknesses and on this basis set instructional priorities. Too often teachers learn to interpret results from single standardized or criterion-referenced tests without obtaining a comprehensive view. Because this text repeatedly looks at cases within the framework of the diagnostic model, it facilitates the development of comprehensive diagnostic thinking.

Our case presentations reflect our belief that diagnosis must lead directly to instructional planning. An elaborate diagnosis is unnecessary if few instructional alternatives exist; the purpose of diagnosis is to provide the basis for deciding among instructional alternatives. Accordingly, case presentations include discussion of how reading evidence is transformed into an instructional plan.

These strengths of a systematic training program have resulted in the omission of many topics that are often developed in traditional texts on reading diagnosis. For example, this book contains no systematic treatment of intelligence testing or perceptual testing, only limited discussion of the nature of standardized tests, and no discussion of school-based remedial reading programs. The omission of these topics stems from the decision to cover a limited number of topics in considerable depth. Moreover, these topics are already amply covered in existing textbooks on reading diagnosis.

Like all projects that involve the development of ideas over an extended period of time, this one has depended on the support and critical insight of many people. We owe a great debt to a number of graduate students in the Department of Education at the University of Chicago, the Graduate School at National College of Education, and the Reading Department at Chicago State University. These students contributed the case studies that we have modified for inclusion in the text, provided important insights into the diagnostic process, and helped us evaluate the manuscript in its many stages. Some students went beyond the requirements of the courses we taught in order to provide us with additional case materials and help us refine the text; we are especially indebted to Katherine Morsbach, Nancy Lamia, Bobbie Johnson, Carol Cain, and Alice Heiman.

Our efforts were encouraged by our colleagues at National College of Education and Chicago State University. In particular, Camille Blachowicz and Darrell Morris provided instructive comments on earlier drafts; and Genevieve Lopardo and Donna Ogle created a climate of intellectual and practical support that facilitated the completion of the manuscript. In addition, we benefited from the clinical experiences and insights that Judith Daskal shared with us, as well as from the many comments and suggestions of James Cunningham, Linda Gambrell, Catherine Hatcher, and Peter Johnston. We also thank Therese Chappell, who typed both an earlier and the final draft of the entire manuscript.

Finally, we owe a special debt of gratitude to Helen Robinson. Our thinking about diagnosis and instructional planning builds directly on the knowledge about reading problems and their correction that she imparted.

Acknowledgments

The authors and publisher gratefully acknowledge the following sources in Appendix C.

Pages 15–16: From "Beginning Readers' Concept of Word" by D. Morris. In E. H. Henderson and J. W. Beers, *Developmental and Cognitive Aspects of Learning to Spell: A Reflection of Word Knowledge*, 1980, pp. 99–100. Reprinted with permission of International Reading Association and D. Morris.

Page 165: From "An Inferential Comprehension Strategy for Use with Primary Grade Children" by J. Hansen. In *Reading Teacher 34*, 667 (1981). Reprinted with permission of International Reading Association and J. Hansen.

Page 251: Adapted from *Black Pioneers of Science and Invention* by Louis Haber, copyright © 1970 by Harcourt Brace Jovanovich, Inc. Reprinted by permission of the publisher.

Page 254: From *The Outsiders* by S. E. Hinton. Copyright © 1967 by S. E. Hinton. Reprinted by permission of Viking Penguin Inc.

Page 256: Adapted from "East Anglican and Essex Witches" by E. Maple. In Richard Cavendish, ed., *Man, Myth, and Magic: An Illustrated Encyclopedia of the Supernatural* (Vol. 6), pp. 753–758. New York: Marshall Cavendish Corp., 1970. Copyright Marshall Cavendish Ltd., London. Reprinted by permission of British Printing and Communications Corp., London.

Page 258: Adapted from "How One Town Solves Pollution and Saves Water" by J. Gentry and "Who's That Polluting My World?" by L. Gott. In *The Plain Truth, A Magazine of Understanding*, Jan. 1973.

Page 261: From *Dave's Song* by Robert McKay, 1969. Reprinted by permission of E. P. Dutton. All rights reserved.

Page 263: Adapted from *Black Pioneers of Science and Invention* by Louis Haber, copyright © 1970 by Harcourt Brace Jovanovich, Inc. Reprinted by permission of the publisher.

Page 265: Adapted from "Robyn Smith" in *The Lincoln Library of Sports Champions* (Vol. 12), 1974, pp. 32–35. Columbus, Ohio: Sports Resources Co. Reprinted by permission of The Frontier Press Co.

Page 267: Adapted from "Vampires" by D. Hill. In Richard Cavendish, ed., *Man, Myth, and Magic: An Illustrated Encyclopedia of the Supernatural* (Vol. 21), pp. 2922–2928. New York: Marshall Cavendish Corp., 1970. Copyright Marshall Cavendish Ltd., London. Reprinted by permission of British Printing and Communications Corp., London.

Page 269: Adapted from "To Save A People" by H. L. Hoeh. In *The Plain Truth, A Magazine of Understanding*, Jan. 1975.

Model for Reading Diagnosis

HISTORICAL PERSPECTIVE

Much of what we know about reading disability and its diagnosis comes from clinical studies of the 1920s and 1930s. Although earlier studies by physicians had described certain extreme cases (Fisher, 1905; Jackson, 1906; Morgan, 1896; Thomas, 1905), two developments in the field of education converged to support the scientific study of reading disability: *(a)* investigations into the psychological processes of reading (Dearborn, 1906; Dodge, 1905, 1907; Huey, 1898, 1900, 1908; Quantz, 1897) and *(b)* advancements in psychometric theory, which laid the foundation for the development of instruments to measure human traits.

Considerable testing of school populations had occurred between 1910 and 1915. In 1916, Uhl published a report describing the use of test results to diagnose the reading needs of individuals (see also Zirbes, 1918). It may surprise some readers to find that the earliest diagnostic work was conducted in the school setting by teachers and other school personnel. The first professional book on reading diagnosis, *Deficiencies in Reading Ability: Their Diagnosis and Remedies,* written by Clarence T. Gray in 1922, relied in large part on what had been learned from school-based studies of reading difficulty.

Concurrently, it became apparent to educators that more detailed study of students experiencing difficulty with reading would provide insight into reading processes and how they become disrupted. Further, detailed case studies would promote the design of appropriate testing procedures and the development of effective remedial instruction. Special educational laboratories and reading clinics were established, mainly in university settings (Clowes, 1930; Dougherty, 1929; Fernald & Keller, 1926; Monroe, 1928, 1932). In order to appreciate the knowledge acquired during this early period, the reader should examine the classic study conducted by William S. Gray and his associates at the University of Chicago Educational Laboratory (Gray *et al.*, 1922). The purpose of the investigation was threefold: to diagnose the nature and causes of reading difficulty, to classify types of poor readers, and to test experimentally the efficacy of remedies.

Other research in the 1920s and 1930s served to expand and develop the knowledge gained through clinical case studies. Pelosi (1977) notes several developments during this period that contributed to the refinement of reading diagnosis. First, case study investigation, which continued to be the dominant method of research, became more elaborate and sophisticated (see, e.g., Baer, 1926; Gates, 1927; Hincks, 1926; Monroe, 1928, 1932). Second, precise diagnostic instruments and procedures were developed (see, e.g., Betts, 1934; Dolch, 1936; Durrell, 1936; Ford, 1928; Gates, 1926, 1935; Monroe, 1932). Finally, there was an ever-increasing interest in the nature of reading processes and the causes of reading disability (see, e.g., Bond, 1935; Dearborn, 1933; Jastak, 1934; Orton, 1928; Robinson, 1937, 1946; Tinker, 1934).

VIEW OF READING DIAGNOSIS

The conception of diagnosis developed in this book builds on this basic knowledge. In addition, it incorporates recently developed understanding of the nature of word recognition and comprehension and the role of background knowledge in the reading process. As discussed in the Preface, we have treated this knowledge in such a way that it might best serve the purposes of teachers working in a school setting.

Our view of reading diagnosis and instructional planning assumes that students are active problem solvers. Therefore, the manner in which they develop reading skill is influenced by the instructional tasks they confront from grade to grade. For example, if students are instructed with a systematic phonics program, they learn to solve a somewhat different set of problems than if they are instructed with an eclectic program that emphasizes comprehension and a core vocabulary of reading words. Similarly, if students are given considerable experience reading and answering questions on expository materials, they develop different comprehension skills than if they read mainly narrative materials.

Two implications follow from this view. First, diagnosis must consider how students currently approach the task of reading in relation to the reading tasks they have encountered in the past. Second, subsequent instruction must build on this foundation. Thus, diagnosis by a teacher who is familiar with the instructional history of students and who tests their response to current instructional materials provides an optimal basis for instructional planning.

What must a teacher know in order to diagnose the nature of a student's reading difficulty? A diagnostician is much more than someone who knows how to administer tests. The diagnostician is like an active explorer whose search is guided by a carefully developed conceptual scheme. This scheme identifies the major decision points in the diagnostic process, and then, once a particular decision is made, certain subsidiary decision points. Through this sequential decision-making procedure, plausible explanations for the difficulty are progressively evaluated.

Major Diagnostic Decisions

The first decision to be made is that of whether a student is experiencing problems in reading. We believe that a student's expected reading level — and whether or not a reading problem exists — should be established in terms of the level of materials used by the class or a subgroup thereof. If a student is able to read and comprehend classroom material, then, within our scheme, we conclude that no reading problem exists. The student can be assigned the appropriate materials and given suitable instruction during the daily reading lesson. However, when there is evidence that a student cannot adequately understand the materials used for regular class instruction, a reading problem is considered to exist and further diagnosis is warranted.

When there is evidence of a reading problem, the second decision point involves identification of the general nature of the problem. The goal of reading is the comprehension of text. Deficiencies in two general areas may interfere with comprehension: *(a)* inadequately developed print translation skills, and *(b)* inadequate word knowledge pertaining to the phenomena described in a passage. In addition, inadequately developed strategies for understanding text may account for poor comprehension (see Figure 1.1).

Print translation skills refer to the ability of readers to efficiently translate printed symbols into spoken language or meaning. This area includes not only such skills as phonics, structural analysis, and syllabication, which permit a student to *identify* previously unknown words, but also the acquisition of a set of words that are *recognized* instantaneously. It includes the proficient integration of word recognition and word identification with contextual information as a student responds to prose.

Most children acquire basic print translation skills in the course of their early reading instruction, and these skills become integrated and automatic through elementary school reading experiences. It should be noted that the emphasis of early instruction can have a profound influence on the particular print skills that students learn. Further, students who have difficulty acquiring print skills that are taught explicitly also have difficulty inferring those skills that are not explicitly taught. For example,

Figure 1.1.   Basic model of reading diagnosis.

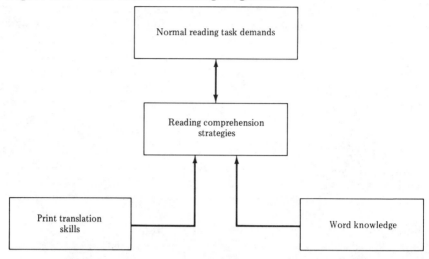

some reading programs emphasize the development of phonic concepts but do not teach the process of blending and the application of phonic knowledge in context. For those students who do not spontaneously infer how to blend phonic values, good knowledge of phonics may be of little value in identifying unknown words. Print translation skills are more fully described in the next two chapters.

Word knowledge refers to knowledge not only of the key words contained in particular reading selections but also of the encompassing concepts that are being conveyed. For example, to understand a passage about the discoveries of Copernicus and Galileo, students must be familiar with the meanings of such words as *planet* and *telescope,* but beyond these, the encompassing concept of "movement" is central to an understanding of how the solar system works. Students differ in the extent to which they can comprehend a passage despite inadequate knowledge of the concepts presumed to be known. Word knowledge is more fully considered in Chapter 4.

In addition to experiencing problems in print skills and/or word knowledge, students may experience problems in their *comprehension strategies.* That is, a student may have no difficulty with print translation and may be familiar with the meanings of the words and concepts that are central to understanding a passage but may still fail to comprehend. This failure stems from difficulty with the integration of knowledge derived from both within and between sentences. Whereas a writer begins with a conception of the important message to be conveyed in a passage and then confronts the problem of how the message may be parceled into words, sentences, and paragraphs, the reader must reconstruct the message of the author by processing these units and recombining them into one or several arguments or descriptions. Some readers experience difficulty that is unique to this integration process. For example, readers often encounter pronouns, nouns, or phrases that refer back to a previously identified person or topic, and they must realize that a new topic is not being introduced, but, rather, that more information is being provided about the same topic or person. Comprehension strategies are considered in Chapters 5 and 6.

The second step in the diagnosis is, then, to determine whether a student is experiencing difficulty with print skills, word knowledge, and/or comprehension strategies. While these three areas are part of an integrated process, it is useful to consider them separately for several reasons. To begin with, each requires different sorts of information and assessment procedures to determine its status. Print translation skills are typically assessed by having students read passages, words, or word parts aloud, whereas discourse processing is typically assessed by having the reader "retell" the passage content or respond to comprehension questions based on a selection that has been read. Word knowledge assessment does not necessarily involve reading; rather, it uses questions to elicit a student's understanding of selected terms. The three areas are also different in terms of the sorts of instructional procedures that enhance their development. For example, the instruction that is useful for helping a student to develop word identification strategies is quite different from that which is effective in facilitating discourse comprehension.

The model for diagnosis shown in Figure 1.1 assumes not only that these three areas can be considered separately, but also that two of them, print translation and word knowledge, represent conditions that are necessary before the third, comprehension strategies, may be effectively employed. Accordingly, if a student fails to comprehend a passage, it is important to examine the student's print translation strategies and word knowledge in order to determine whether problems exist. When problems in either of these areas exist, they could account for the observed difficulty in comprehension. Thus, it is difficult in such cases to ascertain whether the student is experiencing problems in comprehension over and above those that stem from deficiencies in print skills or word knowledge. Comprehension strategies constitute a residual category within the model: problems are assumed to occur in this area when comprehension is weak *and* both word concepts and print translation skills are adequately developed.

In order to begin thinking in terms of the diagnostic scheme, let us consider the strengths and difficulties of four students who have encountered problems reading classroom materials. The reader is encouraged to consider the evidence and determine each student's relative strength in the areas specified by the diagnostic model. On this basis, it should be possible to specify the area(s) in need of further diagnosis.

CASE 1

John is 11 years and 2 months old and is in the sixth grade. His teacher has found that he has considerable difficulty understanding not only his social studies and science textbooks, but also the stories in the fifth-grade-level reading book used by her slowest-paced group. His oral reading, however, is flawless and he even reads the social studies and science passages with considerable fluency. His teacher first noticed that he has extremely vague concepts pertaining to biological terms and then pursued his understanding of more common terms. She found that he knew only superficially or not at all words from his reading book such as *revenge, comrade, foundation,* and *craftsmen.*

The reader should pause for a moment to consider John's case. In terms of the diagnostic scheme, which are the areas of this boy's strength and difficulty?

Diagnosis. The oral reading evidence indicates strength in the area of print translation. John's inability to answer the questions posed by his teacher is therefore attributable to either inadequate word knowledge or poor comprehension strategies. The possibility that word knowledge is an area of difficulty is suggested by his lack of knowledge about terms known by his classmates. Thus, we tentatively conclude that word knowledge is John's major problem area. It is possible that comprehension difficulties also exist, but this remains to be determined by having him read a passage for which his word knowledge is sufficiently well developed. Word knowledge, then, should be the first area of focus.

CASE 2

Mary is 7½ years old and in the second grade. She is currently in the middle reading group, which uses second-grade-level materials. When she reads aloud during reading instruction, she does so fluently, making few errors. However, many of her answers to postreading questions show that she has not understood major events within the story. Questions about important terms within the story reveal that she has a good command of English and is more knowledgeable than other students in the group.

The reader should consider the following questions. Does Mary have any problems in reading and, if so, in what area(s)? What evidence supports these conclusions?

Diagnosis. Obviously, Mary's reading difficulty is not associated with inadequately developed print skills or word knowledge. Her inability to comprehend what she reads may therefore derive from discourse-level inadequacies. Accordingly, comprehension strategies merit further exploration.

CASE 3

Larry is 10 years old and in fourth grade. He is in the slowest-paced group in the class, which reads from third-grade materials. Larry's teacher had almost immediately noted his difficulty in reading aloud. Although Larry had developed familiarity with some common words, he would wait for the teacher to assist him on many other words, particularly those that were multisyllabic. His comprehension of stories that he read silently was extremely low; however, he comprehended well when others in his group read aloud. He also demonstrated good understanding of key words in the reading selections; indeed, he was one of the most knowledgeable class members when it came to science and social studies.

Again, it is important to consider the nature of Larry's reading. The reader should derive a tentative diagnosis of his reading strengths and difficulties.

Diagnosis. Larry experiences difficulty in the area of print translation but also in comprehension of materials that he has read. He is strong in word knowledge. Therefore, we conclude that his comprehension difficulty reflects his poorly developed print skills. There is evidence to support this conclusion, namely, his good comprehension when he listens to others read. Once he acquires skill in print translation, he should become a proficient reader, given his well-developed word knowledge. The task at hand is further diagnosis of his print translation skills in order to learn how to facilitate his development in this area.

CASE 4

Tom is 7 years and 9 months old and in the third grade. In second grade he was with the middle reading group, and his third-grade teacher has continued that placement. His answers to comprehension questions indicate excellent understanding of what he reads, whether silently or aloud. Further, informal questioning about key vocabulary words indicates a breadth of word knowledge and fluency of expression. However, his oral reading is characterized by frequent substitutions of words. He seems to have developed extremely careless reading procedures.

Again, the reader should consider how we might make sense of these reading characteristics. Does Tom have a reading problem and, if so, what is its nature?

Diagnosis. It is clear that Tom's strengths are his good word knowledge and his adequate comprehension. Nevertheless, his print translation skills appear to be inadequately developed and should be explored further. Note that in terms of the model, Tom's pattern of reading strengths and weaknesses is one that is unlikely to occur. The model suggests that adequately developed print skills are a prerequisite for adequate comprehension, and typically this is true. Exceptions occur, however, among students with extremely well-developed word knowledge. Such students, on the basis of this knowledge and minimal information from print, are able to make sense of a story or passage. While we may conclude that Tom has no reading problem at the present time, his print translation skills will become inadequate to the demands of reading as the materials become more technical and precise in their informational content. Therefore, it is appropriate to treat Tom as having a reading problem in the area of print translation and to diagnose further the nature of his difficulty.

Diagnostic Patterns

These cases show how the diagnostic model may be used to determine whether a reading problem exists and to identify the areas in need of further diagnostic exploration. In a more systematic fashion, Table 1.1 shows the number of different patterns of reading skill that are possible when comprehension, print translation, and word knowledge are considered. For example, John, the first case we considered, with poor comprehension and word knowledge but good print skills, conforms to Pattern 3. The second case, Mary, with adequate print skills and word knowledge but inadequate comprehension, conforms to Pattern 2. The third case, Larry, represents Pattern 5, with his poor print skills and comprehension but good word knowledge. Finally, Tom conforms to the relatively uncommon Pattern 6, with good comprehension and good word knowledge but inadequate print skills.

In Pattern 1, reading comprehension and underlying skills in print translation and word knowledge are all sufficient for the student to cope with the reading tasks normally given him or her. Because there appears to be no reading difficulty, further diagnosis is unnecessary.

Pattern 2 consists of adequate print translation and word knowledge but inadequate reading comprehension: clearly, the potential for adequate comprehension is strong, but the student has not yet acquired some skills or organizing concepts for processing text. Further diagnosis in the area of comprehension is needed to determine the nature of the problem.

Pattern 3 is that of the student often identified as a "word caller"—the student who possesses adequate print translation skill but inadequate word knowledge and reading comprehension. Where we see this pattern we assume that limited vocabulary and concepts interfere with reading com-

Table 1.1. Diagnostic Patterns of Print Translation, Word Knowledge, and Reading Comprehension Proficiency

Skill area	Common patterns					Uncommon patterns		
	1	2	3	4	5	6	7	8
Reading comprehension	+	0	0	0	0	+	+	+
Print translation	+	+	+	0	0	0	+	0
Word knowledge	+	+	0	0	+	+	0	0
Further diagnostic exploration[a]	Discontinue diagnosis	Explore discourse-processing skills	Explore word knowledge		Explore print translation skills			

[a] In Patterns 3, 4, and 5, discourse-processing skills might also be an area of weakness. However, this area is directly explored only when word knowledge and print translation have been eliminated as major factors in reading difficulty.

prehension: the student's limited experiences set a ceiling on what he or she can comprehend through print. Further exploration of the student's language functioning is appropriate. For example, a student may have experienced certain situations or events but failed to acquire the pertinent verbal labels. The instruction recommended for this student would be very different from that recommended for a student who also lacked the experiential base.

In Pattern 4, reading comprehension and both sets of underlying skills are inadequately developed. Further exploration of the student's verbal knowledge and print translation skill is appropriate.

Pattern 5 characterizes the student who has difficulty in translating print into familiar language. Here we assume that poor print translation accounts for poor reading comprehension. The student has the strength of good language development, as indicated by strong word knowledge. Further diagnosis should focus on how the student identifies and recognizes words.

Because reading comprehension typically depends on the development of print translation skill and word knowledge, the remaining three patterns, in which comprehension is good while print translation and/or word knowledge are poor, occur infrequently. Pattern 8, in fact, probably does not occur; or, if observed, it probably reflects invalid measurement in one of the three areas. Pattern 6, as we have seen, occurs mainly for extremely able students with well-developed verbal skills. These students are able to compensate for rather poorly developed print translation skills by using a combination of contextual cues, minimal print cues, and past experience; as a result, they score at an adequate level in reading comprehension. For this pattern, further examination of print translation skills is recommended. Although the student will often tolerate the frustration of the reading task when working with the teacher on an individual basis, he or she may avoid reading tasks when left to work alone. And although it may be possible to compensate for skill deficiencies at this stage, these may later interfere with comprehension of more difficult reading material.

Finally, Pattern 7 rarely occurs. If it is observed, it probably reflects a kind of "production deficiency." That is, a student, although able to summarize a passage or respond to questions based on it, may have difficulty generating definitions of terms or demonstrating their use.

The purpose of the first stage of the diagnosis is to examine each of the three aspects of reading and to determine its relative status. This procedure insures that major problem areas will not be overlooked and that areas for more intensive exploration are identified.

Developmental Flexibility of the Model

The diagnostic model is applicable to all levels of skill, from initial reading acquisition to mature reading proficiency. That is, the model is useful in understanding the strengths and difficulties of a beginning reader as well as of a college student. The flexibility of this diagnostic approach follows from conceptualizing reading as having the three component areas. Each area can be seen as having a different pattern of development, in accordance with the different problems posed by the reading materials that students are expected to understand at successive levels. (See Chall, 1983, for a more comprehensive but somewhat different treatment of developmental stages in reading.) These changing demands of reading materials, considered here briefly, are treated more comprehensively in subsequent chapters.

The first two years of reading instruction usually emphasize the development of skills for translating print to speech or meaning. Some reading programs focus on the development of phonic concepts, others on the development of a sight vocabulary. Most current programs work on both types of skills, through a skills sequence and extensive reading of contextual materials. These contextual materials are generally narrative in form, with the characters (people or animals) performing acts and speaking thoughts that are familiar to young children. Accordingly, most children already possess the relevant word knowledge and have acquired the necessary comprehension strategies through listening to stories read to them. However, when this is not the case, these aspects of reading must become areas of instructional focus along with print translation.

Students refine and integrate their print skills during subsequent years in several ways. They become able to tackle longer and more complex words, some of which they have never heard before. They become so familiar with the characteristics of print that processing becomes almost automatic for "easy" materials. As a consequence, reading rate improves dramatically.

As print skills are becoming refined, however, new problems arise. Beginning with third grade, typically, students encounter new forms of printed materials. They are expected to read texts other than the basal readers—texts that are often characterized by a markedly different paragraph structure. In subject areas such as science and social studies paragraphs are often organized around a major topic plus examples of supporting information or in terms of temporal, spatial, logical, or cause-and-effect relationships. Such a structure differs not only from that of narrative materials but also, of course, from the oral language forms with which students are familiar. Once students encounter expository materials, they must acquire many new skills for processing information.

Simultaneous with these new discourse-processing problems, new demands are being made on word knowledge. In sharp contrast to the primary materials, science, social studies, math, and more advanced forms of literature introduce vocabulary and underlying concepts that go beyond the students' prior experiences and word knowledge. Thus, students must learn how to obtain new knowledge from text.

The problems posed in elementary school continue throughout school and college because students are assigned reading materials that make increasingly difficult conceptual and organizational demands. Further, students must become more independent readers in order to accomplish homework assignments. The increasing amount of reading required demands increasingly efficient print processing. And information from a variety of sources must be evaluated, compared, and integrated in ever more sophisticated reports and projects. This brief discussion indicates some of the ways in which reading demands change over time. And the point to which we return is that despite the changing nature of reading acquisition, the diagnostic model is able to account for reading difficulties at all levels.

SUBSEQUENT DIAGNOSIS

The first stage of reading diagnosis involves assessing the relative strength of a student's print skills, word knowledge, and comprehension in response to the demands of reading materials typically used in his or her class. The second stage is somewhat more complex, for it involves more detailed diagnostic exploration of the areas of reading in which a student is experiencing difficulty. In the next five chapters, we examine the nature of and the diagnostic strategies for assessing print translation skills, word knowledge, and reading comprehension. The third stage of diagnosis, that of developing an instructional plan responsive to the difficulties that a student encounters, is also considered in subsequent chapters.

correspond to letters (graphemes) and series of letters. Establishing the relations between phonemes and letters is complicated for several reasons. First, just as children are not aware of word units in their spoken language, so they are not aware of the phonemes that compose spoken words. In fact, it has been argued that it is experience with letters that sensitizes children to the phonemes of words (Ehri, 1983). Second, although there are only 26 letters, some are easily confused because they are mirror images (b and d) or rotations (n and u) of each other. Finally, in English it is not always the case that one letter is used to represent one phoneme. For example, the pairs sh, th, and ch each represent a single phoneme. Further, particularly for vowels, the correspondence is more complex. A letter may stand for several different phonemes, and a phoneme may be represented by several different letters and/or combinations thereof.

DEVELOPMENT OF KNOWLEDGE ABOUT PRINT

There is much that students must come to understand about print in order to become proficient readers. We have divided this learning into three main types: (a) the physical arrangement of text (writing conventions), (b) word learning or recognition, and (c) word identification (phonic and structural analysis). These three types correspond to the understanding that students must acquire about the relationships between print and speech at letter, word, and passage levels. We identify a fourth type of learning that is synthetic in nature, namely, the proficiency that students achieve when they learn to integrate knowledge from print with background knowledge in order to process print efficiently and flexibly.

Writing Conventions

Learning about the arrangement of text involves knowing where a book begins, where to begin on a page, in what direction to move, what to do at the end of a line, and what to do at the end of a page. Further, it involves learning that printed words — and not just pictures — are reliable cues to speech and meaning.

For some children, learning about books and print begins long before school instruction. At home and in preschool, they have been read to from books, and they examine books themselves, sometimes with the help of a friend or older sibling. They ask questions about reading, try to mimic reading, and sometimes ask a reader to demonstrate reading by pointing to words as the story progresses. Knowledge about the arrangement of print develops through a variety of experiences extended over time. Some children, however, come to school without the advantage of these experiences, and, accordingly, lack much of the knowledge about print that has been acquired by their more fortunate peers. Studies reveal that children differ considerably in their knowledge about print (Clay, 1979a, 1982). Thus,

2

The Development of Print Translation Strategies

When students begin to read, they already possess a well-formed language system. Nevertheless, they have not learned to think about their language in an objective fashion. For linguists, language is a complex, hierarchical system, in which smaller units of language are nested within larger ones. For example, large units of discourse can be divided into sentences, and sentences into words or morphemes. Words are themselves composed of smaller units, syllables, which in turn are composed of sounds (phonemes and phones). Although students do not need to acquire the sophisticated perspective of a linguist in order to learn to read, they must become more aware of the nature of their language in order to understand the various ways in which spoken language corresponds to writing.

The correspondence between speech and writing is complicated because relationships occur on a number of levels and are by no means always obvious. At the most general level, the message of written exposition relates to a spoken counterpart. At a lower level, a printed sentence will correspond to a spoken sentence. But whereas a capital letter and a period indicate the boundaries of the printed sentence, inflectional characteristics may indicate the boundaries of the spoken sentence. Spoken words also relate to printed words; but whereas printed words are marked by spaces, spoken words are not delineated from each other. Indeed, children may begin reading with little awareness of how speech becomes partitioned into word units. As children learn to read and spell, they acquire a representational system that allows them to see what they say. Thus, word learning as a part of reading instruction involves learning about the nature of printed words, but also discovering how language may be segmented into units that correspond to printed words.

Below the level of meaningful words, spoken phonemes

teachers must know how to examine these differences so as to be able to provide appropriate instruction.

Word Learning

One of the most important achievements in reading is learning to recognize printed words instantaneously. In word learning beginning readers must confront two problems. The first is learning to segment oral language into parts that correspond to printed words (word awareness). The second is learning to discriminate among the printed words.

Word Awareness. It is difficult for literate adults to imagine that young children may listen to sentences without being aware of the specific words that compose them. Yet, evidence from research indicates that this is true. Perhaps the study that has most influenced our thinking about the development of word awareness is that conducted by Karpova (1955, as described in Slobin, 1966). Karpova found that the word consciousness of children develops in three stages. In the first, at 3 – 4 years of age, children understand sentences as semantic units, without distinguishing individual words. For example, they report that a sentence such as *Galyla and Vova went walking* contains two words: Galyla-went-walking and Vova-went-walking. During the next stage, prereaders become able to separate sentences into subject and predicate. Finally, during the third stage, children learn to identify the words that compose sentences, although they experience difficulty with compound and multisyllabic words and fail to distinguish some function words as separate units. Other researchers (Ehri, 1975; Holden & MacGinitie, 1972; Huttenlocher, 1964) report findings similar to Karpova's.

The problem of trying to determine which units of speech relate to printed words is a complex one. Not only must children learn the conventions of print — how words in English are ordered from left to right and from top to bottom on a page — but they must begin to segment the flow of speech into units that correspond to printed words. Further, they must learn that the correspondent of a printed word is limited; that is, "bunny" is not an acceptable response to the printed word *rabbit*. They must also learn the conventions of English that pertain to wordness — for example, that "not happy" and "full spoon" are represented by two words in English, whereas "unhappy" and "spoonful" are represented by one.

It may be useful for teachers to be able to assess the extent to which the students they work with have become aware of words as distinguishable units. Morris (1980) describes a diagnostic method that reveals a student's word awareness as well as his or her ability to learn and remember words:

1. The child learned to recite a four-line poem with the help of picture cues and examiner support. One of the two poems used in the study is the following:

Sam, Sam the butcher man
Washed his face in a frying pan
Combed his hair with a wagon wheel
And died with a toothache in his heel.

2. Once the child had demonstrated mastery of the spoken poem, a printed copy of the poem was revealed and the child was informed that the printed copy corresponded to the spoken verse. The examiner modeled a reading of the first line, pointing to each word and reading it aloud. Next, the second line was framed with two index cards and the child was instructed to finger-point read the line (accuracy in pointing was recorded). Finally, the child was asked to locate two target words (responses were recorded). Lines three and four were read in the same manner.

3. The examiner and the child "choral read" (read together) the entire four line poem two times. As they read, the examiner pointed to each word as it was pronounced.

4. After the choral reading was completed, the examiner pointed to individual words within the poem and the child was asked to pronounce the words (see underlined words in poem).

5. The printed copy of the poem was removed, and the child was presented with a list of six isolated words taken from the poem. The words were presented one at a time and the child was asked to pronounce each word [Morris, 1980, pp. 99–100].

Morris derives four scores from this procedure, two of which relate directly to the notion of word awareness (the ability to point to words while reading aloud and to select individual words within a single line).

Failure to develop word awareness during the initial stages of reading is manifest in oral reading that bears little or no correspondence to the printed words being read. The development of such awareness is evident in Clay's (1967) description of the stages through which beginning readers instructed by a sentence method progress:

As [the children] developed skill in matching behavior, fingers were used to point to those parts of the text that were supposed to correspond to the vocal responses. Fluency gave way to word by word reading. At this point the child's reading became staccato as he over-emphasized the breaks between words. He could be thought of as "reading the spaces" or "voice pointing" at the words [p. 16].

Thus, pointing to words during the initial stages of reading indicates the development of awareness of words and of the correspondence between spoken and written language. Voice pointing and, subsequently, natural phrasing reflect increasing familiarity with and control over print. Both finger and voice pointing should be interpreted as signs of progress, and as Clay notes, they are not behaviors to be "hurriedly trained out." Nevertheless, continued use of finger pointing may also indicate difficulty in visual coordination or acuity.

Most children do not encounter difficulty in becoming aware of words and learning them. However, there are some who require explicit instruction before they attend carefully to printed words and understand the nature of the correspondence between print and language. Methods for diagnosing these problems are discussed later in this chapter.

Printed Word Discrimination. Learning words is not simply a matter of memorizing sequences of letters and their aural counterparts, one at a time. Instead, word learning involves comparing new words with previously learned words in order to identify features that are useful for distinguishing among words. For example, in learning the words *red, blue, yellow, green,* and *orange,* children need only attend to the initial letter of each word in order to discriminate among them and give a correct response. If, however, the word *brown* is added to the set, the children will need to consider more than the initial consonant to discriminate correctly, as *blue* and *brown* begin with the same letter.

Thus, a problem with the discrimination learning of printed words is that as the set of words learned becomes larger, features that were initially useful in discriminating among words are no longer sufficient and students must attend to other features. Primary teachers observe this problem most often in the failure of students to distinguish among words with similar beginning and ending letters but different medial vowels (e.g., *but, bat,* and *bit*). Children eventually learn to attend to enough word features so that words are rarely confused. In addition, they learn to use other sources of information, such as phonic and contextual cues, to facilitate rapid word recognition.

As discussed in greater detail later, the word features and other information that children use to discriminate words appear to be influenced by the nature of their reading instruction (Barr, 1975). Children instructed by "eclectic" reading materials tend to depend on visual and/or phonic cues, mainly from the initial and final portions of words, in conjunction with contextual information (Biemiller, 1970), whereas those who are instructed with "synthetic phonics" materials are likely to develop greater sensitivity to phonic cues from medial as well as extreme portions of words and to depend less on purely visual or on contextual information for word discrimination (Cohen, 1974–1975).

Word Identification

Word identification through the use of phonics involves several sorts of learning. First, and least problematic, students must learn to discriminate among the set of letters. Second, they must become aware of the phonemes that compose words. Third, they must learn to associate letters with phonemes. Finally, they must learn to blend phonemes into words. We focus our discussion on phoneme awareness and blending since these aspects of learning phonics are problematic for many students.

Phoneme Awareness. Just as young children process words in sentences without being aware of them as distinctive units, so, too, do they process the segments within words. Various research strategies suggest awareness of phonemes within words is developed only gradually. For example, children below the age of 7 experience considerable difficulty reporting the word that remains when a phoneme is deleted (i.e., when /h/ is deleted from *hill* or /d/ from *card;* Bruce, 1964; Rosner & Simon, 1971). Liberman, Shankweiler, Fischer, and Carter (1974) report that none of a preschool group and only 17% of a kindergarten group were able to segment words into their phonemic components, whereas 70% of a first-grade group were successful.

The problem of distinguishing phonemes within words is complicated by the fact that each phoneme has several sound variants; and these are treated as equivalent in the writing system. This makes it difficult to explain and illustrate the concept of phonemes.

The phonemes of English correspond (more or less well) to graphemes, and these correspondences are referred to as phonic concepts. Almost all beginning reading programs now in common use introduce phonic concepts. Where programs with a heavy emphasis on phonics are used, students' reading progress is heavily dependent on their mastery of phonic concepts. However, in many of the phonic programs, phonemes are introduced in isolated form and students bypass the important learning that words can be segmented into phonemes. Accordingly, students learn phonic correspondences on an item-by-item basis and fail to acquire a general procedure by which to relate word forms and phonemes.

Elkonin (1963) has described an instructional procedure that is used in the Soviet Union to teach students to segment familiar words into their component phonemes. Students are instructed to say words aloud and to place a marker for each phoneme heard. To facilitate this learning, students are sometimes shown the printed word they are pronouncing.

Blending. Not only must students learn phonic concepts, but they must also learn to blend phonemes into words. Many poor readers are unable to make their knowledge of phonics functional because they do not understand the blending process. Teaching blending is easier if students have undertaken the reciprocal process of word segmentation. Through this experience they understand how phonemes are derived in the first place.

Integration and Fluency

Integration refers to the use of information from print in conjunction with contextual and background information. A study by Biemiller (1970), to be more fully discussed in what follows, describes three stages of development in beginning reading skill: first, readers attend mainly to contextual information; second, they focus on information from print; in the final stage, they integrate information from print and context. The balance achieved in the use of print and contextual information can differ and the analysis of oral reading responses gives some indication of the balance achieved by individual readers.

Once students have solved the problems of word learning, word identification, and integration, the major remaining print-processing problem is that of achieving fluency or automaticity. LaBerge and Samuels (1974), in their formulation of automatic information processing in reading, propose that instantaneous processing evolves as component skills become automatic through practice. They suggest that practice facilitates two different developments. First, it results in the consolidation of separate processes. For example, at a basic level phonic associations and blending are consolidated within word identification. At a more advanced level, visual recognition leads immediately to semantic awareness with or without phonological mediation. Readers are no longer aware of the visual forms or sounds of words they read but are aware only of their meaning. Second, practice permits the reorganization of perception into larger units, allowing the reader to go, for example, from word-by-word reading to reading word groups or phrases.

Fluency or the lack thereof is evident when one listens to the oral reading of students. The reading of those who have not yet mastered the component skills of print processing is characterized by long pauses, frequent repetitions, and inappropriate phrasing. Students who have mastered the component processes but not consolidated them through practice tend to read with frequent short pauses.

Reading rate is an indication of fluency. As illustrated in Table 2.1, the oral reading rate of students improves dramatically from first to second grade and thereafter shows steady but more moderate increases. Although a comparison of the average reading rates of students on various reading tests shows wide variation (Harris & Sipay, 1980, p. 556), this variability in part reflects variations in the difficulty of the test material. Some tests consist of extremely easy passages, whereas others include more technical material. The rates for the Gilmore Oral Reading Test, New Edition (1968), given in Table 2.1, are based on passages that are appropriate in difficulty to the grade of the students tested; accordingly, these ranges provide a useful standard against which to compare the reading of students at different grade levels.

Table 2.1. Average Reading Rates on the Gilmore Oral Reading Test

Grade level	Average range[a] words per minute
1.8	30–54
2.8	66–104
3.8	86–124
4.8	95–130
5.8	108–140
6.8	112–145
7.8	122–155
8.8	136–167

[a] The average range includes approximately 54% of students, those in stanines 4, 5, and 6 and in the 23–76 percentile band.

Source: Reproduced by permission from the Gilmore Reading Tests. Copyright © 1968 by Harcourt Brace Jovanovich, Inc. All rights reserved.

INFLUENCE OF INSTRUCTION ON READING DEVELOPMENT

Character of the Reading Program

Beginning reading programs are typically described along a continuum ranging from highly systematic synthetic-phonic approaches to sentence approaches with emphasis on meaning. However, almost all approaches involve contextual reading at some point and introduce word identification procedures. Accordingly, some have concluded that current reading programs differ only in degree of emphasis on phonics or meaning. We believe, by contrast, that important differences exist among reading programs and that these differences are reflected in the materials the students read.

Two characteristics in particular seem important. First, what is the design of the contextual materials read by students? What unit of print is controlled: sentence-type, word, word-pattern, or letter? Does the material preclude or encourage heavy reliance on contextual cues? We argue that the contextual materials establish the parameters of the reading problem that students must solve. If words are controlled, students must learn the set of words introduced in order to cope with contextual materials effectively. By contrast, if letters are controlled but many different words introduced, remembering the word set will not prove effective, whereas learning letter–sound associations and blending strategies will be productive.

Second, how is knowledge about word identification developed and applied? In particular, what phonic skills are introduced and when are they introduced? When do these skills first enable students to identify unknown words? Programs published prior to the mid-sixties tended to place little emphasis on phonics and, as Chall (1967) has noted, the phonics that were taught were often not applied. Evaluations of more recent programs suggest that phonic concepts are being introduced earlier and with more intensive practice (Chall, 1979, p. 31). However, Beck and McCaslin (1978) conclude that in 5 of the 10 reading programs they studied, the "brands of phonics are probably useless" in developing the word identification skills of special groups of students such as those in compensatory education programs.

The 10 commonly used programs reviewed by Beck and McCaslin all fall into two main types. The first, which we refer to as *eclectic programs,* include contextual materials in which a limited set of words are introduced and repeated. These programs also introduce phonic concepts, but they differ from the second type of program in terms of when these concepts are introduced and how much they are emphasized. Eclectic programs tend to introduce consonants first and only later give the vowel associations. As noted by Beck and McCaslin, students are usually not taught how to blend phonemes in these programs. Further, many of the words introduced in the contextual materials do not lend themselves to phonic identification, and therefore, the opportunity for applying newly learned phonic concepts is limited. Instead, a strategy for word identification that involves the joint use of contextual and graphic information is encouraged. Perhaps more important, the design of the contextual materials around a limited set of words, which are often introduced by the teacher prior to reading, creates little need for the development of word identification skills in the beginning stages of reading.

The second type of reading program, which we refer to as *code programs,* is characterized by early, intensive development of phonic concepts. Vowels as well as consonants are introduced early so that students have the capability of identifying a limited set of words. Students are taught to blend phonemes and are expected to practice "sounding" and blending when they encounter unknown words. Contextual materials at each stage usually contain only those words that can be decoded given the phonic knowledge that students have already acquired. In other words, letters or letter sequences are controlled in the construction of the materials, and typically only those for which the phonic associations are known are included. This design often leads to contextual materials that contain similarly patterned words and sentences that offer little potential for word identification on the basis of context. Indeed, word identification on the basis of context is sometimes discouraged. The contextual material is by design optimal for the application of a word identification approach that involves the blending of phonic associations.

While these alternative types of programs are easily distinguished at the first-grade level, they lose their distinctive character thereafter. The second-grade materials of almost all programs are composed of a large set of words that vary in length and pattern, even though the basis of design (letter or word control) often continues well into the intermediate grades. Further, by the end of first grade almost all programs, eclectic and code alike, have introduced the most frequently appearing consonant and vowel associations. Nevertheless, as we discuss in the following section, the early emphasis of reading instruction leaves its mark and can be seen to influence the reading strategies used by students in the upper primary grades — and perhaps beyond in the case of those who encounter some difficulty learning to read. However, students in this latter group, which is of particular interest to us, are sometimes shifted from one program to another, making it difficult to determine what influence particular programs have had.

Influence of Programs on Learning

Several studies have compared the reading of students learning from code versus eclectic programs (Barr, 1972, 1974, 1974–1975; Dank, 1976; DeLawter, 1975; Elder, 1971; Lesgold & Resnick, 1982). Generally, students instructed with a code emphasis tend to make fewer oral reading errors than those instructed with an eclectic emphasis. The substitution errors they make tend to be more closely related to letter–sound associations and, indeed, in many cases are nonsense words. By contrast, most of the word substitutions produced by students reading eclectic materials are real words and many tend to come from the set of words being learned. While the errors of students reading code materials often change the meaning of sentences or else make no sense at all, students reading eclectic materials not only produce errors that are contextually more acceptable but also tend more often to correct those errors that are not.

In order to see these differences more concretely, consider the reading characteristics of two disabled readers responding to the sentence *Now he does not try to take his dog* (Spache, 1972). Kay, 8 years of age, who had been instructed with a code program, read the sentence, "Now *his dose* not *tray* to take his dog." Bill, 10 years of age and exposed to eclectic materials, read ". . . . he *did* not *take* to take his dog." The errors that these two students made on words presented in isolation are similar to those they made in reading text. For example, Kay substituted "erv" for the printed word *every,* "doan" for *done,* "road" for *round,* and "those" for *these.* Bill's responses to the same words were "very" for *every,* "did" for *done,* "about" for *round,* and "what" for *these.* While Kay's responses match the printed words more closely than Bill's, some of them are nonsense words and her errors in textual reading tend to make less sense than do Bill's.

Two studies of beginning readers are particularly useful in revealing the stages that students progress through while learning to read. Biemiller

(1970) describes students reading from eclectic materials, while Cohen (1974–1975) describes those instructed with a code emphasis.

On the basis of oral reading errors made during first-grade instruction, Biemiller identified three main phases of development. Each phase reflected changes in the extent to which students used contextual and graphic information. In the initial phase, the responses of beginning readers showed a predominance of contextually constrained errors (that is, substituted words were appropriate to the preceding sentence context). The second stage was defined by an increase in no response errors — to 50% or more of the total. In addition to this tendency to make no response to words, children made significantly more graphically constrained errors than in the first stage. Specifically, they substituted more words that shared a common initial letter with the printed word. In the third phase, characterized by a drop in words not responded to, children's errors showed the joint influence of graphic and contextual information.

On the basis of this evidence and that from the comparative studies mentioned earlier, we speculate that students taught with eclectic materials solve the problem of learning to read in a distinctive and appropriate fashion. They appear to evolve a strategy for distinguishing among words previously taught as reading words, which involves the coordinated use of contextual and graphic cues.

Of particular interest to us is the fact that among the children Biemiller studied, those who made the slowest progress failed to show an increase in graphically constrained errors during the second phase. That is, although their responses tended to be appropriate to sentence context, they did not use the initial letter of the printed word as a cue to pronunciation. Thus, students who experience difficulty learning to read from eclectic programs apparently use contextual cues to help them select an appropriate response from the set of words that they have learned as reading words, but they fail to refine their strategy through the incorporation of graphic cues. There is some evidence that the reading responses of disabled readers continue to be constrained by words they have learned. Bennett (1942) found that not less than 95% of the substitution errors of older disabled readers were words previously learned, particularly in the primers and preprimers.

Students instructed with a code emphasis show a markedly different set of response patterns. Cohen (1974–1975) found that most children during the initial phase of learning gave no response when a word was unknown. She speculates that this tendency reflects the "learner's early uncertainty as to how to express the relationship between letters, sounds, and words [p. 616]." Whereas the better readers rapidly shifted from no responses to nonsense responses and then to real-word substitutions, poorer readers demonstrated much more gradual progress from not responding, and their errors tended to be real words as well as nonsense words. In addition, while the errors of better readers became constrained by an increasing amount of graphic information, poorer readers continued to use mainly first and last letter cues, and they evidenced less "sounding-out" behavior than the better readers. Finally, Cohen notes that during the beginning months of instruction some poorer readers produced "readings" that were holistic interpretations of the text, revealing that they were not aware of oral–written word correspondences.

Students instructed with a code emphasis appear to solve the problem of learning to read by blending phonemes corresponding to letters and matching the synthesized sequence of phonemes with known words; failure to find a match leads either to the production of a nonword or to no response. Some students who experience difficulty with this approach may do so because they fail to understand how phonemes relate to aural words and how the latter relate to text.

It is not surprising that beginning readers evolve some systematic strategy for translating print to speech. Nor is it surprising that with subsequent reading experience, their strategies become modified and elaborated to cope with the new demands of materials they encounter. The studies of Elder (1971), DeLawter (1975), and Dank (1976) indicate that early error characteristics are observed well into the primary grade years, though they become less distinctive. For example, the substitutions of students instructed with code emphases still tend to be more graphically appropriate but less contextually so than those of students instructed with eclectic emphases. Even so, most students show improvement in the integration of graphic and contextual cues, in their ability to self-correct, and in their general level of accuracy, rate, and fluency (Clay & Imlach, 1971; Y. M. Goodman, 1970, Ilg & Ames, 1950).

At the same time, individual variation also increases, and disabled readers are generally marked by poorly refined strategies. Whereas good readers often infer the relationships between speech and print that are not explicitly taught (Soderbergh, 1971), disabled readers not only fail to make such inferences but often they are unable to incorporate what is explicitly taught (Barr & Dreeben, 1983). They may therefore need a greater amount of direct instruction.

Influence of Passage Difficulty on Error Patterns

The error patterns of students are influenced not only by their instructional programs but also by the difficulty of the material being read (Kibby, 1979; Whaley & Kibby, 1981). Generally, as the material increases in difficulty relative to the proficiency of the reader, more "no response" errors and errors marked by a high degree of graphic appropriateness occur. Further, this tendency occurs for all readers, although less proficient readers are more greatly affected (Biemiller, 1979). In addition, poorer readers make fewer contextually appropriate errors than more proficient readers (Weber, 1968). These results show that in interpreting oral reading responses, it is important to consider not only the characteristics of the reading program through which a student learned to read, but also the relative difficulty of the material being read.

ORAL READING
RESPONSE CHARACTERISTICS

We have shown how detailed consideration of students' oral reading response characteristics provides some understanding of the influence of instructional programs and of the changes that occur as students acquire greater proficiency. Just as the oral response characteristics of students provide valuable data for the researcher, so, too, they can assist the teacher. While it is important to consider a student's correct responses, the characteristics of errors are particularly useful in inferring underlying reading processes and print translation strategies.

Reconceptualization of the Meaning of Errors

Among the oral reading error types commonly studied are substitutions (reading a word that is different from the printed one) and omissions (making no response to a printed word). Substituted words are not, for the most part, random guesses but rather calculated responses cued by print and/or prior sentence context or by other more general cues (pictures, story theme, previous reading in the same book). Thus, two assumptions are implicit in the use of response analysis to infer underlying processes: first, that correct responses to printed words are produced in a systematic fashion; and second, that reading errors reflect, in a manner similar to correct responses, the workings of an underlying process.

Oral reading responses have long been used as evidence of a reader's proficiency. But the concept of what constitutes a correct response has changed over time. Prior to the mid-sixties, reading responses were considered mainly in terms of their match with the printed word stimulus. Thus, in determining reader proficiency, all errors were simply tabulated, regardless of their nature. An exact match between printed text and oral response was expected for good readers. The prevailing conception of the reading process was that the reader's response was — or ought to be — wholly triggered by print.

Goodman's (1965, 1967, 1969) reconceptualization of reading as a constructive process in which the reader is an active hypothesis-tester led to a reconceptualization of errors, or "miscues," as Goodman prefers to call them. Responses are now considered within a broader frame of reference: they are judged in terms of their appropriateness to meaning as well as to print. And they are used to infer the strategies the reader is relying on. In short, responses that previously would have been classified as incorrect are now viewed as partially correct, as miscues. It is recognized that they are not blind guesses but show the use of various cues (prior or subsequent sentence context, pictures, print).

Most students reading their instructional materials produce a high proportion of responses that match exactly with the expected response. Words omitted or inserted into text can be judged in terms of their consequence for meaning but not for their match with print. Substitutions of one word for another can be judged in terms of their match with print and meaning while mispronunciations that are nonwords can be examined for their match with print. Other forms of oral reading behavior, such as pauses and repetitions, must be examined in order to infer their function within the strategies of the reader. For example, one reader may repeat in order to correct a miscue, whereas another may repeat in order to determine the meaning of a sentence or to gain time for identification of an unfamiliar word.

Consider the following sentence: *After riding his bicycle around the block, Danny went into the house to get a glass of milk.* Assume that a student reads the sentence as follows: "After he riding . . . after he rode his bic around the black the block Dan went to his home to get a . . . . . . g– . . . of milk. A teacher listening to the student read could record his oral reading as follows:

Table 2.2 shows the symbols used to record deviations from the expected responses. The deviations here were of several different sorts. The student inserted the word *he* and omitted several word parts (in *Danny* and *into*). He substituted *rode* for *riding, black* for *block, his* for *the, home* for *house.* He mispronounced *bicycle* and *glass,* words that were presumably in his speaking vocabulary. Twice he repeated words, both times to achieve a more meaningful phrase. The first repetition resulted in a substitution error (*rode* for *riding*) whereas the second resulted in a correction (*block* replacing his prior response of *black*).

Substitutions can be examined further to determine their degree of match with print and sentence context. For example, the substitution of *his* for *the* makes good sense within the context of the sentence but fails to correspond with letter cues. The substitution of *home* for *house* both corresponds to print characteristics and makes sense within sentence context. The substitution of *black* for *block* matches in terms of initial and final

Table 2.2.   Symbols for Recording Oral Reading Responses

Omissions. Circle the word, group of words, or part of a word omitted.	Danny ran up to the door.
Insertions. Write in the word or word part inserted. Indicate its position with a carat.	He rode his bicycle. (on)
Substitutions or mispronunciations. Identify the mispronounced word(s) by crossing out or underlining it (them). Write in the substituted word.	He bicycled around the block. (bic) (black)
Repetitions. Underline repeated words using a line and arrow or a wiggly line.	He rode around the block. (black)
Corrections. Indicate corrected responses by a *c* inside a circle.	He rode around the block. (©black)
Pauses. Indicate pauses by a single slash. Pauses that exceed 2 seconds should be recorded by a double slash.	He got a // glass / of milk.
Punctuation. Indicate failure to pause for comma or period by circling.	The milk tasted funny⊙ Danny thought it might be too warm.

letters but violates the sense of the sentence. We note that this substitution was corrected and speculate that the reason for the correction was the failure of *black* to make sense within sentence context.

The oral reading responses of any student can be recorded and analyzed to determine how he or she translates print into meaning (see Hood, 1975–1976, and Wixson, 1979, for further discussion of oral reading error analysis). The following sections describe how oral reading responses during contextual reading and further diagnostic probe can be used to assess knowledge about writing conventions, sight word learning, word identification skill, and reading integration and fluency, and to design appropriate instruction in these areas.

INTERPRETATION OF RESPONSE CHARACTERISTICS

Writing Conventions

Diagnosis: Contextual Reading. The oral reading of students who lack basic knowledge about the arrangement of text is characterized by its lack of correspondence to the text. That is, there is usually no one-to-one correspondence between words spoken and those on the printed page. Typically, students develop a story that is related to the pictures.

Diagnosis: Probe. The most effective way to explore knowledge about the arrangement of text is to use a procedure developed by Clay

(1972, 1979b). Her Concepts about Print Test consists of a series of questions that are used in conjunction with two specially designed storybooks (*Sand* and *Stones*); however, the basic procedure will work with other books as well. The questions asked and knowledge assessed can be classified into three main areas.

In order to examine knowledge about *book organization,* the teacher hands the student a storybook with the spine up, and asks him or her where the front of the book is and where reading should begin. A teacher can thus observe whether the student knows how to hold and open books at the beginning of the story with the print right side up.

In order to assess a student's knowledge of the *arrangement of print and its relation to speech,* the teacher opens the book to a place where there is a picture on one page and print on the other and asks the student to point to where the teacher should begin reading. If the student points to the print at the beginning of the page, rather than to the picture, it is assumed that he or she understands that it is print and not pictures that are read and that one begins reading at the left side of the first line of print. The student is then asked to point to where the teacher should go next and where after that. If the student indicates the correct pattern (left to right along the line, with a return sweep down a line and then left to right), it is assumed that directional knowledge about the arrangement of a page has been acquired. Finally, the accuracy of the pointing indicates the extent to which the student has developed awareness of the relationship between printed and spoken words.

In order to examine a student's understanding of important *terminology and symbols,* the teacher turns to a new page and asks the student to "point to the beginning of the story on this page" and then to the "end," and then on another page, to the "top" and "bottom." The student is then given two blank cards and asked to frame just "one word," "two words," "one letter," and "two letters." In addition, the child's knowledge of upper- and lower-case letters and punctuation is assessed. From such questioning, a teacher learns the extent of a child's knowledge of the terms used during reading instruction.

Instructional Implications. Beginning readers who lack basic knowledge about text arrangement need to be provided with experiences that develop such knowledge. This can be done by reading them storybooks. Large-sized "big" books are particularly useful, since they let students participate in the reading. The teacher should talk about where the story begins and demonstrate with a hand motion the portion of the text that is currently being read. Similarly, concepts pertaining to positions ("top," "end"), print ("word," "letter"), and punctuation can be explained and demonstrated. Language-experience stories, in which students dictate a story or event so that the teacher can record it, help to develop knowledge about the arrangement of print and its relation to speech. The procedures for demonstrating print-to-speech relationships developed by Morris (1980) and described earlier can be used with language-experience stories and with familiar poems and songs.

Word Learning

Diagnosis: Contextual Reading. An analysis of responses made during contextual reading will focus mainly on those errors or miscues commonly classified as substitutions or mispronunciations. Procedurally, it is useful to separate these miscues into two groups: *(a)* those occurring in response to basic sight words (i.e., high-frequency function words, which account for 70% of running text, see Appendix A), and *(b)* those occurring in response to content words. The former group allows assessment of how well a student learns sight words; the latter group allows assessment of how well a student can identify words that are unknown.

In studying the responses made to sight words, it is useful to establish the proportion of such errors in relation to total words read. If only a small proportion of words are sight words that were not recognized correctly (less than 2% of running text), it is possible that word learning is not an area of concern. This is especially likely if the oral reading is fluent and the miscues are consistent with the author's meaning. However, in other cases, further diagnostic work with sight words may be appropriate and may lead to the determination that instruction in the area of sight word development or consolidation is warranted.

Diagnosis: Probe. Sight words missed in context should be printed in isolated form and the student should be asked to pronounce them. Isolated word testing limits readers to the use of graphic information. If words are pronounced quickly in isolation, no further testing of sight words is needed. If, however, a student appears to have problems recognizing these words in isolation (slow or faulty pronunciation), more extensive testing should be undertaken, either with specially developed lists such as the Dolch Word List (Dolch, 1936; see Appendix A) or with a list compiled from the basal reader word lists.

Instructional Implications. Readers who mispronounce sight words tend to fall into three groups:

1. Proficient readers who miss a small number of sight words, with the miscues consistent with author meaning and reading fluency not impaired.
2. Readers who miss sight words during contextual reading but not when they are presented in isolation.
3. Readers who experience difficulty pronouncing sight words in isolation as well as in context.

The first group requires no special instruction, and the instructional implications are different for the second and third groups. Typically, disabled readers at the primary grade level of reading fall into the third category, while the second category contains readers of more intermediate proficiency.

The second group does not need direct work on sight word learning. Their sight word problems often result from other problems of word identification during contextual reading. Nevertheless, the fact that sight words are miscalled under stress indicates that they are not as well learned as they should be. For these students, it is not isolated word drill that is needed; rather, these readers profit most from extensive easy contextual reading. Contextual reading requires the integration of meaning and graphic information in a way that is not possible with isolated drill, and it is this integration that is most needed here. However, contextual reading is usually an unpleasant experience for these students. Thus, the materials selected should be highly interesting to the student; they should be easy at the independent reading level; and charts should be kept of the number of pages read as a visual sign of progress. Where necessary, external incentive should be provided.

For the third group, further testing should be undertaken to determine the sight vocabulary known by the student. New sight words to be taught to the student should be drawn from the contextual materials used by the teacher. Instruction should never involve only development of words in isolation. Rather, contextual reading should be a part of every instructional session so that it serves to reinforce the learning of sight words. The number of new sight words introduced each day should depend on the student's mastery. For example, if five new words are introduced but only two mastered, the teacher should reduce the number to two or three at the next session.

The degree of instructional reinforcement should be adjusted to what is needed by the student for retention. Word-sort activities, writing, and spelling can all be used to reinforce the initial learning of sight words.

1. *Word banks.* The use of word banks is an outgrowth of the language experience approach, in which various reinforcement activities serve to help students learn and remember words (Stauffer, 1970). The word bank consists of words that a student is learning through contextual reading (basal materials or language-experience materials) and other words that are of interest to the student. When a new word is encountered or identified, it is printed on a 3 × 5 card. It is important that the student make his or her own cards because writing serves to reinforce the learning of words. The student can use the back of the card to draw a picture or write a sentence that will cue him or her to the identity of the word. As new words are encountered, the stack of cards accumulates. A box and rubber bands should be provided to help students keep and organize the word cards.

The cards may be used for a variety of reinforcement activities. They may be reviewed by children working individually or in pairs. They may be used to form sentences, as a small group or individual activity.

One of the most productive activities involves sorting the words into various classes on the basis of alternative features (see Gillet & Temple, 1982, for a more detailed description of procedures to be followed during *word sorts*). During small group instruction, children may be asked to go through their cards to find those that exemplify a certain characteristic. For example, they may be asked to select words that begin or end like the word *balloon,* that name an animal, or that are three syllables in length. Alternatively, students may be invited to identify words that conform to a criterion of their choosing. Once they have identified and displayed a group of four to six words to their classmates, they can then see if the other students can determine the characteristic that the selected words share.

2. *Writing and spelling.* Beginning readers who have difficulty learning words are often helped to remember them by being encouraged to spell and write words that have been introduced in their reading materials. These activities seem to prompt children to scrutinize words, particularly the medial portions, and to become more aware of the phonemic correlates of the words. Further, once they have learned to write basic sight words, they often draw on these high-frequency words during their other writing activities. Thus, writing is made easier and basic sight words are reinforced.

3. *Contextual reading practice.* One of the best ways to consolidate sight vocabulary is through extensive contextual reading. Many basal programs are designed to provide practice on words that have been introduced by including them in subsequent stories. However, such practice may be insufficient for students who have great difficulty remembering words. Thus, it is important for the teacher to devise ways to give students more practice on the words they are learning. Some basal series provide supplementary materials for this purpose. Alternatively, students may reread stories that they have previously read. For example, once a book is completed, the teacher may ask students to identify their favorite stories from the book and then have students take turns reading them. The teacher may pose a new question about a previously read story and have children read the story silently to identify information relevant to the question. Some teachers find that a prior edition of a basal series provides a "new" set of stories that includes many of the words introduced in the newer edition. These texts may therefore be useful as supplementary reading for students having difficulty learning words.

One reason that teachers fail to provide supplementary reading is that students in the most slowly paced group proceed at a very slow rate as it is. To take time for additional contextual practice would result in an even slower pace. Thus, in order to provide additional practice, it may be necessary to plan extra small-group instructional time. For example, it may be necessary to meet with the most slowly paced group twice a day (morning and afternoon) rather than once.

Word Identification

Diagnosis: Contextual Reading. Word identification skill can be inferred from an analysis of substitutions and mispronunciations in response to unusual content words. The instructional method used to teach the students to read will influence how they attack unknown words. Typically, where the emphasis has been on comprehension and the development of a sight vocabulary, students will produce meaningful substitutions and few mispronunciations that are nonwords. Substitution miscues also tend to approximate the printed word in length. Usually the initial consonant(s) and sometimes the final consonant(s) agree with the text as well. The majority of substitutions are semantically appropriate, at least within the immediate sentence context. There may also be a tendency to correct semantically inappropriate words.

In contrast, where the instructional method has emphasized phonic decoding, students' reading tends to display the following miscue characteristics: the occurrence of mispronunciations that are nonwords, a high degree of letter–sound correspondence between the printed word and oral response, a tendency for miscues to be semantically inappropriate, and corrections made mainly on the basis of graphic rather than contextual cues.

As indicated by several studies (Barr, 1974; DeLawter, 1975; Elder, 1971), the word identification strategy initially learned by a student becomes refined over time; nevertheless, normal readers at third-grade level and disabled readers even later show signs of their initial reading strategy. Although we are not yet sure of the implications of initial strategy for further instruction in the area of word identification, it would seem that building on a student's strengths might lead to faster gains than attempting to teach a new strategy.

Diagnosis: Probe. Word identification skills used with words in isolation should be compared with those used during contextual reading. When words are tested in isolation, we limit the reader to use of graphic cues. Therefore, the words missed in context should be presented in isolation. By inspecting the responses, we can determine the reader's strategy for word identification using only graphic cues for structural analysis and phonic synthesis. In addition to shifting the task from contextual reading to word reading, we can also shift from word reading to syllable or letter pronunciation by covering all but a syllable or letter(s) of a word. Because letter and syllable tests require nonsense responses and isolated phoneme pronunciation, they may be difficult for some students. But they provide one of the least confounded tests of a reader's phonic skill. Once we determine the phonic skills a reader has available, we can compare phonic competency with application in word and contextual reading. Sometimes students have learned phonic skills but have not learned to apply them during contextual reading. From this type of diagnostic probe, then, a teacher can determine whether students know the common pronunciation(s) for consonants, consonant blends and digraphs, and vowels and vowel combinations, and whether they can use this knowledge to pronounce syllables or words either through blending or through analogizing with familiar words.

Once a problem area has been identified it is sometimes useful to undertake a more systematic analysis of phonic knowledge. Appendix B presents the Blachowicz Informal Phonics Survey, which can serve this function.

Instructional Implications. In considering instruction in the area of word identification skills, we need to distinguish between students instructed by phonic methods and students instructed by eclectic methods. For the first group, diagnosis should serve to identify the associations and operations not yet mastered. These should then be taught systematically. Two common problems among this group are blending and vowel associations and markers.

To teach blending skill, the following procedures can be used. They will work with individual students or with groups. Instruction should begin with the blending of syllables *(but - ter, wag - on, ti - ger)*. If this is difficult for the students, compound words such as *football, doghouse,* and *cowboy* should be presented along with pictures corresponding to the component words; the students should identify the picture that corresponds to the "word-syllable" being pronounced. When students can blend compound words, other two syllable words should be attempted. Next, phoneme blending should be developed. First, a vowel unit should be blended into a final consonant *(ca - t, bo - x, de - sk)*, then a consonant into an ending *(f - oot, h - and, p - en)*, and finally, three units should be blended *(r - a - t, f - a - ce, p - a - ge)*. Many students are helped by seeing the sequence of letters while they hear the teacher pronounce the sounds and by imitating the way the teacher separates and blends sounds within words. Blending should be practiced for short periods every day for several weeks.

In teaching phonic associations, instructional materials should be examined to determine the sequence in which these are introduced. For example, some programs introduce long vowels before short, others short before long. Learning to hear the phonemes (sounds) in a word is the first step in learning phonic associations. Some students may need to develop phoneme awareness, using the activities described earlier. Each phoneme to be taught should then be introduced through a series of words in which it occurs in initial position. If students have difficulty remembering the phoneme, a key word (which contains the phoneme at the beginning) should be introduced in printed form. Whenever students encounter words beginning with the newly learned phonic association, they should be encouraged to pronounce that portion of the word. This activity teaches them that phonic associations provide valuable cues for word identification. Finally, students should be encouraged to use phonic knowledge in conjunction with contextual information during contextual reading.

In teaching phonic associations, it is often necessary to introduce the concept of *markers* (see Venezky, 1970, for discussion of this concept). In certain contexts, vowel letters generally and some consonant letters as well "mark" the pronunciation of another letter in that context (e.g., the *e* or *i* following a *c* marks the pronunciation of *c* as /s/). Students need to learn, for example, that the second of two vowels or a final *e* often marks the pronunciation of a preceding vowel. This concept should not be taught as a rule but rather by presenting examples from which students can infer the generalization. The teacher should begin with the final *e* concept *(can – cane, mat – mate, tap – tape)* and then move to vowel combinations *(pad – paid, ran – rain, bat – bait, man – main)*. Though most students pick up this concept rather easily, they sometimes have problems applying it during contextual reading.

Later problems frequently encountered by students taught by phonic methods and materials also include the application of phonic synthesis to multisyllabic words and the use of context to anticipate words. To learn the concept of syllable, students should listen to the teacher pronounce two-, three-, and even four-syllable words and tap the number of syllables they hear. Next, they should examine the syllables of two-syllable words that are regular in pattern *(butter, rabbit, window, pencil, erase, apron, table, open,* and *paper)* to see if they can figure out what constitutes a syllable (that it contains at least one vowel) and determine typical syllable patterns. (These patterns are consonant – vowel – consonant, consonant – vowel, vowel – consonant, and vowel, where a consonant may be either a single consonant, a consonant blend, or a consonant digraph, and where a vowel may be either a single vowel, a vowel digraph, or a vowel plus vowel marker.)

Students should be advised to pronounce vowels in multisyllabic words as they would in one-syllable words and then to blend the syllables into a word that makes sense. Some students have extreme difficulty with syllable pronunciation because syllables are *nonsense*. One way to help students deal with this is to use a word family approach: students should identify several known words first, then related syllables *(bat, cat — lat, tat)*, next a real word followed by a syllable *(bed – med, rod – fod, cab – pab)*, and finally a list of nonsense syllables.

As mentioned, students instructed by eclectic methods will probably have different needs. Such students tend, in the initial stages of reading, to think of words as units. To identify unknown words, they use cues from the sentence context and from the beginnings and ends of words. Students who are successful in developing a sight vocabulary usually do not experience reading problems until about third grade. Prior to this time they generally read basal selections in which the vocabulary, because it is systematically controlled, is highly predictable. Each story contains only a few new words, and often the teacher introduces these words before students read the story. In third grade, however, students are often expected to read nonbasal materials. Because of their relatively weak word identification skills (typically only consonant associations are used during reading), they have considerable difficulty with unknown words, especially those of several syllables.

Rather than shifting these students over to a new reading strategy involving phonic synthesis, instruction should build on the reading strengths that they have already acquired. Since the students tend to think of words as units, instruction should focus on breaking these familiar units into their constituent parts. In particular, the multisyllabic words that cause considerable difficulty can often be identified rather easily with skills already in a student's repertoire once students are able to segment the word into syllabic units. It is usually not necessary to teach students formal rules for syllabication; most have a good sense of syllabic units, which can be refined through class activities such as those described on page 34.

Once words are divided into syllables, students often need instruction in analogizing in order to see how known words and word parts can be used to identify unknown syllables. Students are encouraged to think of a word that ends the same as the first syllable of the unknown multisyllabic word and then to use a consonant-substitution method to identify the syllable. For example, in identifying the word *barter,* students are first encouraged to split the word into two units *(bar - ter).* Then the teacher asks them to think of a word that ends the same as *bar,* such as *car.* If the students have difficulty thinking of an appropriate word, the teacher should supply one. Finally, the cue word is written on top of the first syllable and students are encouraged to identify the syllable by substituting initial consonants. The procedure continues for the remaining syllable. To begin with, only multisyllabic words with obvious sight word analogies should be selected. Once the procedure is mastered, words without obvious analogies should be attempted under the guidance of the teacher. Often the step of dividing multisyllabic words into units is sufficient to permit their identification.

For students who have considerable difficulty thinking of appropriate cue words, the systematic training procedure described by Cunningham (1978; see also 1975 - 76, 1979) may be effective. In this approach, students are made aware that they are familiar with a large number of sight words that can be used to identify unknown words. In the first step, students write the words *he, went, her, can,* and *car* on index cards. Then they are asked to select two of the cards that match parts of such unknown words as *banter, ferment, meter, barber, percent,* and *garment.* Additional sight words are added during the second and third steps and further matching practice is provided. In the fourth step, students are encouraged to use "the whole store of words in their heads as words to match to unfamiliar [two-syllable] words" (pp. 610–611). In the fifth and final step, the procedures are applied to words of three or more syllables.

Integration: Contextual Information

Diagnosis: Contextual Reading. Reading responses can be analyzed in terms of *how* as well as *whether* they match expected responses. Some incorrect responses may reflect use of information about print; others may be influenced by prior sentence context, that is, they may make sense in terms of the meaning of the passage. Furthermore, some responses may reflect both these factors, whereas others may show the influence of neither. If most miscues show the influence of contextual information, it can be concluded that the reader uses this source of information and is trying to make sense of what has been read.

The number and type of miscues that a reader attempts to correct shed light on his or her ability to integrate contextual and print information. Several categories of correction behavior in oral reading have been identified (Page & Barr, 1975). When a reader corrects a response, he or she gives evidence of dissatisfaction with the original response. Conversely, failure to attempt a correction indicates a lack of dissatisfaction. Consider an oral reading miscue that is semantically and syntactically acceptable but differs in letter–sound correspondence from the expected response, as in "Tim ran down the *road*" for *Tim ran down the **lane.*** If the reader does not attempt to correct the miscue, a reasonable assumption is that semantic and grammatical cues from the context permitted him or her to verify the response and feel satisfied with it. We can also assume that, to some degree, the phonic discrepancy did not cause the reader to feel dissatisfied.

If no pauses or other miscues immediately precede or follow the response, the assumption concerning a lack of influence from phonic cues is strengthened. If *road* and *lane* are used interchangeably by the reader in a semantically acceptable way throughout the passage, the assumption is further strengthened.

If, on the other hand, the reader attempts to correct his or her substitution of "road" for *lane,* we must assume that the phonic cues are operating at this point, because the original response caused the reader some dissatisfaction. The attempt to correct may be successful or unsuccessful.

If it is successful, we may assume that phonic cues are influencing the reader's processing.

The production of a semantically and grammatically unacceptable response, such as "Tim ran down the *lone*," would warrant an inverse sort of interpretation in terms of corrections. Once again, failure to attempt a correction would suggest that semantic, grammatical, and phonic information was inadequately processed. If an attempt yields a vowel change such as "lean" for *lane*, we can assume that phonic cues are generating the correction attempt. On the other hand, a correction attempt with "line" for *lane* suggests all sources of information may be involved. In any event, a careful look at what elicits a correction response and what miscues go uncorrected can yield a great deal of information about the reading process.

Diagnosis: Probe.   If few miscues are contextually appropriate, further exploration must be made, through tasks such as the cloze test, to determine whether the student is able to use context to anticipate words (see, e.g., Blachowicz, 1977; Bortnick & Lopardo, 1973). Using a modified cloze approach, words that students were unable to pronounce during contextual oral reading are identified and students are instructed to read the sentences in which they occurred, saying "blank" for the unknown words. After they have read the sentence with the "blank," they are encouraged to think of words that might make sense in the blank. If they are able to produce words that are semantically acceptable within the sentence, we conclude that they are able to make use of context for word identification. It should be noted, however, that some sentence contexts provide little relevant information to aid word identification.

Instructional Implications.   If students are able to complete a cloze blank correctly but show little use of contextual information during oral reading, we can conclude that the problem is one of application. The students know how to use contextual information but have developed a reading strategy that usually does not draw on context as a source of information for anticipating responses and for correction. This type of strategy development is not unusual for students who have been instructed by phonic methods. Students who are able to complete cloze blanks, once alerted to context as a source of information and encouraged to use it, learn to use contextual information during passage reading quite easily.

Relatively few students have difficulty using context to fill in a blank once the procedure has been demonstrated as a class guessing game. These few require more systematic practice completing sentences where a single word has been omitted. To begin with, nouns should be deleted from the final part of a sentence whose initial part contains an explicit clue, for example, *He hit a home run with his new——.* In such activities, any response that makes sense in context should be accepted as correct. Subsequently, deletions other than nouns from sentences with explicit clues should be practiced.

Integration: Fluency

Diagnosis: Contextual Reading. Fluency can only be assessed when a person reads contextual materials. As described earlier, such characteristics of oral reading as long pauses, frequent repetitions, word-by-word reading, inappropriate phrasing, and poor intonation usually indicate a lack of reading fluency. However, some readers who do not usually read aloud are uncomfortable doing so and thus may appear to be lacking in fluency when they in fact *are* fluent during silent reading. Because oral reading is not always an accurate indication of fluency, it is important to consider other evidence such as reading rate. Reading rates below the ranges that were shown in Table 2.1 indicate lack of fluency.

Diagnosis: Probe. Typically, when students experience difficulty with reading fluency, the cause lies in other problems, such as word recognition and word identification. Yet this is not necessarily the case. A primary fluency problem can be distinguished from one that is secondary to other reading problems by having the student read text that is extremely easy for him or her. If the characteristics of nonfluent reading — poor intonation, inappropriate phrasing, long pauses, and word-by-word reading — persist, then it can be concluded that the problem is primarily one of fluency.

Instructional Implications. Reading practice is the most effective means for developing integration and fluency. However, the material practiced must be easy for the reader. That is, it should pose almost no word identification problems and no comprehension problems. Typically, reluctant readers will also need tangible forms of reinforcement, such as charts showing the number of pages read and rewards for the completion of books.

It is sometimes useful to read to a student, in order to model fluent reading. Having a student read together with a fluent adult (or a tape recording) or slightly after the adult's reading is sometimes effective. The procedure of repeatedly reading the same passages can also help students achieve fluency (Lopardo & Sadow, 1982). Many disabled readers fail to achieve fluency because they are continually asked to read materials that are too difficult. They have little opportunity to experience the pleasure of problem-free reading and to develop reading fluency. It is not inappropriate, when the material is appropriately easy, to encourage students to time themselves to see if they can improve their reading rate.

Table 2.3. Symptoms That May Indicate Problems in Visual or Auditory Acuity

Visual acuity

1. Does the student experience frequent eye infections or pain?
2. Does the student rub his or her eyes or evidence other signs of visual discomfort, particularly when reading?
3. Does the student finger point or use a marker while reading long after other students have discontinued such practices?
4. Does the student hold books in atypical positions or at unusual distances from his or her eyes?
5. Does the student frequently skip words or lines when reading?

Auditory acuity

1. Does the student experience frequent ear infections or pain?
2. Is the student's speech unusual in any way (slurred, monotonic, inarticulate, or loud)?
3. Is the student frequently inattentive?
4. Does the student often either fail to follow directions or ask to have them repeated?
5. Does the student fail to pronounce new words and names correctly?

PHYSICAL CONDITIONS INTERFERING WITH READING

With regard to all areas of reading development, but particularly in the development of print translation strategies, the teacher should keep in mind that certain physical problems may interfere with reading progress. While inadequate nutrition or rest may result in inattention, other physical problems may also cause this difficulty. Most important, the teacher should be aware that inadequate visual or auditory *acuity* may cause extreme discomfort in the beginning stages of reading, as well as later, if uncorrected. Table 2.3 lists some questions that should be asked in order to identify students with problems in visual or auditory acuity. If a student shows any of these symptoms over some period of time, he or she should be referred to the appropriate specialist for a thorough examination.

SUMMARY

When it has been concluded that print translation is a major area interfering with reading comprehension, subsequent diagnosis must identify the specific difficulty. We described four aspects of print translation in which students may encounter difficulty — writing conventions, word learning, word identification, and integration and fluency, and discussed how they are related developmentally. Defining the nature of print translation problems is complicated by the fact that oral reading responses, the main source of evidence regarding print translation skill, reflect not only individual learning but also past instruction. We also described how oral reading evidence can be used to plan appropriate instruction for helping students develop effective print translation strategies. In the next chapter, the procedures discussed will be further elaborated through three case studies.

3

Diagnosing
Print Translation
Strategies

In this chapter procedures for oral reading response analysis are described in considerable detail. Those teachers for whom oral reading analysis is a new skill should follow each recommended step. As always occurs with a new skill, the first attempts to use these procedures will be difficult and time consuming. However, with practice the skills and knowledge involved will become automatic so that oral reading response analysis can be undertaken with ease. Indeed, after listening and interpretive skills have been developed, many teachers can perform a useful diagnosis by simply listening to students' oral reading.

THE DIAGNOSTIC PROCEDURES

The procedures involve six main steps. First, some *preparation* is necessary before the teacher listens to a student read. Following this preparation, the teacher *administers* the passage and records the student's oral reading. Third, the teacher *analyzes* the response patterns. With this third step, the first stage of the diagnosis is completed. Then a second work session may be needed in order to *probe* selected aspects of reading. This fourth step may provide evidence that modifies or supports the tentative conclusions reached. Fifth, the teacher *interprets* the response patterns and integrates the results from the probes with the results from the initial diagnosis. Finally, the teacher translates the diagnosis into an *instructional plan.*

Preparation

The teacher should make a judgment as to the level at which the student is able to read. A trial run with several short selections may be necessary. Oral reading may be from any appropriate book including the student's basal reader. For each selection, a double-spaced typewritten version or photocopy should be prepared. The portion used for analysis should be 50–100 words in length for beginning readers and 100–200 words or more for more advanced readers. The total length should approximate that which students typically read at any one time in the classroom.

The teacher should be familiar with the response-recording system presented in Figure 2.1 (or any other appropriate scheme). It is recommended that the student's oral reading be tape-recorded as well, so that it will be possible to check the accuracy of the recording. The reason for the diagnosis should be discussed with the student.

Administration

The teacher should make sure that the student is comfortable and sufficiently relaxed. If the oral reading will be tape recorded, the student's permission should be obtained. It is important to provide an orienting statement to help the student relate to the content and theme of the selection (see Beck, Omanson, & McKeown, 1982, for procedural suggestions). It is also important to explain to the student what he or she should do. For example, the following may be said:

> This is a story in which . . . [theme-related preparatory statement]. Please read this story aloud for me. If you come to a word you don't know, try to figure it out, guess at it, or skip it. I will not be able to help you, so do the best you can. After you finish, I'll ask you some questions.

The teacher should record the student's responses on the photocopy or typed version of the story. Responses should be recorded by the teacher even if the oral reading is tape-recorded. The time that the student begins and finishes reading the passage should be noted.

If the reader becomes frustrated at some point, the teacher should reiterate that it is all right to guess at a word or skip it. If the reader continues to pause and becomes upset, the word causing difficulty should be provided. If the reading passage proves generally too frustrating, the diagnosis should be discontinued and an easier passage read at some later time.

Analysis

The oral reading record should be examined in order to determine whether the passage is of appropriate difficulty and to assess the student's sight word recognition, word identification strategies, and reading integration and fluency.

Passage Difficulty. This analysis pertains to the level of materials that would be appropriate for various purposes (such as, for reading in-

Table 3.1. Criteria for Determining
Reading Levels

Level	Oral reading accuracy (%)
Independent	98–100
Instructional	95–97
Borderline	90–94
Frustration	Below 90

struction as opposed to independent reading) and is based on the student's overall accuracy and fluency of word recognition. The criteria for judging whether a passage is appropriate, summarized in Table 3.1, derive from those originally recommended by Betts (1954). Betts suggests that more than 1 error for every 10 words read indicates that the material is too difficult for the student. That is, when less than 90% of a passage is read correctly, the material is at the student's frustration level. Betts recommends further that students should make no more than 1 error per 20 words on materials that are read as part of instruction. That is, when instructional support is provided, students should be able to read passages with 95% accuracy or greater. There is, thus, a borderline range of 90 to 94% accuracy. What should a teacher do when students perform in this region? Typically, students are asked to read diagnostic passages with little or no instructional support. Therefore, when students perform in the borderline range, the teacher should study the kinds of problems that are encountered to determine whether instructional support might be developed to bring the student's oral reading accuracy into the acceptable instructional range (95% accuracy or greater).

Betts recommends that materials intended for independent reading should pose very few problems for students. Specifically, he recommends that there be no more than 1 problem per 100 words read. However, this standard is based on testing that involves having students read a passage silently before they read it aloud. Thus, we recommend a slightly lower standard for oral reading on sight: no more than 2 errors per 100 words. Perhaps more important than the number of errors is evidence concerning the student's fluency. The material that a student reads independently should be sufficiently easy so that he or she reads with good intonation and phrasing.

Powell's research (Powell, 1970; Powell & Dunkeld, 1971) suggests more lenient oral reading standards for primary grade readers than those noted above. However, subsequent research (Pikulski, 1974; Ekwall, 1976) shows some inconsistency with Powell's findings. Given this inconsistency and our own clinical experience, we suggest standards that are generally in line with those originally suggested by Betts.

These criteria pertain to oral reading accuracy. Obviously, in judging the appropriateness of materials, comprehension must be considered as well. In Chapter 6, criteria for evaluating comprehension are discussed.

In determining whether a passage is of appropriate difficulty, the teacher should study the entire passage for dialect influence and for repeated errors (i.e., where a character name or word is mispronounced more than twice). It should be noted whether the student ever solves the identification of the word, especially when it is a key word. All but the first two instances of any repeated error and all dialect-influenced responses should be disregarded in further analysis.

The teacher should note the proportion of omissions, insertions, and substitutions (including mispronunciations, and responses that were later corrected) in relation to the total number of words in the passage. The total number of miscues should be divided by the total number of words in the passage to get a percentage figure. For example, if a student makes 7 miscues on a passage of 140 words, the proportion of miscues is 5%. If we then subtract the proportion of miscues from 100, we determine the proportion of the passage that was error free — in this case, 95%. The criterion scores shown in Table 3.1 should be used for judging oral reading performance. The results from this assessment of passage difficulty should be recorded on the oral reading summary form shown in Figure 3.1 in the space provided under A.

Sight Word Recognition. The teacher should separate the sight word errors from the miscues made in response to unfamiliar content words. For miscues in response to sight words, the following questions should be considered:

1. What is the proportion of sight word errors in relation to the total number of words in the passage?
2. Is the reading fluent and do these miscues distort the author's meaning?
3. Are these miscues corrected by the reader?

On the basis of this evidence, the teacher should determine whether sight word errors pose a problem and decide whether word recognition should be checked further during the follow-up probe. Sight word errors and responses should be recorded under B, on the left side of the form. If further testing is necessary, the evaluation section should not be completed until this is accomplished.

Word Identification. In order to study the student's word identification strategies, the teacher should record unfamiliar word miscues in section C of the form in the following way. First, single-syllable words should be separated from multiple-syllable words. Errors on single-syllable words should then be sorted into two groups: *(a)* those that deviate from the printed word in more than one element and *(b)* those that deviate from the

Figure 3.1. Oral reading response analysis form.

ORAL READING ANALYSIS

Name_____ Grade____ Date____

Book/Page_____ Level____

A. DIFFICULTY

____/____   _____% Correct

Level: Independent   Instructional
       Borderline   Frustration

B. WORD LEARNING: Sight Word Errors

Printed Word	Oral Response	Probe	Evaluation
___	___	___	
___	___	___	
___	___	___	
___	___	___	
___	___	___	
___	___	___	
___	___	___	

C. WORD IDENTIFICATION: Content Word Errors

Printed Word	Oral Response	Probe	Difficulty	Evaluation
___	___	___	___	Consonants_____
___	___	___	___	Blends/Digraphs_____
___	___	___	___	Vowels_____
___	___	___	___	Vowel Digraphs_____
___	___	___	___	Markers_____
___	___	___	___	Affixes_____
___	___	___	___	Syllables_____
___	___	___	___	Comments:_____
___	___	___	___	
___	___	___	___	
___	___	___	___	
___	___	___	___	
___	___	___	___	
___	___	___	___	

D. INTEGRATION – FLUENCY

Integration: _____

Fluency: Rate ____/____ = ____wpm Evaluation_____

Phrasing_____

printed word in one element only. Errors on multisyllabic words should also be separated into two groups: *(a)* those involving structural elements (i.e., common prefixes and suffixes) and *(b)* those involving other elements. Classification of miscues in this fashion makes it easier to identify patterns in a student's approach to word identification and hence facilitates further probe of word identification skills.

After the words and miscues are recorded, the teacher should examine them to identify patterns. The following questions should be considered:

1. To what extent do the errors resemble the expected response graphically? Is the reader in command of the following phonic associations: consonants, consonant blends and digraphs, vowels, and vowel digraphs? Is the function of markers understood?
2. Are miscues corrected by the reader and, if so, on what basis?
3. What does the evidence reveal about the reader's ability to identify affixes and syllables?

On the basis of this evidence, the teacher should decide whether the student has difficulty in any area of word identification and whether skill in selected areas should be explored further in the follow-up probe. When further testing is indicated, the Evaluation section on the right side of the form should not be completed until the probe has been undertaken.

Integration and Fluency. The teacher should determine whether the student's miscues evidence use of contextual information. For example, are more than half the errors contextually appropriate and does the student have and use contextually-based correction strategies? The teacher should also describe the student's reading fluency and calculate his or her reading rate. Rate is calculated by dividing the number of seconds that the student took to read the passage by 60, to get the number of minutes involved, and then dividing the number of words in the passage by the number of minutes to get a words-per-minute rate. This information should be recorded in section D of the form.

Probe: Further Testing

Often, following the oral reading analysis, questions about the strengths and weaknesses of a student's print skills remain. Some of these questions can be answered by working with the student during a second session, using probe techniques.

Basic Probe. The probe of sight words is fairly straightforward: the student should be asked to pronounce the words miscued during oral reading after they have been rewritten in list form, and the teacher should note how accurately and rapidly the student is able to respond. If the student does not recognize a word, the teacher may then treat the word as an unknown word and use the probe procedures described for content words. The first step of the probe of content words is to determine whether the student can pronounce the words that were miscued during contextual reading when they are presented in isolation. Correct reading of any of these words suggests that the student knows more about word identification than he or she is able to apply in context. Failure to use this knowledge during contextual reading sometimes results from a strategy that is highly dependent on contextual information to the neglect of graphic information. Other times it suggests that the student has become overwhelmed with the task of contextual reading. When a student identifies words in isolation that he or she is unable to recognize in context, the reading problem is one of application. That is, the student possesses the necessary knowledge, but has not yet integrated this knowledge into his or her strategy for contextual reading.

Advanced Probe.   More often, however, words that are not identified in context are also not identified in isolation. The probe of unknown content words in order to assess the student's skill in word identification then takes the form of assisting the student in his or her attempts to pronounce the tested words correctly. Basically, the procedures involve isolating parts of words in order to facilitate the student's analysis of them, varying the unit or word-part that is isolated to probe different aspects of reading skill. Using such procedures, knowledge of phonic principles, word-structure elements, blending skill, and syllabication can each be examined as necessary.

The advanced probe is quite complicated and should not be attempted until the procedures of the oral reading analysis and the basic probe are mastered. Nevertheless, the following material should be studied to learn more about how error types should be interpreted and for a general overview of procedures that can be acquired at some later time.

The advanced probe procedures differ for *(a)* errors involving multiple elements in one-syllable words, *(b)* errors involving a single element in one-syllable words, *(c)* errors involving structural elements, and *(d)* errors involving elements in multisyllabic words.

Errors involving multiple elements in one-syllable words.   Every oral reading response corresponds to the printed word in some way. Occasionally the match is only in length but usually, at the very least, the response matches the text in both length and the initial or final consonant (e.g., "day" for *deep,* "true" for *towed*). When such errors occur frequently, it is likely that word identification skills are very limited. Even when the response has more than the initial letter in common with the text (e.g., "chase" for *catch,* "snow" for *swam,* "coat" for *crowd*), if the shared letters are not in the same sequence, then word identification must still be considered quite weak. That is, when miscues of this type predominate, it is likely that they reflect a whole-word strategy — a tendency to process words as single units — rather than a letter–sound analysis. This tendency is not unexpected with younger children (first and second grades) whose instruction has emphasized whole-word learning, and in such cases it should be regarded as a developmental stage in reading acquisition rather than a weakness. With older students, however, these errors suggest an overdependence on whole-word strategies and failure to use word identification as a supplemental or alternative technique. In either case, the teacher should explore the possibility that the student actually knows many letter–sound associations as a result of specific instruction but cannot make a letter-by-letter analysis.

The general procedure to be used in exploring the knowledge a student has about letter–sound associations is as follows. The teacher directs the student's attention to a consonant that was mispronounced, then asks the student if he or she knows what sound it stands for. If the student responds correctly to a sample of 8 to 10 consonants, then his or her knowledge of letter–sound associations represents a strength that is clearly not yet functional in reading tasks. Consonant digraphs and consonant blends can be tested in the same way.

For many students who are learning to read, knowledge of letter–sound associations develops into functional reading skill through a process of consonant substitution. When a student has command of a number of letter–sound associations, even though the letter-by-letter correspondence between his or her oral responses and the printed words may be quite limited, the teacher should explore the student's skill or readiness to profit from instruction in this technique. Selecting a mispronounced word that contains a common phonogram (e.g., -ill, -an, -op), the teacher covers the first consonant and asks if the student knows a word that looks like the remaining part of the word. In the event that the student responds appropriately (with a rhyming word), the initial letter is uncovered and the student is encouraged to pronounce the word. If the student is unsuccessful, the teacher may then assist by directing attention to the sound of the initial consonant. In the event that the student does not recognize the phonogram as part of a familiar word, the teacher should pronounce it for him or her, uncover the initial letter, and ask the student to try to pronounce the word.

If the student succeeds in identifying the word in either of these situations, he or she has demonstrated the capacity to blend an initial consonant with a final phonogram; and to the extent that the student recognizes phonograms, he or she is prepared to develop the technique of consonant substitution through practice. On the other hand, if the student proves unable to identify the word after he or she (or the teacher) has identified the phonogram, the teacher should model the blending technique. The teacher pronounces first the initial consonant, then the phonogram, and finally the word itself (e.g., *f – all, fall*). Then the teacher writes another word with the same phonogram *(t – all)* on a sheet of paper and encourages the student to imitate the blending process. If the student is successful, he or she can easily be prepared for the consonant substitution technique; if not, more intensive instruction in blending will be needed.

Errors involving a single element in one-syllable words. When most errors involve only a single element in one-syllable words, greater strength in word identification is demonstrated. In such cases, the teacher should explore the student's mastery of letter – sound associations and phonic principles as distinct from his or her skill in using those associations and principles during contextual reading. A gap between the two may simply be a matter of practice and experience or may represent a more serious difficulty requiring individualized instruction.

- *Consonants and consonant digraphs.* When errors involve only a single consonant or consonant digraph *(beat – beak; shop – chop)*, it is a simple matter to explore the student's knowledge of letter – sound associations. The teacher covers the word, leaving exposed only the element that is in error, then asks the student, "What sound does this letter stand for?" If the student gives the correct sound, the teacher prompts him or her to attempt the word again, saying, "What sound should this word end [or begin] with?" . . . "What is the word?" If the student succeeds in identifying the word and can repeat that success with a few other words, the teacher may conclude that the student has strength in knowledge of letter – sound associations but is weak in his or her application of that knowledge. This is particularly likely to be the case when consonants are in error in final position but not in initial position. However, there is usually no such position bias with consonant digraph errors.

- *Consonant blends.* The procedure is similar to that outlined above. The teacher covers the word except for the blend and asks, "What sounds do these letters stand for?" If the student answers correctly, the teacher prompts him or her to try the word again. If the student cannot answer correctly, the teacher exposes only the first letter of the blend, then only the second letter, and so forth, asking each time for the sound the letter stands for. If the student knows the individual sounds, the teacher asks him or her to say them together; if the student succeeds, the teacher prompts him or her to attempt the word again.

- *Vowels.* When errors involve only vowels, the teacher must explore the student's knowledge of vowel markers as well as his or her knowledge of vowel letter – sounds. The examination of vowel letter – sounds follows the general procedure described above. If the errors are such that the short sounds of the different vowels are confused with one another *(cat – cut; fell – fill)*, then the sounds most commonly associated with each vowel may not be firmly fixed in the student's mind. The teacher probes this possibility by isolating the vowel letter (covering the letters surrounding it) and asking if the student knows a sound it stands for. If the student answers correctly, giving the vowel's short sound, the teacher then prompts him or her to make another attempt at pronouncing the word. If the student gives the long sound of the vowel — which many students do, because it coincides with the vowel name — the teacher should ask if he or she knows another sound for that letter. If the student does, he or she is encouraged to try the word again.

On the other hand, if the errors are such that each vowel is consistently associated with its short sound even in the presence of a long vowel marker (e.g., a vowel digraph such as *ai* or *oa* or a final *-e* in the pattern of CVC*e*), then the student may know only one sound for each vowel. The teacher probes this possibility with the same general procedure as outlined for short vowel confusions.

• *Markers.* If vowel errors are such that both the long and short sounds associated with each vowel are used at times but not used appropriately with vowel markers (final *-e,* vowel digraphs, *r*-controller), then the student may be confused about the situations in which one or the other sound is appropriate. On the other hand, the student may have knowledge of certain vowel markers but have difficulty monitoring for their presence while alternating with ease and fluency among the different sounds associated with each vowel letter. (Students often become habituated to the short sound for each vowel and have difficulty making the variable response function in reading tasks). Each type of marker should be examined separately. The general procedure is, as above, to isolate or point to the vowel and ask for the sound it represents. To test specific knowledge, the teacher then calls the student's attention to the marker and asks if he or she knows what function it performs. Finally, the teacher encourages the student to say the word and notes the fluency with which he or she alternates the sounds as the marker is changed. If the student is not familiar with the vowel marker as such, the teacher should explain it briefly, with examples, to determine the student's readiness to receive such instruction.

• *C and G Markers.* When a student fails to associate the letter *c* with its alternate sound correspondent (/s/) when appropriate (i.e., when *c* is followed by the letters *e, i,* or *y*), the teacher explores, first, whether the student knows that *c* has an alternate pronunciation and, second, whether he or she understands that the presence of *e, i,* or *y* is the governing condition. The teacher points to the letter *c* and asks the student to give the sound it stands for. If the student gives the phoneme /k/, the teacher asks if he or she knows another sound for the letter *c.* If the student recalls that the letter *c* sometimes stands for the *s* sound, the teacher may demonstrate and explain the principle and then ask the student to apply it to a few appropriate words, in an effort to assess how readily he or she can learn to make this new response. Errors involving the alternative sound of the letter *g* (/j/) should be dealt with in the same way.

Errors involving structural elements. A structural error involves the substitution of one affix for another or the omission of the affix while the base word is correctly identified *(brings – bringing, shipping – ship).* Only when such errors occur repeatedly should they be of concern. The teacher tries to determine whether they are caused by a lack of familiarity with particular affixes or by a failure to monitor affixes carefully while reading difficult words. The teacher covers the base word and asks the student to identify the affix. If the student recognizes the affix, the teacher suggests that he or she correct the error, although this may be done spontaneously in many cases. If the student does not recognize the affix, the teacher identifies it and asks him or her to try the word again.

Errors involving elements in multisyllabic words. Examples of such errors include "country" for *century,* "cherry" for *chimney,* "conferation" for *conversation,* "invention" for *invitation,* "coming" for *company,* and "downcade" for decade. The identification of multisyllabic words is greatly facilitated when they are broken down into smaller or even one-syllable units (provided, of course, that the student is skilled in identifying these smaller units). When errors involving multisyllabic words occur, the teacher first explores whether the student is able to divide words into pronounceable units. As a second step, to determine whether the student can pronounce syllables, the teacher covers all but the first syllable of the word. If the student identifies it, the second syllable is exposed, and so on. Finally, the student is encouraged to put the syllabic parts together to form the word.

If the student is unable to divide words into pronounceable units and the teacher's aid enables the student to succeed in identifying a number of words, then it is likely that he or she will profit from instruction in syllabication techniques. If the student lacks sufficient skill to identify the first syllable, the teacher should explore his or her mastery of letter – sound associations just as was described for one-syllable words and his or her ability to analogize from a known word to identify an unknown syllable. The division of words into syllabic units is perhaps one of the most useful features in the diagnostic probe, as it often serves to teach the skill as well as to test it.

Finally, it should be emphasized that if the informal diagnostic probe is to be of value, care and good judgment must be used. The teacher should keep within the limits of the student's patience and endurance and should avoid pursuing specific skills once it is clear that they are too difficult for the student. Only a few problem areas should be probed, with the aim of identifying where instructional focus is needed. The informal probe is *not* designed to be an inventory of known and unknown blends, digraphs, and so forth — such an inventory can be taken another time (see Appendix B). The major purpose of the informal probe will be served if the teacher becomes aware of particular skills the student needs to develop, understands the way in which the student organizes printed words, and can judge wisely where the student can profit from carefully chosen practice exercises and where he or she needs more intensive personal instruction.

Interpretation

Evidence on print-processing skill must be used together with evidence on comprehension and word knowledge in order to determine whether the student has a reading problem and, if so, in what major area(s). Oral reading response evidence alone can be interpreted to answer the following questions:

1. Does the passage represent an appropriate level of difficulty in terms of the reader's print translation skills?
2. Is the reader developing a sight vocabulary or are there problems in this area?
3. Has the reader evolved a successful strategy for identifying unknown words or is further development needed?
4a. Has the reader evolved a strategy that is based on the integrated processing of graphic and contextual information?
4b. [When few print processing problems exist, it is appropriate to pursue the final question.] Is the reader's rate of reading in accord with that of his or her classmates or are there problems of reading fluency that need correction?

Instructional Recommendations

Recommendations for instruction follow directly from the interpretation of the reading response evidence. They involve both an evaluation of the appropriateness of the current reading materials and the identification of any areas in need of instructional support. The focus of instruction should be specified along with appropriate methods and materials for the initial stages of instruction.

CASE STUDIES

The purpose of the case presentations is twofold: first, to demonstrate more concretely the procedures for diagnosing print translation skill and, second, to describe problems that occur in the acquisition of print-processing skill at three different stages of development. The first case is discussed in considerable detail; the second and third are described more briefly.

CASE 1: EVA

Eva's teacher was concerned about her lack of interest in classwork and wanted to know how she could help Eva improve her reading. For this reason, the teacher decided to analyze Eva's oral reading. Eva was 9 years, 5 months old at the time and in the second month of fifth grade. She had changed schools four times in the past four years and there was little in her record to help the teacher understand her achievement problems. It should be noted that although Eva is fluent in English, Spanish is sometimes spoken in her home.

Preparation

Eva was tested on a passage from *Discovering Treasure,* a third grade reader in The New Open Highways series (Scott Foresman). This book was being read by the lowest reading group in the class, the group to which Eva belonged. The story selected was "The Picnic Mystery." Although Eva read the entire story, only a representative portion is analyzed here. Eva was told that the story was about a boy and his uncle who was a detective. She was asked to read the story to see if she could solve the picnic mystery. Eva's oral reading, which was both tape-recorded and recorded by the teacher on a typed double-spaced copy of the story, is shown in Figure 3.2.

Oral Reading Analysis

After recording a student's oral reading and checking the accuracy of the record, the first task is always to determine whether any errors reflect dialect. In Eva's case, one error is suspicious: She tends to drop the final *s* during conversation, and here has mispronounced *Lee's* as "Lee." This was therefore not counted as a miscue. In order for an error to be counted as one of repetition, it must occur more than twice. No such errors occurred in the segment analyzed. The numbers at the right of each line in Figure 3.2 indicate the number of miscues per line. It should be noted that miscues that are subsequently corrected are nonetheless counted as errors, the reason being that they are indications of difficulty. That they were subsequently corrected is noted by a © on the oral reading analysis sheet, and these corrections are considered a sign of strength.

    Difficulty. In all, Eva committed 10 miscues while reading this portion of the story. The length of the selection is 115 words. If we divide 10 by 115 (and multiply by 100), we find the percentage of miscues, which is 9%. Accordingly, 91% of the passage is read correctly. When we compare this level of accuracy with the criteria levels in Table 3.1, we find that it falls

Figure 3.2.   Record of oral reading: Eva.
(Passage from *Discovering Treasure,* pp. 46–50, in *The New Open Highways,* published by Scott, Foresman, 1973. Story entitled "The Abandoned Picnic," from THE SECOND BAFFLE BOOK by Lassiter Wren and Randle McKay. Copyright 1929 by Doubleday & Company, Inc. Copyright 1929 by Clues, Inc. Reprinted by permission of Doubleday & Company, Inc.)

"The Picnic Mystery"

Lee's uncle was a famous detective. During the ride Lee asked him $\frac{10}{×\ 1}$ *

dozens of questions about his work. At last the detective laughed, "You ask |

more questions than I do during a police case," he said. "Let's stop and rest |

for a while."

He drove until he came to a grape group of shade several trees in a field forest. As he parked 3

the car, he saw something sparkling strange. |

Spread under one of the trees was a white paper tablecloth. Picnic food

was set out on the cloth. But there was no one in sight.

"When Where is anyone everyone?" asked Lee. "I don't see a place where anyone 2

could hide. Why was would people go off and leave their picnic?"

* Dialect-based miscues were not counted.

---

below an acceptable instructional level, in the borderline range. We can now complete section A of the oral reading analysis form (the section pertaining to passage difficulty), as shown in Figure 3.3.

Word Learning.   The next step is to record the miscues in response to sight words in the first two columns of section B of the form. (The probe and evaluation columns are completed later.) As shown in Figure 3.3, three of the miscues are in response to high-frequency words. (The Dolch Basic Sight Vocabulary, contained in Appendix A, may be used as an aid in identifying sight words.) All three miscues were corrected, apparently on the basis of subsequent contextual information. The fact that they were corrected is indicated by a © in the second column under B.

Although most of the sight words in the passage were read correctly, the three errors represent about 2% of the total passage (3/115). Because the sight word errors are few in number and because they were corrected

Figure 3.3. Analysis of oral reading responses: Eva.

ORAL READING ANALYSIS

Name *Eva W.*   Grade *5*   Date *4/15/83*

Book/Page *Discovering Treasure*   Level *gr. 3*

A. DIFFICULTY

10 / *115*   *91* % Correct   Level: Independent   Instructional
                                         (Borderline)   Frustration

B. WORD LEARNING: Sight Word Errors

Printed Word	Oral Response	Probe	Evaluation
where	when ©	✓	*Sight word errors are few in number*
everyone	anyone ©	anyone ©	*and were corrected during contextual*
would	was ©	✓	*reading. Thus, no major problem*
			exists. However, the miscues
			seemed to interfere with obtaining
			the author's meaning. Eva needs
			to consolidate her sight
			vocabulary.

C. WORD IDENTIFICATION: Content Word Errors

Printed Word	Oral Response	Probe	Difficulty	Evaluation
shade	several	should	Digraph-Vowel-Cons. © ©	Consonants *Can't produce sound / only a word*
field	forest	fill	Vowel-Blend	Blends/Digraphs
strange	sparkling	NR*	Blend-Vowel-Cons.	Vowels *Not*
case	care	care	-Cons.	Vowel Digraphs *tested*
group	grape	grape	Vowel	Markers
famous	[omitted]	NR		Affixes *Seems to know*
dozens	[omitted]	NR		Syllables *Doesn't know*
				Comments: *Eva lacks the*
				most basic knowledge of
				phonics. She seems to
				recognize words on the
				basis of visual cues and
				context. She does not
				attempt unknown
				multisyllabic words.

* NR = no response

D. INTEGRATION – FLUENCY

Integration: *Overreliance on prior context; most miscues violate author meaning. Effective use of repetitions and pauses to correct errors.*

Fluency: Rate *115* / *1.8* = *64* wpm   Evaluation *Slow – even for a second grader*

Phrasing *Rapid reading interspersed with long pauses for word recognition* spontaneously during contextual reading, we conclude that there is no major problem in this area. However, the fact that such errors were made at all suggests that Eva has not consolidated her sight vocabulary.

Word Identification.   The next step is to record in section C miscues in response to unfamiliar content words. We begin first with miscues that deviate from single-syllable printed words in several elements, followed by those that deviate in a single element, then with errors that reflect a problem in affixation, and finally with miscues in response to multisyllabic words. Errors of omission are then listed following the substitution errors, as shown in Figure 3.3. In contrast to sight word recognition, Eva makes no successful corrections of unfamiliar content words.

Three of the seven miscues deviate from the printed word in more than one element and involve substitution of multisyllable for single-syllable words. The next two miscues, which show a close correspondence, are also in response to single-syllable words. Finally, Eva omits rather than attempts two words that are two syllables in length. This pattern of response suggests that Eva has serious difficulty in word identification.

Although almost all Eva's miscues show an initial consonant match, she erred on two of three initial consonant blends and digraphs. Vowels in miscued words are more often mispronounced than not, and she seems to have no knowledge of vowel digraphs and markers. The nature of the mismatch that occurs for each miscue is recorded under "Difficulty" in the fourth column of C. Affixed words were, however, an area of strength, with *laughed, during, asked,* and *parked* all correctly pronounced. Overall, the evidence suggests little skill in word identification. This possibility should be explored through a follow-up probe with the miscued words.

Integration and Fluency.   Eva is lacking in integration, in that she relies heavily on context in identifying unknown content words. With few exceptions, her substitutions in response to content words are plausible with respect to prior sentence context, but they show low correspondence with print. Although Eva shows an effective use of repetition to correct sight word errors, she is unable to correct her content word miscues.

Her reading is not fluent, as it is characterized by many pauses before unfamiliar words. She read this portion of the story in 108 seconds. By dividing the number of seconds by 60, we get a time of 1.8 minutes, as shown in Figure 3.3. By then dividing the number of words in the passage — namely, 115 — by 1.8, we determine Eva's reading rate — 64 words per minute.

This rate is extremely slow; it is even below the average range for second-graders shown in Table 2.1. We would expect, however, that Eva's rate would be faster on easier materials that posed fewer word identification problems for her. Because word identification difficulties are seriously interfering with her reading fluency, we will not make further exploration of this aspect of her reading at this time. Rather, the probe will focus on the development of her sight vocabulary and her word identification skills.

Probe and Interpretation

Sight Words. Eva's response to the three sight words that she missed during contextual reading was rapid. Further, all but one of the sight words was pronounced correctly, (indicated by a check in the third column of B), and when she was asked to look at *everyone* again, she was able to recognize it.

The results from the probe suggest that Eva knows most basic sight words, even if she at times confuses certain similar sight words. These results support the hypothesis that Eva's main problem in word learning is not in knowing the words but, rather, in being able to recognize them quickly when under the pressure of difficult contextual reading. Eva needs to consolidate her existing set of sight words through contextual reading of easy materials as summarized under "Evaluation" in B.

Word Identification. Most of the probe focused on Eva's ability to deal with unfamiliar content words. As shown in Figure 3.3, when words that were miscued during contextual reading were presented in isolation, Eva was still unable to recognize them.

During the probe that followed, she was first asked to respond to initial consonants, in order to confirm their apparent effectiveness as a cue system. Surprisingly, she experienced extreme difficulty producing the sounds that corresponded to the initial consonant letters identified. This finding suggests that she uses initial consonants as effective visual cues to search for known words in her memory but not as elements that cue an appropriate initial sound.

Because of her extreme difficulty with initial consonants, no further probe was undertaken at this time to assess her knowledge of other letter–sound associations. That will come later, once initial consonants become an explicit part of her knowledge about print. Further probing did reveal that with support, Eva is able to segment off the initial phoneme of a known word. This is probably the point from which instruction should begin.

Assessment of Eva's knowledge of the structural characteristics of words revealed that she is familiar with most common word endings (e.g., -ing, -ed, -er, -est). She has no knowledge about how to segment multisyllabic words into pronounceable units. However, when some of the words were divided for her, she was able to pronounce a few syllables correctly because they resembled known words. This facility suggests that Eva may be able to use her relatively well-developed sight vocabulary to help her identify syllables through an analogizing procedure.

Instructional Plan

Reading Materials. Eva should be reading from materials at two levels of difficulty. First, in order to consolidate her sight vocabulary, material should be at a level that poses few word identification problems. Whether second-grade-level materials would be appropriate for this purpose needs to be established. Second, Eva's teacher should experiment with instructional support prior to and during the reading of basal stories in order to determine whether the current (third-grade) materials can be used. It is important to keep Eva involved in ongoing class activities if at all possible. However, if the third-grade basal materials are still too difficult with instructional support, the teacher will need to establish an individual reading program for Eva with somewhat easier materials.

Sight Vocabulary. Eva's sight vocabulary is quite well developed, as indicated by the large number of sight words she recognized during contextual reading and the fact that she was able to recognize all miscued sight words correctly when they were presented in isolation. However, the fact that she miscues on sight words during contextual reading means that they are not yet learned to the level of immediate and automatic recognition. In order to consolidate her sight vocabulary, Eva should be encouraged to read easy, highly interesting materials. Charts should be kept to let Eva see her reading progress.

Word Identification. Eva's teacher will focus on three objectives in the area of word identification: (a) making explicit Eva's knowledge of initial consonant associations, (b) developing procedures for helping Eva divide multisyllabic words into pronounceable chunks, and (c) developing strategies for pronouncing syllables. The teacher will work with Eva individually to achieve the first goal, since all other members of Eva's reading group already possess this knowledge. The other two objectives will be worked on as part of small group reading instruction in conjunction with the introduction of unfamiliar words.

As a first step in helping Eva acquire explicit knowledge of consonant correspondences, her teacher will pronounce words and have her listen to them and identify their component sounds. Once Eva is aware of the phonemic composition of words, the teacher will present known sight words, all beginning with the same consonant, in order to have Eva identify the initial consonant correspondent. If Eva has difficulty remembering the consonant association, it might be helpful to have her select a key word as a means to retrieve the phoneme. For example, if she has difficulty remembering the phoneme corresponding to *d*, she might use the key word of *dance*. Whenever she sees a *d*, she can think of *dance* and abstract the initial sound. Typically, this sort of memory aid is not needed for many consonants and where needed is not needed for long.

Teaching syllabication and syllable pronunciation can easily be incorporated into small group reading instruction. After introducing a new story but before reading it, the teacher should present any unfamiliar content words. Using certain of these words, the teacher can conduct the following two-part exercise. The words are written on the board, one at a time. After a word is written, students should speculate about how it might be divided into "chunks" that can be pronounced. A line should be drawn after each chunk and the teacher should proceed to the right until the word has been completely divided. Even when the final product does not conform exactly to what is specified by rules for syllabication, the teacher should proceed to the task of pronouncing the syllables. If students wish to revise their prior decisions, they should be allowed to do so.

The second part of this exercise consists of teaching analogizing. After examining the first chunk, the students are asked if it looks like any word they know. This word should then be written above the syllable to see if students can use it to identify the syllable. If they are unable to think of a word, the teacher should supply one or provide the phonogram with which the syllable ends as an alternative. The students should then use a consonant substitution (word family) approach to identify the syllable. Correct and incorrect attempts should be presented to the group for their evaluation.

This procedure can be used for three or four of the multisyllabic words appearing in the story or as long as the attention of the group is sustained. Other unfamiliar words should simply be pronounced by the teacher, as part of a discussion of the meaning of all unfamiliar words and how they pertain to the theme of the story.

Integration and Fluency. Eva's overreliance on contextual information indicates that integration is a problem for her. Her difficulty stems from the lack of a proper balance between the use of contextual information and attention to graphic information. Therefore, integration should be reexamined as she develops greater proficiency with word identification.

Eva read this third-grade material at an extremely slow rate. It is appropriate to emphasize fluency only with much easier materials that pose no word identification problems for her. In fact, the easy reading she does to consolidate her sight vocabulary may have the consequence of improving her reading rate and fluency.

CASE 2: ANN

We now consider the case of a younger child. Ann, now in second grade, has experienced considerable difficulty learning to read. Whereas Eva had little difficulty learning basic sight words, Ann's major problem is in this area.

Ann's teacher was confused by her slow reading progress and decided to undertake a more detailed analysis of her print-translation skills in order to determine how she might help her make better progress. Ann currently reads with the lowest reading group in a departmentalized grade two and three reading program. The group reads from a first-grade primer, *Sun and Shadow* from the Bookmark Reading Program (Harcourt Brace Jovanovich). There are ten students in the group. Three of them, including Ann, are having particular difficulty learning to read.

Preparation

Ann was tested on a story from her reader entitled "Sun Down." She was asked to read only the first two pages of the story because she is not used to reading more at one time and reading is, for her, a frustrating experience. The sample of her reading shown in Figure 3.4 is typical of her oral reading during small group instruction. Before proceeding, the reader is encouraged to examine the oral reading record in Figure 3.4 in accordance with the procedures described on page 42ff. First of all, a decision should be made as to whether the passage is of appropriate difficulty. Next, basic sight words should be separated from unfamiliar content words. Names of characters should be treated as content words. The reader should then draw some tentative conclusions about Ann's sight recognition and word identification skills. Finally, it is important to consider Ann's fluency and integration and also to decide whether these areas can be properly assessed when the reading material poses so many problems.

Oral Reading Analysis, Probe, and Interpretation

Once this analysis is completed, the reader should compare his or her results with the corresponding parts of Figure 3.5.

Difficulty. Ann made 20 substitutions and 1 omission when she read the passage. However, 2 of the substitutions were not counted because they were the third occurrence of a miscue. This means that only 72% of the passage was read correctly; clearly the story is too difficult for her given her current knowledge of print translation.

Word Learning. Of the 19 words that were counted as miscues, 14 were basic sight words. These words alone account for 21% of the passage. This high proportion of sight word errors indicates that Ann is having considerable difficulty in the initial stages of learning to read. She is confusing a substantial proportion of the function words, which account for about 70% of the text.

Although Ann has developed an understanding that each printed word has an aural counterpart, she has not identified the cues that constitute reliable information in word identification. Thus, of the miscues on

Figure 3.4. Record of oral reading: Ann.
(Passage from "Sun Down" in SUN AND SHADOW, *HBJ Bookmark Reading Program*, Second Edition by Elizabeth K. Cooper, copyright © 1974 by Harcourt Brace Jovanovich, Inc. Reprinted by permission of the publisher.)

"Sun Down"

19

Down, down, down went the sun.

The sun went down in the \sky. [*Key*] |

The sun went down ~~over~~ the pond. [*for*] |

The sun went down ~~over~~ the hill. [*for*] (

The afternoon was ~~over~~. [*down*] + o*

\\ ~~Jill~~ was at ~~Stan's~~ house. [*Jan*] [*night*] 2

~~Stan~~\and Jill sat on the grass. [*happy*] |

~~They~~ looked up at\the sky. [*When*] [*Jan key*] 3

"The sun ~~is~~ down," ~~said~~ Stan. [*see*] [*for*] 2

"~~It will~~ get dark." [*then was good*] 3

"Yes," ~~said~~ Jill. [*did*] |

"~~It will~~ get dark(fast)" [*see the did*] 4

* Miscues occurring more than twice were not counted

sight words, 6 matched the printed word in neither the initial nor final consonant. One word *(fast)* was not attempted, and two miscues ("see" for *is*, "them" for *it*) may have been cued from the end of the printed word. The remaining 5 substitutions did show a match in either the beginning (e.g., "was" for *will*, "good" for *get*) or end ("did" for *said*, "for" for *over*). It is clear from this analysis that Ann is having considerable difficulty learning sight words. However, as indicated by her correct recognition of some sight words, she has made some progress.

The results from the probe indicate that Ann was able to recognize

Figure 3.5. Analysis of oral reading responses: Ann.

ORAL READING ANALYSIS

Name _Ann M._ Grade _2_ Date _1/30/83_
Book/Page _Sun & Shadow_ Level _gr. 1 (primer_

A. DIFFICULTY

_19_ / _67_   _72_ % Correct

Level: Independent Instructional
Borderline (Frustration)

B. WORD LEARNING: Sight Word Errors

Printed Word	Oral Response	Probe	Evaluation
they	When	NR *	_Sight words are a major problem._
the	Jan	✓	_Only two of 15 words are cued_
is	see	✓	_by the initial consonant and_
said	for		_these are inconsistently known._
said	did	NR	
it	then		_However, some sight words_
it	see	✓	_seem to be known (e.g.,_
will	was		_down, went, the, was, dark)._
will	the	was	
get	good		
get	did	NR	
② over	for	NR	
fast	[omitted]	NR	

* NR = no response

C. WORD IDENTIFICATION: Content Word Errors

Printed Word	Oral Response	Probe	Difficulty	Evaluation
② sky	Key	NR	Beg.+Middle	Consonants _Seems to know_
Jill	Jan	NR	Middle + End	Blends/Digraphs _Doesn't know_
Stan's	night	NR	Little	Vowels ⎫
Stan	happy		Correspondence	Vowel Digraphs ⎬ Not tested
				Markers ⎭
				Affixes _Doesn't know_
				Syllables _Not tested_
				Comments: _Not much_
				about phonic and structural
				analysis is known – but
				not much has been
				taught in this area.

D. INTEGRATION – FLUENCY

Integration: _Cannot assess given the difficulty of the material._

Fluency: Rate _67_ / _2.3_ = _29_ wpm Evaluation _Low-average for first grade_
Phrasing _Many pauses, poor intonation_

only 3 out of 9 words that she did not know during contextual reading *(the, is, it)*. The 6 errors (including omissions) on sight words presented in isolation confirm that she is having considerable difficulty in word recognition.

Word Identification. Ann seems to have an easier time with the content words in the passage *(sun, pond, hill, afternoon, house, grass)* than with the function words. Other than the names of characters, she missed only one content word — *sky*. Moreover, both the word *sky* and the character names were new words, introduced for the first time in this story. In general, her content word miscues resemble those of basic sight words in terms of their degree of letter – sound correspondence.

During the probe of word parts, Ann correctly identified all initial consonants tested *(s, j, w, g, f)*. However, she knew neither the blends nor the digraph tested *(sk, st, th)*. Vowels, vowel markers, and vowel digraphs have not yet been taught to her and, therefore, they were not tested. Limited testing of affixed words was done. She pronounced both *looked* and *looking* as "look" even though during contextual reading, she pronounced *looked* correctly. Syllabication was not tested. The probe shows that her knowledge of phonic and structural analysis is limited but is in accord with what she has been taught. However, she does not apply the knowledge that she does possess (initial consonant associations) in word recognition and identification.

Integration and Fluency. Ann's miscues show little integration of graphic and contextual information in the recognition of words. She reads in an extremely halting manner, with many long pauses. Her serious difficulty in word recognition causes her rate of reading to be extremely slow. However, it is not really possible to draw conclusions about the development of her contextual reading strategies. Because of the number of errors that she made, there is little intact context on which she might rely. Generally, when passages are at a student's frustration level, it is inappropriate to examine the degree to which substitutions are contextually appropriate and whether they are corrected.

Instructional Plan

Reading Materials. Ann is currently reading at the primer level in first-grade materials. As these materials are at her frustration level, a change must be made in the materials that she uses.

Instruction. Every so often, a teacher will encounter a student who is experiencing extreme difficulty learning to read. In the early stages of reading this problem is often manifested in an inability to remember sight words. When this occurs, it is important that the teacher refer the student to an experienced reading clinician for more detailed diagnostic analysis and teaching. In Ann's case, at least a part of her reading instruction will have to be individual and the classroom program can be designed to reinforce this individual instruction.

Because Ann has been experiencing extreme difficulty for over a year, it is important that her parents be notified so that they can work together with the school in implementing a more effective instructional plan. There are limits to what classroom teachers can provide in the form of individual instruction, as their main responsibility must be to provide quality instruction for all students in their class. However, teachers *are* responsible for knowing when a problem is severe and when outside help is required for the design of effective instruction.

CASE 3: STAN

The final case to be discussed is that of a junior high student. The other two cases, Eva and Ann, were experiencing difficulty in the basic print translation areas — word learning and word identification. Stan's major problem, by contrast, is in neither of these areas, even though a cursory examination of his oral reading record might suggest otherwise.

Stan is an eighth-grade student who lives in an affluent suburb. He achieves well below average in his school, and usually students in his academic situation suffer greatly in this achievement-oriented community. At various times during his schooling, he has received remedial help in reading. Unfortunately, there has been little evidence of application of newly learned strategies. Stan's reading teacher has decided to examine his reading, in order to see whether he is applying the skills that they have been working on and to determine whether a new set of materials are appropriate for Stan's subsequent reading instruction.

Preparation

Stan read a selection entitled "Two American Girls in a Turkish Jail," from *Topics for the Restless* (Jamestown Publishers). According to the Raygor Readability Measure, this selection is of ninth-grade-level difficulty. A portion of the record of Stan's oral reading is shown in Figure 3.6. His oral reading was frequently unsteady and his voice often lacked expression. The reader should examine the record in order to draw tentative conclusions about the difficulty level of the passage and the development of Stan's sight vocabulary, word identification strategies, and fluency.

Oral Reading Analysis, Probe, and Interpretation

Before proceeding, the reader should compare his or her analysis with the summary of the results from the analysis shown in Figure 3.7. As can be seen, Stan had difficulty with only two types of words: a small number of sight words and multisyllabic words.

Figure 3.6.   Record of oral reading: Stan.
(Passage from *Topics for the Restless* (BROWN series), by Edward Spargo (Ed.) pp. 73–75. Providence, R. I.: Jamestown Publishers, 1974. [Originally published in *People* Magazine, 1974, Time Inc.])

"Two American Girls in a Turkish Jail"

/2

con finedent② ©
confined①   Cal–
At first the girls were ~~confident~~, even ~~cavalier~~, pressing close to the   2

© s
barred window_∧of their cell to smile for a guard who wanted to take their   /

picture. Then came the shock of the verdict: the young tourists from Amer-
McDayel ←
ica, Kathy Zenz and JoAnn ~~McDaniel~~, were found guilty last December of   /
← hashes
smuggling ~~hashish~~ into Turkey. Their penalty: death, later commuted to life |

imprisonment.

Kathy and JoAnn are among the 1,000 or more Americans — largely
young ful   the
~~youthful~~ white and middle class/— currently being held ~~in~~ jails overseas on   2

various drug charges. There are fifteen others in Turkey alone. Most are
© have②
are①
serving relativ(ly)short/terms of five or ten years, but Kathy and JoAnn ~~had~~   2

the misfortune to be arrested shortly after the United States had brought
the
pressure to bear on the Turkish government to crack down on ~~that~~ country's |
Opinyum
~~opium~~ trade, one of its principal cash crops. The Turkish courts were in no |
© lenent
mood to be ~~lenient~~ toward Americans. |

Difficulty. While oral reading affords the opportunity to observe how well Stan translates print, his nervousness may have increased the number of errors that he made. Thus, while the analysis may accurately reflect the strengths of his print processing, it may underestimate his general proficiency. However, on the basis of this oral reading sample, this selection seems to be of borderline difficulty. Clearly, the material is too difficult for him to read without initial preparation.

Sight Words. Stan missed three sight words or slightly less than 2% of the words in the portion of the selection analyzed. Two of the three did not distort the author's meaning and the third was corrected. On the basis of this evidence it is concluded that sight word learning and recognition of

Figure 3.7. Analysis of oral reading responses: Stan.

ORAL READING ANALYSIS

Name _Stan G_ Grade _8_ Date _2/15/83_

Book/Page _Topics for the_ Level _9 (?)_
Restless, p. 73

A. DIFFICULTY

_12_ / _157_ _92_ % Correct

Level: Independent Instructional
(Borderline) Frustration

B. WORD LEARNING: Sight Word Errors

Printed Word	Oral Response	Probe	Evaluation
in	the	⎫	_Although an occasional sight_
had	are/have ©	Not tested	_word miscue is not contextually_
that	the	⎭	_appropriate, sight word errors_
			are few in number and tend
			not to interfere with meaning.
			Thus, sight words do not
			pose a problem.

C. WORD IDENTIFICATION: Content Word Errors

Printed Word	Oral Response	Probe	Difficulty	Evaluation
window	windows ©	✓		Consonants ⎫
youthful	youngful	✓		Blends/Digraphs ⎬ No
relatively	relative	✓		Vowels ⎪ problem
confident	confined/confinedent	con-fi-'dent	accent vowel	Vowel Digraphs ⎭
cavalier	cal - ©	✓		Markers ⎭
McDaniel	McDayel	McDayneel	vowel	Affixes _Some difficulty in context_
hashish	hashes	✓		Syllables _OK in isolated words_
opium	opinyum	opinyum	consonant inserted	Comments: _Stan has_
lenient	lenent ©	✓		_well-developed word_
				identification strategies,
				particularly with isolated
				words. May need
				practice applying this
				knowledge during
				contextual reading.

D. INTEGRATION – FLUENCY

Integration: _Many nonsense word miscues; most other miscues are contextually appropriate. Many repetitions - to make corrections and to get meaning_

Fluency: Rate _157_ / _1.92_ = _82_ wpm Evaluation _Slow - caused by pauses for word inden_

Phrasing _Not fluent - poor intonation and phrasing_

sight words in context do not pose problems for Stan. Accordingly, no further probe of this area is necessary.

Word Identification. As noted earlier, Stan had no difficulty with one-syllable words. Three of nine miscues of multisyllabic words involved affixed words. In one ("windows" for *window*) an affix was added and then corrected; in a second ("relative" for *relatively*) the ending was omitted; and in the third, ("youngful" for *youthful*) the root word was miscued. It is surprising that the second and third were not corrected, on the basis of contextual information *(relatively)* or vocabulary knowledge *(youthful).*

The remaining six miscues of multisyllabic words represent minor deviations from the printed words, and two of these were corrected *(cavalier, lenient).* The degree of correspondence suggests well-developed word identification skills. Nevertheless, in order to confirm this assumption, Stan was asked to identify the nine words in isolation. He correctly identified six of them and, in the process, demonstrated a highly refined application of his print-processing strategies. Two of the words he failed to identify — *McDaniel* and *opium* — were words that were unfamiliar to him. The fact that *opium* is not a familiar term suggests that word knowledge (vocabulary) may be a more general problem and one that interferes with his word identification. While he derives a close phonemic approximation, because many words are only vaguely familiar to him he may have difficulty making a match — particularly under the pressure of contextual reading.

The analysis of Stan's word identification skill reveals well-developed knowledge of phonic and structural analysis. However, he is less proficient in the application of this knowledge. This difficulty may simply reflect lack of practice; more likely, it also reflects inadequate word knowledge. Such a deficit could pose a problem not only in the identification of specific words, but also in the general comprehension of a selection (see Chapters 4, 5, and 6).

Integration and Fluency. The analysis indicates that many of Stan's miscues are not contextually appropriate (many are nonwords) and that in spite of this, he only rarely corrects miscues. He reads extremely slowly, with many short pauses and repetitions. While the function of these may be for word identification, they also seem to reflect an attempt to clarify the meaning of phrases. Evidence on comprehension and word knowledge is particularly crucial for determining the basis for Stan's lack of fluency. If comprehension is adequate, then the fluency problem would appear to result from lack of reading practice. On the other hand, if comprehension is inadequate because of limited word knowledge, then further assessment of Stan's reading integration and fluency should be undertaken with easier materials.

Further testing using procedures described in the next three chapters did reveal that Stan's knowledge of vocabulary contained in the selection was inadequate, as was his comprehension. Nevertheless, even on materials (eighth-grade level) that posed no vocabulary difficulties, Stan's oral reading showed many of the same pause and repetition characteristics and his rate of silent reading, though somewhat faster, was normal for fourth- or fifth-grade readers. Thus, we may conclude that Stan's reading fluency needs to be improved through extensive practice with easier material.

Instructional Plan

Stan's immediate instruction should focus on two objectives: *(a)* the development of reading integration and fluency, and *(b)* the development of word knowledge to facilitate comprehension.

Difficulty.   Stan's reading materials should be on two levels of difficulty: extremely interesting materials on the sixth- or seventh-grade level and materials on the eighth- or ninth-grade level (such as that used for the initial testing) for the development of word knowledge.

Integration and Fluency.   It is particularly important to find materials that match with Stan's interests and that are easy enough so as not to pose any print-processing problems. Stan should be encouraged to keep his attention on the meaning of the story or article and increase his reading rate. Techniques for directing students' attention to the meaning are described in Chapter 6.

The best way to encourage rapid reading is to have the student keep track of how many minutes it takes him to read a 10- or 20-page selection and then to record this figure on a chart. Thus, if Stan reads an established number of pages each day and records the time it takes, over a period of weeks his reading rate should improve. To focus on comprehension, he could be asked to retell interesting portions of the selection.

Word Knowledge.   Procedures for the development of word knowledge are described in the next chapter.

SUMMARY

As this chapter includes a great deal of information, it should be referred to and read closely until the procedures become well learned. In order to master these procedures, it will be necessary to reread sections while diagnosing the reading problems of individual students. The case presentation of Stan clearly shows the difficulty involved in trying to assess print translation skill without examining word knowledge and comprehension at the same time. In the next chapters, we consider these important topics.

4

Vocabulary Knowledge

Words are the basic units of meaning in a language. It seems self-evident, therefore, that understanding a message which is made up of words should require some degree of familiarity with those words. And in fact, when we examine the relationship between word knowledge and reading comprehension, we typically find a very high correlation (Davis, 1968; Thorndike, 1973). Yet recent attempts to demonstrate a simple causal relation between knowledge of specific words and the comprehension of texts containing those words have not been uniformly successful. Markedly increasing the number of difficult words in a text leads to poorer comprehension, just as decreasing the number of difficult words leads to better comprehension (Wittrock, Marks, & Doctorow, 1975); but teaching students the difficult words before reading does not necessarily result in comprehension gains (Jenkins, Pany, & Schreck, 1978; Tuinman & Brady, 1974). One explanation of this latter result is that knowing words well enough to select appropriate synonyms on a multiple-choice vocabulary test is not necessarily sufficient for the comprehension of discourse. The reader must also be somewhat familiar with the cultural context or domain of knowledge in which the words occur. For example, a high school student may know that a geologist studies the history of the earth through its rock formations; but this student will have difficulty comprehending the function of a geologist on a deep-sea expedition unless he or she is also aware of recent technological advances that make it possible to study the earth beneath the ocean floor. Thus, it is important to recognize a distinction between word knowledge as traditionally conceived (and measured) and the cultural or general knowledge that may be necessary for understanding a given text. This distinction is somewhat analogous to the difference between a dictionary and an encyclopedia, between a definition and a full-fledged concept. Nevertheless, it is through words that readers gain access to their relevant stores of knowledge — their mental encyclopedias as well as their mental dictionaries — and through them that we assess that knowledge in diagnosing comprehension difficulties.

When a student fails to show good comprehension of a diagnostic passage and print translation is not the primary source of difficulty, the problem can often be traced to lack of familiarity with a particular word or words. In this chapter we will discuss and illustrate some procedures for investigating this possibility. But first we will offer some general insights into the nature of words and meanings and provide an overview of the "state of the art" of teaching word meanings.

WORDS, MEANINGS, AND CONCEPTS

The words of a language comprise its *lexicon*. Different languages have different lexicons in the sense that they use different sequences of *sounds* (phonemes) to express the same *meanings*. But languages also differ in the meanings or concepts, the aspects of experience, that they have words for, reflecting the different concerns and interests of the communities that speak them. For this reason, the lexicon of a language is never static. Words are constantly being added to express new thoughts and conditions; and some words fall into disuse while others undergo changes in primary meaning or intent. In a very real sense, the lexicon is an inventory of the concepts available to a language community, a map of the categories into which reality has been segmented and organized. For, though words are the names we give to objects and actions, events and experiences, and so on, this naming activity involves, in the first place, the construction of concepts that determine the way in which the environment is subdivided into parts and the parts grouped into categories. For example, in English we divide the color spectrum in such a way that the colors blue and green are placed into separate categories designated by the words *blue* and *green*. Other languages, however, do not distinguish between the colors blue and green and use a single word to designate this portion of the color spectrum. To take another example, some languages have words for individual kinds of trees but lack a general term for the entire class analogous to the English term *tree* (Langacker, 1973). These differences are not just linguistic curiosities. They reflect differences in the categorization of experience and illustrate the important principle that the categories of objects, actions, and properties labeled by words are not "given" by the nature of things. That is, these categories do not present themselves directly to the senses. They are, rather, a manifestation of the human capacity for analyzing and organizing the world of experience and "reifying" that organization in words (Bronowski & Bellugi, 1970).

Words and Meanings

What does it mean to know a word in the lexicon? It means, first of all, knowing how the word sounds when it is spoken and, in the case of literate speakers, how it looks in printed or written form. Proficient readers occasionally have the latter knowledge but not the former. We have all had the experience of discovering, upon hearing a word for the first time after years of encountering it in print, that it is pronounced quite differently from what we had thought. Bolinger (1968) cites the following example: "When someone pronounces *pulpit* to rime with *gulp it,* it is a fair inference that he did not acquire the word from hearing it [p. 95]." The spoken or printed form of a word provides direct access to the listener/reader's stored knowledge of its meaning. That is, the pairing of word with meaning is virtually instantaneous.

Second, knowing a word means knowing the aspect of reality to which it refers — which entities in the universe of entities it serves as a verbal label for. In the case of a noun, this means knowing the objects or ideas, persons, and places to which it refers. In the case of a verb, it means knowing the actions it denotes. And, in the case of adjectives and adverbs, it means knowing the qualities of objects and actions which these words designate. When we tell students that a *snare* is a trap or that a *squabble* is a quarrel, we are identifying the real-world referents of these words, the known objects or ideas they name (on the assumption that traps and quarrels are familiar as real-world entities).

Yet, it should be clear that words are not simply verbal labels for particular experiences or individual segments of reality. They are, rather, labels for *categories* of things. The child who believes that the word *dog* refers only to the family pet does not know the meaning of the word, for that entails understanding that the word applies to all other animals of a similar kind.

To be sure, we use words to refer to specific things — the *car* we drive, the *meal* we ate, the *anger* we feel. That is their central function, enabling us to talk of things in their absence, of events in the past or future, of thoughts and feelings that cannot be seen. But the meaning of a word is not so much embodied in its referents as in the attributes of its referents that are criterial in distinguishing them from the referents of other words. That is, it consists of the properties that determine whether something is or is not an instance of a category. The meaning of the word *story,* for example, does not begin and end with any particular story, or type of story, or even all the stories in the world. It consists, rather, of what a thing must be like in order to be considered a story, as distinguished, for example, from a poem or essay.

There is a sense, then, in which words are verbal labels for specific entities. This is their referential, or *extensive,* meaning. And there is a sense in which words stand for the defining attributes of classes of things. This is their *intensive* meaning (Anglin, 1977). But, of course, the one implies the other. When we use a word to refer to a specific thing (its extensive meaning), we identify that thing as a member of a category and so attribute to it the properties common to all members of that category (its intensive meaning). When we refer to an object as a *chair,* we mean that it is like all other chairs in certain essential respects. When we refer to that same object as an *armchair,* we give it some additional characteristics not shared by all chairs. And when we refer to it as *furniture,* we exclude those qualities that distinguish it from tables, beds, and so forth. We could even refer to it as *junk,* giving it an entirely different set of attributes.

Because words have both intensive and extensive meanings, the act of using them to name things is more than a matter of convenience in talking about things. It provides a "shorthand" for communicating information. This was illustrated above in the possibility of referring to a chair as *junk.* Similarly, in telling a child that a certain strange-looking animal is a *dog,* we make available much information that is not immediately apparent — for example, that it barks, chases cats, and chews on bones. By the same token, if someone tells us that an object we are unfamiliar with is a *fruit,* we immediately know that it is edible and grows on plants (Anglin, 1977).

The notion of words as designating categories of referents is relatively clear-cut in the case of common nouns. We are accustomed to organizing "persons, places, and things" into hierarchical systems according to their shared properties (e.g., animal → human → adult — child). But a moment's reflection makes it evident that verbs are also category labels. The verb *build,* for example, may refer to a baby in relation to blocks, a brick-layer in relation to a wall, an entrepreneur in relation to customer goodwill, and so on. It is a generic term for actions that are different in many ways but alike in terms of the meaning of *build,* to construct something from elementary parts. To illustrate with a less obvious example, even the simple act of walking differs from time to time for each individual and from one individual to another, so that the verb *walk* actually designates a range of locomotive behavior.

Adjectives also refer to categories. The *red* of one apple is different from that of others; oranges and apples are two different forms of *round;* and a *happy* coincidence and a *happy* child are different varieties of *happy.* In the process of segmenting reality into manipulable parts and naming them, we necessarily ignore much detail. Otherwise, the number of words needed to map reality would become unmanageable. More importantly, words could cease to serve an important function of naming, which is to establish the equivalence among items in a class (Bolinger, 1968).

What we have described thus far as the meaning of a word may be seen as closely akin to what dictionaries attempt to record. The typical dictionary definition gives the essential properties of a category of objects, actions, or qualities, which may be used to identify word referents, or instances of that category. And it does this in a most economical way, by naming the extensive, or superordinate, category to which the word referents belong and then setting forth the special characteristics that distinguish them within this more extensive category. This system eliminates the need for specifying for each word the properties of the extensive category to which it belongs.

That word meanings and (dictionary-type) definitions are more or less coterminous, at least in common parlance, is nowhere more evident than in the responses people make to questions about meaning. When adults are asked "What does —— mean?" or "What is (a) —— ?" they most commonly use the dictionary format — that is, they name the superordinate and the differentiating features, or give a word with similar meaning (a synonym). Students aged 9 or 10 also use this definitional form more often than any other (and this tendency increases with age). Younger children, on the other hand, are most likely to define words in terms of function or salient physical characteristics. Thus, an adult will say that *straw* is "dried grass," *gown* is a "long dress," and *orange* is "a fruit," whereas a young child will say of *straw*, "It's yellow"; of a *gown*, "You wear it, what you sleep in"; and of an *orange*, "You eat it." Similarly, a young child will say that *puddle* is "what you step in," while an older child will say that it is a "small pool of water" or "water that gathers after a rain." An explanation type of response (e.g., *skill* is "being able to do something"; *priceless* means "worth a lot of money") is infrequent among younger children but occurs at age 11 or 12 as the second most frequent response though still considerably less frequent than the superordinate or synonym response (Feifel & Lorge, 1950).

It has long been believed that these age-related differences in definitional form reflect developmental changes in conceptual processes. Accordingly, "functional" definitions, which seem to be more personal, less generalized, than explanations, superordinates, and synonyms, are considered less mature. However, Anglin (1977) points out that adults and older children often include use, or function, in their definitions, "the difference being that children mention only use whereas adults mention a superordinate category as well [p. 21]." Nelson (1974) has also argued that function is an important aspect of word meaning for adults as well as children. Moreover, all types of definitions are found at all ages, and the shift from predominantly functional to categorical meanings is a gradual one (Wolman & Barker, 1965). If the form in which children defined words were primarily a manifestation of their "stage" of cognitive development, each stage being qualitatively different from the preceding one, we would expect the transition from one form to another to be more sudden. It may be that children's definitions gradually become more like those of adults mainly as a reflection of their gradually increasing knowledge about the nature and origin of things. In other words, as children gain in knowledge of where things come from and how they are made, their definitions are likely to include such information. After all, one must know that straw *is* dried grass in order to define it that way.

An alternative explanation for the fact that children do not typically give superordinate terms when asked to define a word is that many superordinate terms are not frequently used and are, therefore, not known to them (Cocks, 1974). Thus, when asked to define such words as *robin, apple,* and *dog,* a large majority of children are likely to give "mature" definitions (e.g., "A robin is a bird."), because the superordinate terms for these objects are well known. In contrast, when defining words with low-frequency superordinate terms (e.g., *pencil, umbrella, cup*), children are likely to use "semantically empty" superordinates, such as *something* (e.g., "A pencil is something to write with."). Cocks argues that definitions that take this latter form reflect a high level of understanding of the requirements of the definitional task.

Meanings and Concepts

We tend to think of concepts as precisely formulated ideas concerning the essential attributes of classes of things. This tendency stems in part from the close association between concepts and scientific thought and also from a long tradition in psychological research. In this tradition, concepts are generally considered to involve a limited set of stable features (e.g., red geometric figures that have four sides and are surrounded by dots). However, it is mainly scientific concepts that are so well defined. Most "natural" concepts — the ones we use in everyday thought and action — do not have clear-cut boundaries. Is a wooden shoe "clothing"? Is coffee "food"?

A further complication is that the various members of a category are not necessarily considered equivalent: some members seem to be much more central or dominant than others. For instance, people are much more likely to name a sparrow or a robin as an example of a bird than they are to name a penguin or a duck. Similarly, it is easier to verify statements of category membership for central instances or "good examples" of a category than for peripheral instances. That is, it takes less time to verify that a doll or a ball is a toy than to verify that a swing or a skate is one. These phenomena are not merely artifacts of word frequency or familiarity — *doll* and *swing* occur with equal frequency in the language. They appear, rather, to reflect a general awareness of differences in the extent to which individual members of a category exemplify that category. Thus, when college students in an experiment were asked to rank the degree to which various objects were "good examples" of a category, they not only found the task meaningful (i.e., they could respond to it without confusion or wonder) but tended to agree with one another as to the "best" and "worst" examples of the various categories used. For instance, almost 100% of the 117 subjects gave chemistry, football, and carrot the highest rating as examples of a science, a sport, and a vegetable, respectively; while history, weight-lifting, and pickle, respectively, were given low ratings in these same three categories by a majority of subjects (Rosch, 1973).

It appears that the pattern in which children develop knowledge of categories is also from central to peripheral. When 9–11-year-old children were asked to verify category membership by answering "yes" or "no" to statements like "A chicken is a bird," they made no errors on the items that were rated as "central" by adults, whereas 25% of their responses were incorrect on the items rated peripheral (Rosch, 1973). In a somewhat similar study (Anglin, 1977), it was found that even very young children — preschoolers — tended to include the "good examples" as members of a category and exclude the less exemplary ones. What is particularly interesting about Anglin's results is that the good examples did not have to be familiar to the children in order to be classified correctly: pictures of a wombat, an aardvark, and an anteater were identified as animals just as frequently as pictures of a cow, a horse, and a cat. Anglin interprets this as evidence of the "inferential or generative nature of the child's concepts, for they will consistently include in concepts various kinds of instances which they have never seen before, provided they are central instances [p. 156]." On the other hand, familiar items were sometimes misclassified (though not by the majority of children) if they were peripheral. For example, an ant, a butterfly, and a starfish were not considered animals by a few children. This tendency seemed to be related to the fact that the children had another name for these familiar objects — they would say, "That's a tree, not a plant"; "That's a butterfly, not an animal."

What these studies suggest is that concepts are much more than definitional. They include (at least when reasonably well developed) not only the attributes necessary for category membership (i.e., the criteria for determining what is or is not a category member) but also what is *characteristic* of most members — information about the people and places, objects and actions, with which they are commonly associated as well as information about origins, internal constituents, and functions of category members. Thus, an adult's concept of flowers is not limited to the idea that they are the part of a plant in which seeds are formed. Rather, it includes the knowledge that flowers wilt, are considered pretty, are likely to be seen at funerals as well as weddings and parties, and much more.

In sum, words are the names we give to categories of objects, actions, and the qualities of objects and actions, and their meanings lie in the set of properties that distinguish one category from another. A statement of these properties constitutes a definition, and the things to which a word applies by virtue of having these properties are its word referents. Thus, words are terms of reference for specific objects as well as units of the language with intrinsic meaning. But, as we have seen, the properties that define a category are only part of what an individual knows about that category, only part of his or her word knowledge. Underlying each word in an individual's lexicon is a concept, and this may be thought of as comprising all of the significant knowledge an individual possesses in association with that word (including its definition). *Word knowledge, then, involves the meaning of words in the strict sense and in the broader sense of the concepts underlying words.* It is the sum total of knowledge associated with words. We can also refer to this as "verbal knowledge."

Finally, as noted at the beginning of this chapter, it is conceptual or word knowledge, and not definitional knowledge alone, that is implicated in the comprehension of discourse. For we do not use words merely to refer to things or identify their category of membership. We use words in sentences to describe situations — that is, the relations between objects and actions and the qualities of objects and actions. Even a simple sentence such as *John pulled Mary's hair* involves a series of relationships, between *John* and *pull,* between *hair* and *pull,* and between *Mary* and *hair.* More importantly, sentences are used in discourse, so that the situations they describe become part of a larger complex. It is here that conceptual knowledge is likely to play a role. One cannot understand the following vignette:

> John pulled Mary's hair. She ran home crying, and he was sent to the principal's office.

unless one's concept of hair includes the fact that it is painful to have it pulled.

Multiple Meanings

Many words in the English language have more than one meaning. In fact, there are relatively few words that do not. This normally causes little difficulty in communication, however, as the reader or listener can usually tell which meaning is intended from the immediate context or the topic of discourse. For example, the word *cell* is almost sure to refer to the cells of the human body in a biology text and to a small room or apartment in a treatise on monasteries. In a book on reading, the word *passage* will generally refer to a portion of printed text rather than to a hallway. But it is only true, of course, that words with several meanings pose no special problem if the intended meaning is known and readily accessible in memory. If the word *passage* has never before been encountered in reference to written material, a "reading passage" might be construed as a "hallway in which to read." Thus, a word with several meanings is more likely to cause confusion and misunderstanding if one of its meanings is known and this is not the intended one than if the word is completely unfamiliar. In the former case, unaware of his or her ignorance, the reader will be tempted into an erroneous interpretation. In the latter case, the reader simply faces the ordinary problem of an unknown word.

Extended Meanings and Metaphor

The several meanings of a word sometimes have little in common. *Bat* is an example. The fact that two entirely different entities — a small rodent and an item of equipment used in baseball — have the same verbal label seems to be purely coincidental. The word *fair* in the sense of "just," and *fair* in the sense of "light colored; blond" is another example.

On the other hand, what we think of as the several meanings of a word can often be seen, upon closer examination, to be closely related. Think of the word *sharp.* In *sharp mind,* it means "quick, intelligent"; in *sharp picture,* it means "not blurry"; a *sharp outfit* is "stylish"; and a *sharp knife* is one that "cuts well." Yet, all of these senses seem to share a common core of meaning:

> On purely intuitive grounds, one could maintain that *sharp* in the sense of 'having an edge that cuts well' is somehow basic and that the other versions of *sharp* are secondary, being derived from it as essentially metaphorical creations. A mind is sharp in that it cuts with ease through difficult problems; a picture is in sharp focus when the lines are thin and well defined, like the blade of a keen knife; a sharp outfit is one that stands out in sharp focus against the background of mediocrity [Langacker, 1973, p. 86].

Such extensions of meaning are extremely frequent in the language. They are closely related to metaphor in the sense that they involve attribution of a quality commonly associated with one kind of thing to another, completely different kind of thing. That is, comparisons are drawn across different realms of experience. If it is common to speak of *pure* water, *pure* food, *pure* air, and so forth, then we can also, by extension, speak of a *pure* heart or mind. And we can have *strong* evidence as well as *strong* muscles. The difference is that in extension the quality we wish to impute is specified, whereas in true metaphor we merely liken one thing to another and the reader must infer which property (or properties) of the one is shared by the other. When Romeo says Juliet is "the sun," we must understand that he is referring to the sun's warmth, brilliance, and life-sustaining qualities (and not to its shape or color).

Research on the comprehension of metaphor is not extensive, but a few interesting observations have been made. For example, many adjectives describing physical sensations are also used to describe psychological characteristics (e.g., *sweet, warm, cold, rough, hard,* and *loud*). In one study, children ranging in age from 3 to 12 were first asked about the literal meanings of some of these dual-function words (to verify mastery at this level); and then they were asked about their figurative meanings (e.g., "Are people cold? What do they say or do when they are cold?"). It was not until the age of 7 or 8 that children showed some understanding of the psychological meaning of these terms. But even then they were unaware of the connection between psychological and physical meanings, believing the words to be entirely unrelated. By 9 and 10, children were more sensitive to this connection; and 11- and 12-year-olds were often actually able to explain the connection (e.g., "hard things and hard people are both unmanageable"; Asch & Nerlove, 1960, cited in Gardner et al., 1978, p. 8). To summarize, the physical or concrete meanings of dual-function adjectives are generally understood even by preschool children; the psychological meanings are mastered during the early years of schooling; and recognition of the metaphoric connection emerges during preadolescence (Gardner et al., 1978).

This pattern of development holds true for metaphoric comprehension in general. That is, children of 8 or 9 can understand the meaning conveyed by a metaphor, but only on an intuitive basis: they can match a picture to the statement "He has a very heavy heart" but cannot easily paraphrase the statement. This may be related to the fact that children of this age tend to avoid figurative usage in their own speech and, perhaps because of their concern with dictionary definitions, tend to prefer ordinary, established meanings and comparisons, occasionally protesting that figurative expressions are "silly": "A tie can't be loud"; "A person can't be a rock." This may be a necessary stage of development; one must understand what words usually (and literally) mean before one can appreciate the departures and extensions of metaphoric comparisons (Gardner et al., 1978).

This point was recently demonstrated, to some extent, in a study of instruction in the comprehension of metaphors and similes (Readence, Baldwin, & Rickelman, 1983). The investigators hypothesized that the key to comprehension of these expressions is vocabulary knowledge. More specifically, they pointed out that one must be sufficiently familiar with the "vehicle" term to know which of its features is being predicated of the "topic," the thing being described. For example, in *his hands were sandpaper, hands* is the topic and *sandpaper* the vehicle; that is, *sandpaper* is the means for conveying the idea that his hands were rough. In order to understand this metaphor, one must be familiar enough with sandpaper to know that roughness is its most significant characteristic. To cite another example, *The smoke from the forest was pea soup* can only be understood if one knows that pea soup is thick; knowing that it is green or edible provides no help. The investigators found that when fifth- and sixth-grade students misinterpreted metaphors and similes, it usually turned out that they did not associate the necessary attribute with the vehicle term. For example, they might not think of pea soup as thick. However, when these students were given lists of attributes (including the one being predicated of the topic) for the vehicle terms of the metaphorical statements they had misinterpreted, they were able to correct 77% of their misinterpretations (Baldwin, Luce, & Readence, 1982).

Similar results were obtained in a related study of similes (cited in Readence *et al.*, 1983). In this study, one control group simply practiced interpreting similes; a second control group studied paragraphs that described the vehicle terms in the experimental materials but that did *not* include the specific attributes necessary for their interpretation. The experimental group read descriptions of the vehicle term that included the necessary attribute. As expected, subsequent performance on the test of simile interpretation was considerably superior for the experimental group.

These studies suggest that failure to understand metaphorical language is not primarily due to lack of the necessary reasoning powers or inability to recognize the type of comparison involved. Consequently, "drill exercises in discriminating between literal and metaphorical statements or matching interpretations with metaphors and similes may have little effect [Readence *et al.* 1983, p. 111]." Rather, direct instruction in the critical attributes of word referents seems more appropriate.

Nevertheless, the difficulty of understanding figurative language must not be underestimated. Familiarity with the terms used is certainly essential, but it is not sufficient. In order to determine which of the possible attributes of a metaphoric vehicle is the intended one, the reader must understand the situational context. We understand what Romeo means when he says Juliet is "the sun" because we know from what has gone before how he feels about her.

The following teacher–student dialogue exemplifies the difficulty that students may have in identifying the intended metaphorical attribute:

TEXT: "When he lands, he alternately tugs on vent lines and burner throttle to waft the balloon at heights of only 10 or 20 feet right over slight ridges, up gully inclines, and across ponds to the dime he has in mind. An error of a few feet could butt the basket against a rock or put it in the water ["A Love of Flight," in *Chicago Tribune*, 11/18/83]."

TEACHER: What does the pilot do to land the balloon?

STUDENT: Tug on the lines and burner throttle.

TEACHER: What is difficult about this landing?

STUDENT: He could hit a rock or fall into the water.

TEACHER: Yes. And why is it difficult to avoid the rocks and water?

STUDENT: You have to steer it.

TEACHER: Yes, he has to steer very carefully. But why?

STUDENT: (No response.)

TEACHER: What is meant by "the *dime* he has in mind"?
STUDENT: The place he wants to land . . . open spot.
TEACHER: What about the dime? What does that tell you about the open spot?
STUDENT: . . . it's round?
TEACHER: What other quality of a dime would relate to this situation? For example, compare a dime to a quarter.
STUDENT: It's less.
TEACHER: Think of another quality.
STUDENT: It's smaller.

Thus, although a dime is an extremely familiar object, its small size was not immediately recognized as the relevant attribute, in part, it seems, because the student had little grasp of the fact that the size of the landing area might be important.

By the time students reach the age of 10 and 11, they can paraphrase as well as understand metaphors. Evidently, their conceptual and lexical knowledge is sufficiently consolidated that they do not resist or protest against comparisons between animate and inanimate objects, physical and psychological properties, etc. However, it is not until adolescence that students are likely to fully appreciate the nature of metaphor, to recognize the links between sensory, physical, and psychological realms and perceive the significance of comparisons drawn across them (Gardner *et al.*, 1978).

How Are Words Learned?

An eminent psycholinguist, George Miller (1977), recently observed that young children seem to learn the words that name colors before they learn to match those words to specific color stimuli. That is, they will answer "red," "blue," "green," (or some other color word) in response to the question, "What color is this?" even though the color they name is not the correct one. And when asked to point to all the blue things in an array of objects, they may point to all the tan ones, showing that they can distinguish between colors without knowing which color-name to apply. The same phenomenon has been observed with respect to time words: children will give time units in response to questions about time, but the numbers they give are often quite bizarre in relation to the questions (e.g., in answer to the question, "When was your daddy little?" a 3-year-old will respond, "Last week.").

These observations led Miller to reflect on his own word knowledge, and he recognized that he, too, knew many words whose specific referents he could not identify or did not understand. For example, he knew the words *camellia, nasturtium,* and *marigold* were the names of flowers but he did not know what these flowers looked like. Many adults are probably in a similar position with regard to tree names like *sassafrass* and *cottonwood* or animal names like *wombat* and *aardvark*.

What these observations suggest is that both children and adults often learn the general domain of knowledge or experience to which a word belongs before they understand its precise meaning. It should not surprise us, therefore, when students can give only the most general of information about certain words — that *anxiety* means "feeling"; *soliloquy* is "a statement"; *penance* means "punishment" (Drum, 1983). This probably represents a first stage in the process of learning words. With further experiences in a variety of contexts, word meanings become more differentiated.

The phenomenon of overgeneralization of word meaning is well documented among very young children (Clark, 1973). They commonly use the term *dog* as a label for other animals (horses, cows, sheep), *baby* for young children, *tick-tock* for instruments with round dials (gas meter, bathroom scale), *ball* for spherical objects (marbles, balloons), *Christmas tree* for all evergreens, and so on. One child used *open* for both the untying of shoes and the peeling of fruit! We can understand these overextensions as stemming from the perceptual similarity of "correct" and "incorrect" word referents. And, to some extent, it may be that the child is aware of the difference between babies and children, a clock and other dialed instruments, and so on, but has not yet acquired the appropriate verbal labels. This would also explain the child's use of the terms *big* and *little* to cover all dimensions of size — long and short, wide and narrow, thick and thin, high and low. In other words, some overgeneralizations undoubtedly stem from the fact that children must use the terms that are available to them to refer to new objects and ideas.

More difficult to explain is the common confusion between antonym pairs such as *more* and *less, before* and *after, same* and *different.* One theory (the Semantic Feature Hypothesis) is that the meanings of words can be broken down into smaller units or elementary components of meaning (semantic features) and words that share many features are likely to be confused. More specifically, the meaning of one word in an antonym pair is likely, at first, to be extended to cover the meaning of the other as well because the contrastive feature of the second word has not yet entered the child's "mental dictionary." In other words, the meaning of *less, after,* or *different* has not yet been differentiated from (respectively) *more, before,* or *same;* the lexical entry for these words is incomplete (Clark, 1973). Perhaps this same notion of incomplete entry accounts for the confusion, found even among adults, between *affect* and *effect, imply* and *infer.*

The Semantic Feature Hypothesis represents just one attempt to understand the development of word meaning, and much can be said about its limitations (cf. Anglin, 1977; Nelson, 1974). From our point of view, one serious limitation is that it is based on observations of preschool children. Nevertheless, we believe it is sometimes useful to think of words as "bundles" of semantic features and to understand students' partial or vague knowledge of words in these terms.

Possibly more frequent than overgeneralizations of word meanings are undergeneralizations. These tend to go unnoticed in spontaneous speech (upon which much of the research on child language is based) because they do not result in erroneous verbal labels — the child merely applies a word to a more restricted range of objects than is necessary. Consequently, undergeneralizations have been relatively neglected in the study of word meaning. They are, however, much in evidence when observations are based on comprehension tasks (Anglin, 1977). Whether a word is overgeneralized or undergeneralized appears to depend somewhat on its level of generality. The reason for this is that perceptual similarity plays an important role in children's categorizing behavior. General terms tend to refer to an assortment of dissimilar items and therefore to be undergeneralized. Thus, Anglin found that with the general terms *food, plant,* and *animal,* atypical instances such as ketchup, trees, and insects, respectively, were excluded. Rarely were these terms overgeneralized. Specific terms, on the other hand, were often overgeneralized to perceptually similar items — *apple* to tomato, *flower* to other plants (cacti, philodendron). In general, then, children's acquisition of word labels cannot be said to progress either from specific to general or from general to specific. Rather, "vocabulary development is characterized by the complementary trends of differentiation and of hierarchic integration [Anglin, 1977, p. 237]."

In conclusion, we have argued that underlying the meaning a student attaches to a word is a concept. This includes, even for young children, knowledge of what instances of the concept look like, smell like, taste like, etc., where they are found, the uses to which they can be put, and what they can do. With development, a concept comes to include knowledge of the relations of instances to other things, their internal constituents, and their origins (Anglin, 1977). But it should be clear that there can be concepts without words just as there can be words without conceptual underpinnings. The distinction between words and concepts is an important one for vocabulary instruction; it implies that teaching definitions is not the same as teaching concepts. The teaching of definitions (or synonyms) makes sense when words pertain to well-developed concepts. Even then, new words must be practiced in a variety of verbal contexts if they are to be useful in comprehending discourse. But when the concepts underlying words are somewhat unfamiliar, definitions will be inadequate; instruction must also provide the verbal and nonverbal experiences necessary for concept development. In the following section we will review recent research on vocabulary instruction and describe some innovative instructional practices.

INSTRUCTION IN WORD KNOWLEDGE

It was noted earlier that the high correlation between vocabulary and comprehension is not well understood. There is currently some controversy over whether word knowledge is directly "instrumental" in understanding text or is itself a reflection of "deeper and broader knowledge of the culture [Anderson & Freebody, 1981, p. 81]." That is, on the one hand, students who score high on a vocabulary test may simply "know more of the words in most texts they encounter"; on the other hand, it may be that "possessing a certain word meaning is only a sign that the individual may possess the knowledge needed to understand a text [p. 81]." The second position assumes that students who select the right responses on a multiple-choice test know more about words than their definitions (though that is all that is demonstrated on the test). This position is consistent with the view of verbal knowledge that we have proposed.

Unfortunately, as Anderson and Freebody (1981) point out, there is little besides logic and intuition to support the view that vocabulary scores primarily reflect conceptual or background knowledge. The tendency among reading researchers has been to study background knowledge as separate and distinct from vocabulary. However, there is a kind of support for the vocabulary-as-background-knowledge view, by default, in the finding that simply teaching definitions does *not* tend to improve comprehension. Out of eight studies recently reviewed by Mezynski (1983), four resulted in comprehension gains due to vocabulary instruction and four did not. In each of the four that proved unsuccessful, students were taught simple definitions or synonyms, accompanied in some cases by illustrative sentences. By contrast, in each of the successful studies, instruction went beyond this narrow type of drill.

In one of the successful studies, the additional instruction amounted to little more than answering two questions about each word. For example, in addition to learning that *altercations* are "fights," students answered these questions: "Do you have altercations with your teacher? Do you have altercations with a tree? [Kameenui, Carnine, & Freschi, 1982]." One wonders why this should make the difference between success and failure. Perhaps the questions helped students associate the new word with an underlying concept — meaningful experiences or knowledge — rather than with a rote definition. In any case, since this study is possibly unique in effecting gains in passage comprehension through short-term instruction in difficult passage words, further research is necessary before we can have full confidence in the efficacy of its instructional method.

Whereas Kameenui *et al.* (1982) taught a small number of words (six) and used a short experimental passage incorporating these words to assess the effect of instruction on comprehension, the other successful studies involved large numbers of words taught over a period of many months and assessed the effects of instruction through standardized comprehension tests. Thus, there is evidence in favor of instruction that is geared toward improving students' *general* vocabulary as well as support for direct instruction in difficult passage words. More significantly, in the general vocabulary studies, words were not only taught (i.e., defined, illustrated, explained, and discussed), but they were also presented in rich contexts. The Draper and Moeller (1971) study constituted a veritable "barrage" of new words — 1,800 in all — presented in the context of fables, folktales, and Greek and Roman myths. The Lieberman study (cited in Mezynski, 1983) used social studies and English curriculum materials as the context for new words. A slightly different approach was taken by Beck, Perfetti, and McKeown (1982). Instead of providing narrative or expository contexts for newly learned words, they designed activities in which the meanings of words were explored and refined. For example, students completed sentences or answered multiple-choice questions about the situations, behaviors, or events in which word referents might be involved. To illustrate, for the word *accomplice,* students were asked, "Would an accomplice be more likely to (a) squeal to the police in return for not having to go to jail? (b) rob a bank by himself? (c) enjoy babysitting? [p. 510]." Also, the words taught in the Beck *et al.* study were grouped into semantically related sets, eight to nine words per set, and some questions were designed to probe the overlap among words in a set. For example, *accomplice, novice,* and *hermit* were in the "people" set of words, and the questions asked were: "Could an accomplice be a novice? Would a hermit likely be an accomplice? [p. 510]."

If there is any lesson to be learned from this body of research, it would seem to be that instruction in definitions alone does not adequately prepare students for the task of comprehending discourse. Most children can learn definitions well enough if given sufficient practice — indeed, most instructional studies are quite successful in this regard. But a broader range of experiences seems to be necessary before newly learned words can be understood in novel contexts. Such experiences can evidently be provided through exploratory questions as well as through traditional contextual materials. These experiences make definitions "come alive": they enable students to associate words with real-world events, situations, and behaviors — with existing conceptual knowledge.

It should be noted, however, that the successful general vocabulary studies discussed here also included practice with definitions — that is, workbook-type exercises in matching synonyms and filling in sentence blanks. So the claim is not that word meanings are better learned if direct instruction is followed by contextual reading (or exploratory questions) alone. On the contrary, students also need repeated opportunities to associate words with their meanings.

In general, then, the results of research suggest that effective instruction in vocabulary should incorporate the following:

1. *Definition.* Briefly worded explanations or synonyms of words to be learned should be provided by the teacher. Alternatively, students can look the words up in a suitable dictionary. For variation, the teacher might present sentences from which target words have been omitted and replaced by blanks. Students then fill in the blanks under the guidance of the teacher. The sentences should describe situations that make the meaning of the words quite clear.

2. *Discussion.* The concepts underlying words should be developed through discussion of illustrative situations; meanings should be expanded and clarified through association with familiar people, places, objects, and actions. Students' own experiences are of course elicited wherever possible. But when students' experiences are limited, the teacher should invent appropriate scenarios.

3. *Application.* Concepts should be reinforced and refined through further interaction with illustrative contexts. This can take the form of exploratory questions similar to those used by Kameenui *et al.* (1982) and Beck *et al.* (1982), or it can involve instructional materials regularly used in reading or the content areas. In addition, when time permits, students may be given writing assignments in which they generate sentences or paragraphs around newly learned words.

4. *Practice.* Included here are the traditional crossword puzzles, anagrams, and synonym-matching and sentence completion tasks. These are primarily aids to memory, reinforcing the associative bond between words and their meanings. As such, they seem to be suitable for use right after definitions are introduced as well as for final "wrap-up."

One final study should be mentioned before we conclude this discussion of instructional research. It concerns the special importance of vocabulary instruction for less able readers. Roser and Juel (1982) selected children in first through fifth grades who were either average or poor readers (i.e., who were reading either at or one year below grade level). Each group read two stories from their classroom reader, one with vocabulary instruction and one without. The words taught were those identified in the teacher's manual as "new words," and the instructional method emphasized the relationship of each new word to the children's lives. Specifically, new words were presented along with sentences in which blanks were substituted for the new words, and the teacher guided the group in selecting the appropriate word for each sentence, centering the discussion on students' knowledge and previous experiences. The results showed a marked increase in passage comprehension after vocabulary instruction only for the poorer readers in third, fourth, and fifth grades. The average readers in all grades performed just about as well without instruction as with it. In first and second grades, not only did instruction have no effect, but the poorer readers performed as well as the average readers. These results are not unexpected, given the fact that beginning reading materials make fewer demands on students' word knowledge, as was discussed in Chapter 1. A noteworthy feature of this experiment was the use of instructional-level materials in regular reading lessons conducted by the classroom teacher. The study seems to indicate that the introduction of unknown words before reading may be most essential for students beyond second grade who are reading below grade level.

Instructional Techniques

Within the framework of effective instruction outlined above, a wide variety of techniques and activities are possible. For example, students can "guess" the meanings of unknown words from sentence or paragraph contexts before looking them up in a dictionary. Alternatively, the concept underlying each unknown word can be discussed before the word itself is introduced. For example, to introduce *assassination,* discussion would begin with the idea of "kill" or "murder" and lead toward the murder of a political figure (Vaughan, Castle, Gilbert, & Love, 1982). Described below are three additional strategies for introducing words. They are designed primarily for showing the interrelationships among word meanings and thus are particularly suitable for developing conceptual knowledge in the content areas or for learning words that share a common theme.

1. *Structured overview* (Barron, 1969). The teacher identifies the words to be taught and shows how they are related to each other in a diagram. But the teacher does not present a finished diagram to the students. Rather, the diagram is built *with* the students as the teacher explains and discusses each new word. Students participate by recalling prior knowledge, relevant experiences, examples, and so on. The diagram then remains on display as a reference point and an aid to memory while instruction proceeds. Thus, the structured overview is actually an "advance organizer" for the key concepts, as represented by the technical vocabulary, to be taught in a content area lesson or unit. As such, it may contain familiar as well as unfamiliar words, relating what is to be taught to what is already known about a particular topic.

2. *Capsule words* (Crist, 1975). Like the structured overview, this technique involves the introduction of a set of words related to a single topic or idea (the capsule). However, the relationship is not graphically displayed. Instead, words are listed on the board and the teacher discusses the meaning of each word in relation to the topic, giving examples of how it is used in speaking and writing. One capsule suggested by Crist (1975) consists of words related to money: *affluent, austerity, avarice, fiscal, indigent, lucrative,* and so on. After the words are discussed, their meanings are reviewed and briefly noted in writing. Then, for practice, working in pairs, the students attempt to use the words in conversation. They are given a limited amount of time (5 minutes, say) in which to use as many words as they can, each member of the pair keeping track of the words used by the other. For additional practice, students are directed to incorporate the words into a written story or essay.

3. *Brainstorming* (Vacca, 1981). In this activity students create what might be called a "concept map," a representation of what they already know in relation to a given word. Working in small groups, students are given a limited amount of time to list as many related words as they can. The teacher then combines the students' contributions into a master list, and the students group the words on the list into categories. The categories may be provided by the teacher, or the students may derive their own. This technique is often recommended as an interesting way of introducing a major concept related to a unit of study. Concepts associated with terms such as *propaganda, pollution, nutrition,* and *revolution* lend themselves to this technique, since students are likely to have a degree of knowledge in these areas.

Once words have been introduced and discussed, students need opportunities to relate them to real-world contexts. The following are suggested.

1. *Insult or compliment?* (Lake, 1971). This activity works well with adjectives, as it deals with the favorable or unfavorable connotations of words. A list of words is prepared by the teacher and given to the students. The words may be unfamiliar, in which case the use of the dictionary will be involved; or they may be words that have already been defined and discussed, in which case the activity may be considered an application of word meanings. The students' task is to decide whether the use of these words to describe them personally would be a compliment or an insult. A teacher-led discussion follows.

2. *Sentence meaning exercises.* These can be in the form of yes–no questions, true–false statements, or fill-in-the-blank sentences. The following examples are from Hafner (1977):

Few people make favorable impressions by making _____ remarks.
Would a *motley* group be interesting?
Are street urchins likely to be *squalid*? [pp. 118–119].

3. *Word sorts.* In this activity students organize words into categories. The teacher can provide the categories, or the students may be required to search for the relationships among word concepts in order to derive their own.

4. *Post–structured overviews.* This activity is somewhat similar to a word sort, but it allows greater freedom in portraying relationships. Students must be familiar with structured overviews or various diagram formats, however, before they can exploit this freedom. Small groups are each given a list of words and a set of 3 × 5 cards; each word on the list is written on a card. The students then "work together to decide upon a spatial arrangement among the cards which depicts the major relationships among the words [Vacca, 1981, p. 251]." Discussion of each group's solution follows, the teacher recognizing that more than one solution is possible.

Learning Word Meanings from Context. An early study by Gray and Holmes (1938) showed that fewer words are learned in a given period of time through independent reading than through direct instruction. Indeed, a great many studies since then have shown that almost any method of word study is superior to simply reading text for the acquisition of word meanings (Petty, Herold, & Stoll, 1968). This is not really surprising. When we encounter unfamiliar words in a text, we are not, in general, inclined to develop and commit to memory precise meanings for them. Because we are attending to passage meaning rather than to individual words, we are more likely to infer vague meanings consistent with the text, or else read around unknown words as long as the passage remains comprehensible. In unusual circumstances we may consult a dictionary. Nevertheless, many of the words we know — perhaps most — have probably been learned spontaneously in the course of general reading experiences. It is important, therefore, that students develop facility in the process of inferring word meanings from context. The following steps represent one instructional approach (Cunningham, Cunningham, & Arthur, 1981).

1. The teacher prepares for the lesson by creating one or two sentences for each word that will be taught before a passage is read. The sentences should provide clues to word meaning. (For examples of the many different kinds of clues commonly found in written discourse, see Ames, 1966).

2. The words alone are listed on the chalkboard, and students are asked to write a meaning for each word. If a word is completely unknown — as many will be — students are told to make a guess.

3. The teacher elicits a few meanings for each word and writes them on the chalkboard.

4. The sentences prepared by the teacher are displayed and students again write a meaning for each word. This enables them to see the difference between pulling a meaning "out of thin air" and using contextual information.

5. Students now volunteer their context-based guesses, explaining how other words provided clues. These explanations enable "the students who do not know how to use context clues to 'look into the minds' of those students who do know how [p. 27]."

6. Each word is looked up in the dictionary; context-based guesses are verified or revised as necessary. In this way, students "discover that while the context does not 'tell the whole story' about a word, it does give important clues to its meaning [p. 27]."

7. Students read the passage which contains the words taught.

As students gain insight into the use of context for deriving word meaning, the teacher may omit the specially prepared sentences designed to illustrate the variety of such clues found in texts. Instead, the teacher identifies the words in students' texts whose meanings can readily be inferred from text information. These are written on the chalkboard along with the page numbers where they will be found, and students are directed to derive meanings for them, as in Step 4. Steps 5, 6, and 7 follow.

A Mnemonic Device for Learning Definitions. Acquiring word knowledge may be seen as a twofold task. It involves an initial mastery of a word's core or basic meaning — in the form of a brief definition — and it involves elaboration of that core into a full-bodied concept. We have, up to this point, emphasized the latter part of the process, because it is complex and often overlooked in the design of vocabulary instruction. Here we are concerned with the simpler task of associating words with brief definitions.

We are all familiar with mnemonic devices. We use rhymes, alphabetic and numerical sequences, and well-known dates to help us remember names, lists, telephone numbers, and the like. They involve the use of extrinsic cues to facilitate rote learning. A mnemonic for vocabulary learning was recently introduced and found more effective than simple drill or contextual reading (Pressley, Levin, & Miller, 1981). Students generate a "keyword," which will serve as a mnemonic for the definition of the to-be-learned word. The keyword is a familiar word that is in some way similar in sound to the target word. It may, for example, rhyme with it or begin with the same syllable. The keyword is then used to construct an image (or verbal cue) that represents the meaning of the target word. For example, to remember the definition of *carlin* (an old woman), one might select *car* as the keyword and visualize an old woman riding in (or atop) a car. Then, the word *carlin* would bring to mind *car,* and this in turn would bring to mind the image of the old woman and, hence, the meaning of *carlin.* Keywords and images are sometimes difficult to create, especially for abstract words. However, the activity is likely to be interesting as well as useful to students, at least for some words or in some learning situations. It should be introduced to students accordingly — as one possible strategy for remembering definitions.

DIAGNOSIS OF
WORD KNOWLEDGE DIFFICULTY

We have seen, from the review of experimental research above, that knowing the definitions of words in a passage does not always lead to increased comprehension. By the same token, *not* knowing word meanings does not necessarily interfere with comprehension. Why should this be so? Clearly, much depends on how many unknown words there are and on how important they are to the central content (Freebody & Anderson, 1983a). The influence of these factors on comprehension will depend, in turn, on the familiarity of the content (cf. Freebody & Anderson, 1983b). A large number of unknown words may present no obstacle to comprehension in a highly predictable context. For example, a simple 100-word fairy-tale-style story was readily understood by a fifth-grade group of average readers even though 10 of the words were taken from an eighth-grade list and, moreover, an average of 7 of those words were marked incorrectly by the experimental group on a multiple-choice test given after instruction (Stahl, 1983). On the other hand, even a few unknown words can severely disrupt comprehension if they represent key concepts in an expository passage on an unfamiliar topic.

In the usual case, however, unknown words tend to result in losses or misinterpretations of information that are more limited in scope. By way of illustration, a child who did not know the meaning of *snare* and *clipped* read a story that began as follows: "A miller laid a snare, and a baby eagle flew into it. The miller tied him to a pole and clipped his wings. [Hughes, Bernier, & Gurren, 1979, p. 19]." The unknown words prevented her from answering questions about the *causes* of the bird's predicament; but the *facts* of its predicament — captivity and inability to fly — were clearly understood from ensuing events. In general, students appear to tolerate unknown words as long as other, compensatory sources of information are available to them, either from the passage itself, in the form of redundant information, or from their own store of knowledge.

In the following section we present two case studies illustrating the way in which word knowledge and topic familiarity influence comprehension. The first case represents the moderate loss in comprehension likely to be observed when passages are not overly demanding relative to the reader's conceptual knowledge. The second shows a more severe loss, due to a more demanding (relative to the reader) passage. The presentation of cases will, in addition, demonstrate the diagnostic procedures useful in assessing word knowledge and evaluating its effect on comprehension.

Diagnostic Procedures

The general procedure for reading diagnosis, as discussed in Chapter 3, involves the preparation of materials, test administration, a preliminary analysis of test results, an informal probe, an interpretation, and finally, an instructional plan. It is during the preparation stage that words are selected from the passage for the assessment of word knowledge. Comprehension questions are also constructed at this time (specific procedures are discussed in the next chapter). Then, after a preliminary analysis of the results, additional words may be selected and presented during the probe. The purpose is to determine whether word knowledge is a major source of difficulty in reading — more specifically, whether uncommon words could have interfered with comprehension and whether unknown words represent unknown concepts as well.

Step 1: Preparation: Selection of Words. Three to eight words (depending on passage length) are selected for an initial appraisal of word knowledge. The words should be important to the passage — that is, they should convey information pertaining to the main ideas and essential details. Figurative expressions and phrases of a technical nature should also be selected, as they, too, represent possible obstacles to comprehension. Basic to this step, then, is a careful reading of the passage to identify its central content. The teacher must also be alert to the occurrence of common words used in uncommon or metaphorical senses.

Step 2: Administration: Presentation of Words. The words selected are presented to the student in isolation after the comprehension questions have been asked. The teacher simply asks, "What does —— mean?" or "What is a —— ?" In the case of words with multiple meanings, the context in which the word occurred may also be provided. If the student cannot formulate a definition, or the response leaves some doubt as to the accuracy or fullness of the student's word knowledge, the teacher probes further, asking for an exemplary object or situation to which the word would apply or requesting that the student use the word in a sentence. Examples as well as sentences often have to be explored still further. For example, Raymond (Case Study 1 in what follows) suggested that the word *sophisticated* could be applied to a truck. Although this is potentially correct, further questioning indicated that he thought it was motion (rather than modern design or engineering) that made a truck sophisticated.

Step 3: Preliminary Analysis of Results. In this step the teacher notes the degree of success achieved in defining the words presented in Step 2. If as many as half the words presented are unknown, the teacher should consider word knowledge an area of general weakness. But the diagnosis does not end there. The teacher must also determine the extent to which unknown words constituted a specific impediment to comprehension. This involves scrutiny of incorrect responses to comprehension questions. In particular, the teacher must determine, for each question that was answered incorrectly, whether the information needed to answer it was unavailable to the student because of an unknown word. If this is true for a majority of incorrect responses, then reading difficulty can be attributed to inadequate word knowledge.

Obviously, the words and ideas that will cause confusion and misunderstanding cannot always be anticipated during the initial selection of words; often the student's responses to questions reveal difficulties that were entirely unexpected. In Case Study 1, for example, the word *crude* was not recognized as a possible source of difficulty in the teacher's first analysis of the passage and was not, therefore, included in the initial set of words presented. In such cases, the additional words are selected for presentation to the student during the next step, the probe.

Performance on the comprehension questions is also examined at this point for evidence that the student lacked the conceptual knowledge or specific information necessary for general comprehension of the passage. If such evidence exists, questions to explore this possibility are formulated and then presented during the probe. This procedure is particularly important when overall comprehension is poor — say, 50% or less — and specific words do not seem to be directly implicated.

Step 4: Probe. The additional words identified in Step 3 as potential obstacles to comprehension are presented to the student as in Step 2. The results enable the teacher to complete the determination, begun in Step 3, as to whether particular questions were answered incorrectly because the meanings of certain words were unknown. The questions devised to explore conceptual knowledge and information are also administered. These results provide further insight into the source of comprehension difficulty.

Steps 5 and 6: Interpretation and Instructional Plan. The results of Steps 3 and 4 combined serve as the basis for final evaluation of the role of word knowledge in the student's reading difficulties. If questions about the passage cannot be answered for lack of word knowledge, then word knowledge represents an area of weakness in reading and warrants instructional emphasis. Whether the passage should be considered too difficult for instructional purposes on account of word knowledge will depend on the severity of the comprehension loss. If the loss is limited in scope, as in Case Study 1, then passages of equivalent difficulty will probably be suitable for instruction as long as important words are taught before reading. On the other hand, if the loss in comprehension is widespread, extending to information not specifically related to unknown words, as in Case Study 2, then the student should be assigned an easier level of materials.

CASE 1: RAYMOND

Raymond is a seventh-grader whose work in school is generally above average. But he is ambitious and expresses some concern about his reading ability. The diagnosis was undertaken in an attempt to identify areas of performance that might be strengthened through specific instruction.

Preparation

An expository passage from his seventh-grade reader, entitled "Kinds of Housing," (275 words in length) was selected for Raymond to read. It is shown here in Figure 4.1. Using the procedures that have been described, the reader should examine the passage to identify key vocabulary items that would interfere with Raymond's understanding of the passage if they were unknown to him.

Figure 4.1. Diagnostic reading passage: Raymond.
(From EXPLORING PATHS: READING SKILLS WORKBOOK, *HBJ Bookmark Reading Program,* by Margaret Early, Donald Gallo, and Gwendolyn Kerr, copyright © 1979 by Harcourt Brace Jovanovich, Inc. Reprinted by permission of the publisher.)

Kinds of Housing

With a few exceptions, environment determines the kinds of shelter people choose. So, houses are usually built from materials that are most readily available in the surrounding area.

The temporary dwelling, as its name suggests, is not built to last. Nomads, people who are always on the move, build temporary dwellings. For example, Native Americans of the plains developed the tepee made of buffalo hides. When buffalo were plentiful, they were an important food source. To avoid waste, Native Americans found a practical use for the hides of the animals. When the tribe moved on, the tepees were left behind.

The grass lean-to is favored by the Bush people of the Kalahari Desert. It is made from grasses and sticks found in the area in which they live.

There are two kinds of permanent housing: crude and sophisticated. Igloos, log cabins, and adobe huts are crude permanent housing. They are built to last. The surfaces, however, are rough and unfinished.

The igloo is a dome made of blocks of hard-packed snow. The snow acts as an insulator. It makes the igloo surprisingly warm.

Log cabins were common during America's westward expansion. As settlers headed west, the thick forests provided timber for housing.

Adobe is sun-dried mud. Adobe huts are found in warm, dry areas, such as parts of Mexico and the American Southwest.

Sophisticated permanent housing can be made from many materials. Homes with concrete foundations are built to last from owner to owner. Very often, these houses have a framework of wood, iron, or steel. The location of steel mills and ironworks often determines the areas where this housing is found.

The reader should then compare his or her selections with those made by Raymond's teacher. She selected six words. The first, *environment,* is important for understanding the thesis of the passage. The second word, *determines,* was included because it is central in understanding the main idea of the passage, that environmental conditions influence the nature of housing. The third, *available,* is a general vocabulary word that is important for understanding why kinds of housing vary according to the locale. The fourth, fifth, and sixth words — *temporary, permanent,* and *sophisticated* — represent major concepts that distinguish major types of housing. The word *insulator* was not included because the insulating property of snow was deemed incidental to the main point of the passage. Furthermore, the meaning of *insulator* was explained in the sentence following the one in which it was introduced. The words *adobe, igloo, tepee,* and *nomads* were excluded because they, too, were explained in the text.

The preparation stage involved not only the selection of key vocabulary items but also the development of comprehension questions (to be discussed in the next two chapters). These are shown, together with the vocabulary items, in Figure 4.2; the expected answers are in parentheses. The first nine questions can be answered from information either stated or implied in the text; the remaining three require interpretation or application of text information.

Figure 4.2.   Comprehension and word knowledge questions: Raymond.

Comprehension

1. a.   What determines the kind of shelter people choose? (environment; available materials)

    b.   Where do we usually get the materials we build houses from? (environment; surrounding area)

2. What is a temporary dwelling? (one that is not built to last)

3. What are the people called who build temporary dwellings? (nomads)

4. Why do some people build temporary dwellings? (they are always on the move)

5. What are the two types of permanent housing? (crude and sophisticated)

6. What is the difference between crude and sophisticated permanent housing? (crude are rough and unfinished; sophisticated are made from modern materials)

7. Name some types of crude permanent housing. (igloo, adobe, log cabin)

8. What are some materials sophisticated permanent housing is made of? (wood, iron, steel)

9. What determines where sophisticated permanent houses are built? (location of materials)

*10.   If you had the choice between living in an igloo, a log cabin, or an adobe hut, which would you choose and why? (discuss climate and comfort)

*11.   Of all the types of housing mentioned in the passage — temporary and permanent, crude permanent and sophisticated permanent — which type do you live in? (permanent sophisticated)

*12.   Do climate and environment still govern what materials we use to build houses today?

* Beyond-text question

Word Knowledge

1. environment	4. temporary
2. determines	5. permanent
3. available	6. sophisticated

Administration

Raymond read the passage aloud while the teacher recorded his errors and noted the amount of time he took to read it. The comprehension and word knowledge questions were administered immediately thereafter. Raymond's responses are shown in Figures 4.3 and 4.4. The reader should study his answers in order to make a tentative judgment about the adequacy of his comprehension and word knowledge.

Figure 4.3. Responses to comprehension questions: Raymond.

$\frac{1}{2}$ **1.**   a. $\frac{1}{2}$ What determines the kind of shelter people choose? (environment; available materials)
RESPONSE: It can be the grounds, maybe grass or sand; and like if it's cold or sunny.

      b. $\frac{1}{2}$ Where do we usually get the materials we build houses from? (environment; surrounding area)
RESPONSE: Sometimes we can make it. Like the log cabins, you could get it from the trees around you. The igloos you could pack the snow yourself.

✓   **2.**   What is a temporary dwelling? (one that is not built to last)
RESPONSE: It's not built to stay long.

✓   **3.**   What are the people called who build temporary dwellings? (nomads)
RESPONSE: Nomads.

✓   **4.**   Why do some people build temporary dwellings? (they are always on the move)
RESPONSE: They are always moving around.

✓   **5.**   What are the two types of permanent housing? (crude and sophisticated)
RESPONSE: Crude and sophisticated.

✗   **6.**   What is the difference between crude and sophisticated permanent housing? (crude are rough and unfinished; sophisticated are made from modern materials)
RESPONSE: Not sure—crude are built to stay longer and sophisticated is not that long.

✓   **7.**   Name some types of crude permanent housing. (igloo, adobe, log cabin)
RESPONSE: Log cabin, adobe hut, igloo.

✗   **8.**   What are some materials sophisticated permanent housing is made of? (wood, iron, steel)
RESPONSE: I think one of the houses are igloos made out of snow—or I think wood. [Anything else?] Steel.

$\frac{1}{2}$ **9.**   What determines where sophisticated permanent houses are built?
RESPONSE: Well, if they were wood, they would be by a forest.

(Continued)

Figure 4.3. *(Continued)*

½*10. If you had the choice between living in an igloo, a log cabin, or an adobe hut, which would you choose and why? (discuss climate and comfort)

RESPONSE: Igloo, or log cabin. . . . Well, I would choose an igloo because it keeps you warm. Maybe a log cabin; it was built like a house — and that's what we mostly live in, like in cabins in the woods. [So which would you choose?] Log cabin 'cause it's built like a house.

✓ *11. Of all the types of housing mentioned in the passage — temporary and permanent, crude permanent and sophisticated permanent — which type do you live in? (permanent sophisticated)

RESPONSE: I think sophisticated. [Is it permanent or temporary?] Permanent.

✗ *12. Do climate and environment still govern what materials we use to build houses today?

RESPONSE: Not sure. [Do you think people can build any kind of house no matter what the climate is?] Well, not exactly — don't know how to explain it.

* Beyond-text question

Figure 4.4.   Responses to word knowledge questions: Raymond.

✓ 1. *environment*
RESPONSE: The things around you.

✗ 2. *determines*
RESPONSE: They . . . say it, they predict.
TEACHER: Can you use the word *determines* in a sentence?
RESPONSE: He determined that the number was gonna be five.

✓ 3. *available*
RESPONSE: That it's . . . I can't explain it.
TEACHER: Then use it in a sentence.
RESPONSE: This pen is available for anybody that wants to use it.

✓ 4. *temporary*
RESPONSE: It's not built to stay long.

✓ 5. *permanent*
RESPONSE: That it stays there . . . the house stays up longer.

✗ 6. *sophisticated*
RESPONSE: I don't know the meaning of that word from the other thing, but I think I know another meaning.
TEACHER: O.K. Tell me the meaning you know.
RESPONSE: Well, I don't know how to explain it.
TEACHER: Could you put it in a sentence?
RESPONSE: This is a sophisticated truck.
TEACHER: What does that mean about the truck?
RESPONSE: That it's in a kind of motion or something. A kind of way.

Preliminary Analysis

Print Translation. Raymond had difficulty with only three words, or fewer than 1% of the words in the passage. Two miscues involved inserted and omitted sight words that did not alter the meaning of the passage. The third was potentially more serious; it involved the mispronunciation of the word *determines,* with the third syllable pronounced like the word *mines.* Raymond read the passage in 2 minutes and 12 seconds, at a rate of 125 words per minute. This is within the average range for seventh graders. On the basis of this evidence, it is possible to conclude that Raymond's print-processing strategies represent an area of strength.

Comprehension. Of the nine questions that pertained to text information, Raymond answered five correctly and two incorrectly (Items 6 and 8). His answers were only partially correct on the remaining two questions (Items 1 and 9). The partially correct answers involved use of examples rather than the more general formulations called for by the questions. Thus, Raymond's comprehension score (6 out of 9) was below 75%. Is there a possibility that his incorrect (or incomplete) answers were due to unknown words? We believe it will be useful for the reader to consider this issue before reading on; in particular, it is important to examine the way in which information pertinent to the questions Raymond missed was presented in the passage.

Raymond's incorrect responses to the comprehension questions suggested confusion over the terms *crude* and *sophisticated.* In response to the question of the difference between these two types of housing (Item 6), he replied that "crude is built to stay longer and sophisticated is not that long." In addition, he could not remember the kinds of materials used in sophisticated housing (Item 8), a plausible consequence of unfamiliarity with this term. Again, to gain experience with the diagnostic process, the reader should examine Raymond's responses on the word knowledge assessment at this point. Is there corroborating evidence that word knowledge interfered with comprehension?

Word Knowledge. Of the six words selected for assessment, there were only two that Raymond could not define — *sophisticated* and *determines.* For *sophisticated,* he thought that he knew "another meaning" for it — other than the one intended in the passage — but the meaning he gave ("a kind of motion") was incorrect. Note that the passage characterizes *crude* permanent housing (as in igloos, log cabins, and adobe huts) as "rough and unfinished" and later states that *sophisticated* houses have concrete foundations and frameworks made of wood, iron, or steel. Thus, the meaning of *sophisticated* in the sense of smooth, finished, and involving advanced technology is not given; this must be inferred from the contrast with *crude.* Raymond was evidently unable to make this inference; possibly he did not know what *crude* meant.

Because Raymond's difficulties on the comprehension questions seemed to be caused by his limited understanding of such terms as *determines, crude,* and *sophisticated,* his teacher decided to focus the subsequent probe on his word knowledge. In addition to determining his understanding of *crude* and further specifying his knowledge of *determines,* she planned to explore his understanding of the words *plentiful, readily,* and *insulator.*

Probe

The next day, after having Raymond reread the passage, the teacher asked what *crude* meant. He replied that *crude* "was a kind of housing" (as stated in the text) and he recalled the three examples that were given in the passage. Further questioning revealed that he had never before heard the word used nor could he use it in a sentence himself. It now seemed reasonable to consider Raymond's difficulty with Item 6 on the comprehension test as stemming primarily from the unfamiliarity of *crude* and *sophisticated.* Without prior knowledge of these two words, Raymond could only assume that the difference in the materials used in these two types of housing made for a difference in degree of permanence. Although the terms *rough* and *unfinished* were used in the passage to describe crude housing, he evidently failed to relate these words to the meaning of *crude.* Consequently, he could not, in turn, grasp the idea that *sophisticated* was the opposite of rough and unfinished.

In the case of *determines,* Raymond seemed to know what it would mean in the context of people making decisions or predicting outcomes, but he seemed unable to grasp the idea that existing conditions could (so to speak) do the same:

TEACHER: The passage states that environment determines the kinds of housing people choose. What does *determines* mean?
STUDENT: If they lived in a cold place, that would show that they lived in an igloo. If it was hot, that would say that they would live in a hut maybe.
TEACHER: O.K. Then what would *determine* the kind of shelter people choose?
STUDENT: Well, like the people who run the city, they can choose if they wanted brick or wood.
TEACHER: Yes. But what does *determine* mean?
STUDENT: They . . . say it, predict.
TEACHER: Can you use the word *determines* in a sentence?
STUDENT: He determined that the house was gonna be wood.

Thus, it was not so much the meaning of the word itself that gave Raymond difficulty; it was rather the underlying concept, that environmental conditions could set limits on people's choices, that escaped him. His failure to grasp this concept could explain his inability to give generalized answers to the questions, "What determines the kind of shelter people choose?" and "Where do we usually get the materials we build houses from?"

To explore further the possibility that word knowledge was a limiting factor in Raymond's comprehension, the teacher asked him to define several other words. He knew that *plentiful* meant "there is a lot." However, for *readily*, he said, "that it's done, finished, used . . . I'm not sure." And for *insulator*, he understood that it was related to keeping warm but thought it was "a type of machine, a heater." Although unfamiliarity with these latter two words did not interfere directly with overall passage comprehension, they provided additional evidence that word knowledge was somewhat inadequate.

Interpretation

Raymond's responses to the word knowledge and comprehension questions are summarized in Figure 4.5. The summary indicates that Raymond's comprehension (67%) is somewhat below the instructional range (75–89% comprehension) but not at his frustration level (less than 50%; see Table 7.1). When comprehension falls within the borderline range between instructional and frustration levels, it is appropriate to consider whether additional instructional support, directly in the major area of reading difficulty, may enable Raymond to read passages similar to this one with adequate comprehension.

Raymond's performance on the initial administration of the questions and during the probe indicates that his major difficulty is in the area of word knowledge. Generally, he is able to process text with good understanding. However, when the text and/or the questions used to assess comprehension involve terms that are unfamiliar to him, his comprehension is not entirely adequate. For example, he misconstrued the difference between "crude" and "sophisticated" housing. Similarly, although he understood the use of available materials in the specific instances cited in the passage, he did not grasp the general principle or concept that these instances exemplified. In both these failures of comprehension, unknown words were directly implicated. This evidence suggests that Raymond should be able to cope with passages similar to this one in difficulty if special instruction focuses on developing his knowledge of the words they contain.

Instructional Plan

In conclusion, the passage represents an appropriate level of difficulty for instructional purposes as long as important word meanings are discussed before reading. Raymond's instruction should focus on two major areas. First, using procedures discussed earlier in this chapter, the development

Figure 4.5. Summary of responses to comprehension and word knowledge questions: Raymond.

COMPREHENSION – WORD KNOWLEDGE SUMMARY

Name __Raymond__ Grade __7__ Date __2/84__
Book/Page __Exploring Paths 82-83__ Level __13__

COMPREHENSION

__6__ / __9__   __67__ % Correct

Level: Independent   Instructional
    (Borderline)   Frustration

A. RETELLING: Complete   Main Idea   Partial   (Inadequate)

Comments: _Missed main idea_

B. TEXT-RELATED COMPREHENSION

Item #	Response	Probe (Comments)	Item #	Response	Probe (Comments)
1	½	Examples rather than general idea	6	X	
2	✓		7	✓	
3	✓		8	X	
4	✓		9	½	
5	✓				

C. BEYOND-TEXT GENERALIZATION

Item #	Response	Probe (Comments)	Item #	Response	Probe (Comments)
10	½		12	X	
11	✓				

WORD KNOWLEDGE

__5__ / __10__   __50__ % Correct

Item Tested	Response	Comments	Item Tested	Response	Comments
environment	✓		crude (P)*	X	never heard of word before
determines	X	"predict"	plentiful (P)	✓	"a lot"
available	✓		readily (P)	X	defined "ready"
temporary	✓		insulator (P)	X	knew relation to warmth
permanent	✓				
sophisticated	X				

* Prefers to probe items

EVALUATION

A. COMPREHENSION: _Remembered examples and details but did not grasp the main idea of the passage; problems are directly related to unknown words._

B. WORD KNOWLEDGE: _Deficiencies in word knowledge currently interfere with comprehension; prereading activities focused on vocabulary development should improve comprehension._

of word meanings should be emphasized during prereading. Second, systematic instruction should be developed in the area of using text information to infer word meanings.

CASE 2: TANYA

Tanya is a seventh-grader assigned to a seventh-grade basal text. Her performance in class was erratic, and she was generally reluctant to participate in group discussions. The teacher decided to use diagnostic procedures to investigate the appropriateness of her basal assignment as well as the nature of her difficulty.

Preparation

Tanya's teacher selected a passage entitled "And Then There Were None" from the Bookmark Reading Program, which was being used for class instruction. The passage, 342 words in length, is shown in Figure 4.6. The reader should examine the passage in order to select words that would appear to be central to the understanding of this passage.

Figure 4.6. Diagnostic reading passage: Tanya.
(From EXPLORING PATHS: SKILLS READER, *HBJ Bookmark Reading Program,* by Margaret Early, Donald Gallo, and Gwendolyn Kerr, published by Harcourt Brace Jovanovich, Inc., 1979. Passage by Mark Wexler, copyright 1974 by the National Wildlife Federation. Reprinted from the April–May issue of National Wildlife Magazine.)

And Then There Were None

In 1534, a French sea captain reported that his men had killed more than a thousand "northern penguins" in a single day. But the bird to which the captain referred was not a penguin at all. It was the great auk, which at one time nested safely by the millions from Newfoundland to Scandinavia. Today the only specimens are in museums.

Like the penguin, the great auk could not fly but was a powerful swimmer. Each season, a female laid only one enormous egg, measuring about five inches long. Fully grown, a great auk stood three feet tall.

Originally, the great auk's largest nesting ground was an island off the eastern coast of Newfoundland. But by the early 1800's, fishermen had completely destroyed them. They used the birds' bodies for food or rendered them into cooking oil.

While the Napoleonic wars were raging across Europe, ships were sailing from Reykjavik, Iceland, to nearby Penguin Island, the second largest great-auk nesting colony, to kill the birds for food. There, using only large sticks, sailors slaughtered the proud birds by the thousands. Then, in the spring of 1830, another terrible blow struck the few great auks still at Penguin Island. The island just disappeared beneath the frigid ocean waters.

(Continued)

Figure 4.6. (*Continued*)

Most of the surviving great auks took refuge on the small island of Eldey. This island was not far from where their home had been.

But Eldey was not to remain their home for long. The birds had become famous in Europe. Collectors paid immense sums for great auk skins throughout the 1830's. In 1884, Carl Siemson of Reykjavik, an agent for prospective buyers, offered a large cash reward in hopes of getting just a few more skins of the almost extinct bird. A daring Icelandic fisherman answered the challenge and went to Eldey with a small crew. There, he looked for and finally discovered two great auks. He promptly killed them both. Soon after, he returned to Reykjavik to collect his reward; 100 crowns ($60) for the last two great auks on earth.

Tanya's teacher prepared both word meaning and comprehension questions to be administered following the reading of the passage. Before proceeding, the reader should compare the words that he or she selected with those chosen by the teacher: *specimens, slaughtered, surviving, refuge, prospective, immense,* and *extinct.*

Administration

Tanya read the passage in 3 ½ minutes, a rate of 98 words per minute. The record of her oral reading is given in Figure 4.7. Examine the evidence in order to decide whether print translation represents an area of reading difficulty for her.

Figure 4.7.   Record of oral reading: Tanya.
(From EXPLORING PATHS: SKILLS READER, *HBJ Bookmark Reading Program,* by Margaret Early, Donald Gallo, and Gwendolyn Kerr, published by Harcourt Brace Jovanovich, Inc., 1979. Passage by Mark Wexler, copyright 1974 by the National Wildlife Federation. Reprinted from the April–May issue of National Wildlife Magazine.)

And Then There Were None   18

In 1534, a French sea captain reported that his men had killed more than

a thousand "northern penguins" in a single day. But the bird to which the

captain referred was not a penguin at all. It was the great auk, which at one
                                                                    est

time nested safely by the millions from Newfoundland to Scandinavia.

Today the only specimens are in museums.

Like the penguin, the great auk could not fly but was a powerful swim-

mer. Each season, a female laid only one enormous egg, measuring about five

                                                                    at
inches long. Fully grown, a great auk stood three feet tall.

Figure 4.7. (*Continued*)

Originally, the great auk's largest nesting ground was an island off the

eastern coast of Newfoundland. But by the early 1800's, fishermen had com-

pletely destroyed them. They used the birds' bodies for food or ~~rendered~~ them   I

reneered

into cooking oil.

While ⟨the⟩ ~~Napoleonic~~ wars ⟨were⟩ raging across Europe, ships were sail-   3

Nupolentic

ing from ~~Reykjavik~~, Iceland, to nearby Penguin Island, the second largest   I

Reja

great-auk nesting colony, to kill the birds for food. There, using only large

sticks, sailors slaughtered the proud birds by the thousands. Then, in the

spring of 1830, another terrible blow struck the few great auks still at Pen-

guin Island. The island just disappeared beneath the frigid ocean waters.

Most of the surviving great auks took ~~refuge~~ on the small island ~~of Eldey~~.   3

rē-uge   *at Italy*

This island was not far from where their home had been.

But ~~Eldey~~ was not to remain their home for long. The birds had become   I

Italy

famous in Europe. Collectors paid immense sums for great auk skins

through ⟨out⟩ the 1830's. In 1884, Carl ~~Siemson~~ of ~~Reykjavik~~, an agent for   3

Simmons   Reja

prospect ⟨ive⟩ buyers, offered a large cash reward in hopes of getting just a few   I

more skins of the almost ~~extinct~~ bird. A daring Icelandic fisherman answered   I

estic

the challenge and went to Eldey with a small crew. There, he looked for and

finally ⟨discovered⟩ two great auks. He promptly killed them both. Soon after,   2

found

he returned to ~~Reykjavik~~ to collect his reward; 100 crowns ($60) for the last   I 0 *

Reja

two great auks on earth.

* *Miscues occurring more than twice were not counted.*

Her comprehension and word knowledge responses are shown in
Figure 4.8. The reader should examine this evidence in order to formulate
tentative answers to the following three questions. First, is Tanya experiencing difficulty with reading comprehension? Second, is her knowledge
of word meanings limited? Third, if she is experiencing difficulty with both
comprehension and word knowledge, is there evidence that her inadequate knowledge of word meanings accounts for her comprehension difficulty?

Figure 4.8. Responses to comprehension and word knowledge questions: Tanya.

Comprehension

½ **1.** What is this passage about? (the great auk; its extinction)
   RESPONSE: About two auks.

✕ **2.** In what part of the world did the great auks live? (Newfoundland, Scandinavia, Iceland, etc.)
   RESPONSE: On an island. [Do you know where it was?] No.

✕ **3.** When did the events in the story take place? (1500–1800)
   RESPONSE: Don't know.

½ **4.** ✕ a. What did the great auks look like? (penguins)
   RESPONSE: Like hawks; big birds.
   ✓ b. How big were they? (3 feet)
   RESPONSE: Three feet.

½ **5.** What problem did these birds have? (hunted and killed)
   RESPONSE: They couldn't stay in one place. The place where they were at would disappear under the ocean.

½ **6.** Why were the birds hunted and killed? (for food, cooking oil, skins)
   RESPONSE: For the money. If they caught two hawks, they get $50 worth, get 50 coins each. So they got 100 coins, they got $60.

½ **7.** What happened to Penguin Island in 1830 and what did the birds do? (it sank into the ocean; the birds swam to another island)
   RESPONSE: It disappeared under the ocean. [What did the auks do when this happened?] They flew away.

½ **8.** Why did Carl Siemson offer a large sum of money for the birds? (he was an agent for prospective buyers of skins)
   RESPONSE: He wanted to get some money for himself for the birds. So if he got 'em, then he would kill them. Then he would get some money for them and they both would have been even about the money.

✓ **9.** How much were the hunters paid for the last two great auks? ($60)
   RESPONSE: (not asked; answered in response to Item 6)

✕ **10.** What happens when animals are hunted and killed with no protection from the law? (extinction)
   RESPONSE: They'd be kind of scared. They'd be dead. Men would go to jail.

Word Knowledge

✕ **1.** *specimens*
   RESPONSE: Leaves. [Tell me more about it.] Not sure.

Figure 4.8. (*Continued*)

✓ **2.** *slaughtered*
RESPONSE: Kill someone.

✓ **3.** *surviving*
RESPONSE: They lived on.

✗ **4.** *refuge*
RESPONSE: Don't know.

✗ **5.** *prospective*
RESPONSE: You're looking at it . . . thinking about it.
TEACHER: Can you use it in a sentence?
RESPONSE: The prospective was easy.

✗ **6.** *immense*
RESPONSE: Clever.

✗ **7.** *extinct*
RESPONSE: Don't know.

Preliminary Analysis

Print Translation. The results from Tanya's oral reading are summarized in Figure 4.9. A total of 18 oral reading errors were tabulated. Of these, 5 were sight word errors, mainly insertions and omissions. A few of the sight word errors seemed to result when a difficult name was being attempted; the others are typical of mature readers and do little harm to meaning. The majority of miscues were in response to content words, and almost half of these were responses to somewhat unusual names. The others involved important content words (e.g., *extinct, rendered, refuge, prospective*). These errors may indicate some difficulty with the pronunciation of multisyllabic words. On the other hand, there were many difficult content words that she pronounced accurately (e.g., *Scandinavia, specimens, slaughtered, frigid*). Thus, the hypothesis that her apparent print translation difficulty may actually reflect unfamiliarity with these words should be considered.

Comprehension. The results from the comprehension questions are summarized in Figure 4.10. Of the 9 text-related comprehension questions that were asked, only one (Item 9) was correctly answered and 6 were only partially correct, yielding a comprehension score of 44%. Tanya showed some understanding of the destruction of the last two great auks but seemed unaware that this was the culmination of a series of destructive events. Her grasp of the details of time and place and the auks' resemblance to penguins was also quite limited.

It is not always possible to identify specific words that might be implicated in failures of comprehension. And so it was in this case. An examina-

Figure 4.9. Analysis of oral reading responses: Tanya.

ORAL READING ANALYSIS

Name _Tanya_ Grade _7_ Date _10/83_

Book/Page _Exploring Paths_ Level _13_

A. DIFFICULTY

_18_ / _342_ _95_ % Correct

Level: Independent (Instructional)
Borderline   Frustration

B. WORD LEARNING: Sight Word Errors

Printed Word	Oral Response	Probe	Evaluation
of	at		No problem.
finally	found		
the	[omitted]		
were	[omitted]		
at	[inserted]		

C. WORD IDENTIFICATION: Content Word Errors

Printed Word	Oral Response	Probe	Difficulty	Evaluation
great	greatest	✓		Consonants _____
throughout	through	✓		Blends/Digraphs _____
prospective	prospect	✓	meaning	Vowels _____
				Vowel Digraphs _____
refuge	rē-uge	re-fuge	meaning	Markers _____
rendered	reneered	✓		Affixes _____
Napoleonic	Nupolentic	Nā-pol-e-nic		Syllables _____
③ Reykjavik	Reja	Rē-ka-vik		Comments: _____
② Eldey	Italy	✓		
Siemsan	Simmons	Simson		
extinct	estic	✓	meaning	
discovered	[omitted]	✓		

D. INTEGRATION – FLUENCY

Integration: _Most sight word and affixed word errors are contextually appropriate. No use of correction strategies._

Fluency: Rate _342_ / _3.5_ = _98_ wpm Evaluation _Slower than average_

Phrasing _Fluent except when she encountered unknown words_

Figure 4.10. Summary of responses to comprehension and word knowledge questions: Tanya.

COMPREHENSION – WORD KNOWLEDGE SUMMARY

Name _Tanya_ Grade _7_ Date _10/83_

Book/Page _Exploring Paths_ Level _13_
_334-335_

COMPREHENSION

_4_ / _9_ _44_ % Correct

Level: Independent   Instructional
Borderline   (Frustration)

A. RETELLING: Complete   Main Idea   Partial   (Inadequate)

Comments: _Remembered only minor details._

B. TEXT-RELATED COMPREHENSION

Item #	Response	Probe (Comments)	Item #	Response	Probe (Comments)
1	1/2		6	1/2	
2	X		7	1/2	
3	X		8	1/2	
4	1/2		9	✓	
5	1/2				

C. BEYOND-TEXT GENERALIZATION

Item #	Response	Probe (Comments)	Item #	Response	Probe (Comments)
10	X				

WORD KNOWLEDGE

_2_ / _8_ _25_ % Correct

Item Tested	Response	Comments	Item Tested	Response	Comments
Specimens	X		extinct	X	unknown concept
Slaughtered	X		penguins(P)*	X	"tiny creatures"; unfamiliar
surviving	✓				
refuge	X				
prospective	X				
immense	X				

*P indicates a probe item

EVALUATION

A. COMPREHENSION: _Not probed because basic concepts were unfamiliar._

B. WORD KNOWLEDGE: _Lacks much background knowledge presumed by this material (e.g., didn't know what penguins looked like; could not locate Newfoundland, Scandinavia, or Iceland on globe; completely unfamiliar with concept of animal extinction._

107

tion of the passage in relation to incorrectly answered questions provided few good "leads" regarding specific words that might be sources of difficulty. There were, however, two words central to the general topic or theme of the passage that could have interfered with overall comprehension. The word *specimens* in the first paragraph provided an important clue to the fact that the birds were now extinct; unfamiliarity with this word would certainly make the rest of the passage more difficult to understand. Similarly, the word *extinct* in the last paragraph, if unknown, would represent a significant loss of information about the topic at large. In addition, there were a number of place-names mentioned in the passage that could have been unfamiliar; and the auks' resemblance to penguins would have little meaning without some knowledge of the latter. The teacher planned to explore these items during the informal probe. In the meantime, she examined the results of the vocabulary assessment.

Word Knowledge.   As summarized in Figure 4.10, Tanya was able to define or use in a sentence only two of the seven words she was asked about. On this basis, word knowledge was definitely an area of weakness. However, the unknown words alone could not fully account for her low comprehension score, as they were not directly related to incorrectly answered questions. Further questioning was undertaken, therefore, during the informal probe which followed, to determine whether Tanya's general information and conceptual knowledge were adequate for this passage.

Probe

The probe focused on Tanya's knowledge of a few key terms (e.g., *penguins* and *extinct*) and on her knowledge of the places mentioned in the passage. When asked if she knew anything about penguins, Tanya replied that they were tiny creatures, but she did not know what they looked like. With regard to the problem of extinction, Tanya did not know of any other animals that were hunted and killed until there were none left on earth; and she was unaware that anything was currently being done to protect wildlife from extinction. For example, she assumed that hunting and fishing licenses were primarily for the purpose of raising money and that wildlife preserves were designed to make it easy for people to see the animals. Finally, she did not know where Newfoundland, Scandinavia, or Iceland could be found on the globe.

Interpretation and Instruction

Tanya's comprehension of the diagnostic passage was extremely limited, as was her knowledge of important words in it. But lack of word knowledge was only part of the problem. She lacked, as well, the basic concepts necessary for understanding the significance of the events described. The teacher decided that passages at this level of difficulty were inappropriate for Tanya and that she should be assigned to an easier basal text. The teacher also planned to focus on important concepts and background knowledge during prereading instruction.

SUMMARY

We have described procedures for investigating the influence of unknown words on reading comprehension. And we have illustrated the application of those procedures in two case studies. The studies demonstrate how the assessment of word knowledge is related to the diagnostic process as a whole; they also highlight the way in which unknown words may underlie incorrect responses to comprehension questions. It was seen, in the first case study, that specific words may lead directly to incorrect answers. But, in the second case study the relationship was less direct and unknown words took their toll in fragmentation of overall comprehension. This latter phenomenon, in turn, reflects the important principles discussed in the first part of the chapter regarding the nature of word knowledge. It reflects the fact that we ordinarily know much more about word referents than just their definitional attributes and that it is this sum total of knowledge that "drives" the comprehension process. If this knowledge is inadequate with respect to the major theme of a passage, overall comprehension is likely to be disrupted. (In other words, had Tanya been aware of the *problem* of extinction, even though she did not know the word itself, she might have been able to recognize the events described in the passage as instances of that problem.) This view of word knowledge has clear implications — supported by recent research — for the design of instruction. In general, instruction in word meanings must go beyond definitions and include experiences that relate words to real-world situations and events.

5

Comprehension: Its Nature and Assessment

We assess comprehension by asking students questions about a passage they have read, or by having them retell the passage. If they perform well on these tasks, we assume that reading skills are adequate for the passage in question and for others like it. If performance is poor, we hypothesize a deficiency in either word knowledge or print translation skill — possibly both — and explore further as discussed in Chapters 3 and 4. If further examination reveals that these two aspects of reading are not deficient, we assume that the difficulty is specific to the process of comprehension itself — to the process of integrating and organizing information within and between sentences. In other words, a diagnosis of specific difficulty in the area of comprehension is made when word identification and word knowledge have been ruled out as major factors.

Thus, the assessment of comprehension plays a central role in the diagnostic process. It enables the teacher to estimate the level of materials that would be appropriate for instruction; and it serves as a backdrop against which word-level skills and knowledge may be evaluated. Hence, it is extremely important that the assessment itself be valid. The questions we ask must be reasonable, reflecting expectations that derive from an enlightened view of the nature of comprehension. The purpose of this chapter is to provide such a view and to offer suggestions for constructing questions that will be consistent with that view. Also included are brief remarks on the scoring and evaluation of students' responses. Further diagnosis and interpretation of comprehension performance will be taken up in the chapter that follows.

THE NATURE OF COMPREHENSION

There are many ways to view comprehension. It is "thought-getting and thought-manipulating" (Huey, 1908, 1968); it is "reasoning" (Thorndike,

1917); it is the "construction . . . and progressive refinement of hypotheses in order to comprehend, interpret, or evaluate text information [Mason *et al.,* 1984, p. 31]." These are all apt descriptions of effective reading, but they are *process* oriented—they pertain to the mental activities of the reader as he or she interacts with written language. We are concerned, instead, with the outcome, or *product,* of a reader's encounter with text—with the proficiency with which a reader engages in these activities. And we measure that proficiency by the ability to answer questions. Therefore, we will consider below those aspects of the reading process that seem directly to impinge on that ability.

Reading and Language

Reading is intimately related to language at many levels. Words that look alike tend to sound alike, and words and sentences have the same meaning when they are written as when they are spoken. Indeed, reading is commonly characterized as "a language process." But what is language? Is it the words we use when we speak? Or the sounds that make up the words? Or is it the organization of words in sentences? The very fact that we can ask these different questions suggests something about the answer: language involves all of these—sounds, words, and sentences.

Words, of course, have both sound (i.e., phonemes) and meaning. Thus, we can say that language is a system of sounds that conveys meaning. To know a language is to know that system, its *phonology.*

But the sequence of sounds that make up a word conveys meaning only to those who already know what thing, or action, or quality of things or actions, the word stands for. Knowing a language, then, involves some knowledge of its *lexicon* as well as its phonological workings.

Finally, the sequence of words that make up a phrase or sentence is meaningful only if one knows the third component of language, its *syntax.* Language, then, is not speaking or listening—these are language *behaviors.* It is, rather, a three-level system of *knowledge* that we use when we speak or listen (and when we write or read as well). It is this knowledge that enables us to express our thoughts and feelings (in speech or writing) and to understand others (in listening and reading). In other words, we use our *knowledge* of language in reading and writing just as we do in speaking and listening. And it is in this sense that we can say, "Reading is a language process."

The fact that reading and language are so closely related is sometimes taken to mean that reading comprehension—the comprehension of written language—is neither more or less than the comprehension of spoken language. That is, it is assumed that a student need have no difficulty understanding a written passage so long as the words and sentence structures in it are familiar and express ideas that are within his or her cognitive grasp. But this is only partly true. Reading differs from listening in a number of important ways, and accommodating to these differences is part of the process of learning to read. For one thing, except in the special case of oral reading in the classroom, reading is a solitary activity whereas spoken language generally involves the presence of another human being. This may be one reason many children find it difficult to concentrate during independent (silent) reading. For another thing, written language provides less information: the stress, pause, and intonation of spoken language are absent in reading, as are the relevant social and physical contexts, which supply important nonlinguistic clues. Thus, reading places the burden of comprehension more squarely on language alone. Finally, children must become aware that written language is processed in much the same way as spoken language — that it relates to real-world situations and can be understood by reference to prior knowledge and experience. A primary purpose of language-experience stories, it may be noted, is to help children develop this awareness.

For the child in the primary grades, then, the transition from spoken to written language entails a major adjustment over and above the adjustment to the print translation task. This adjustment is facilitated by the traditional practice of simulating in beginning reading materials the language of ordinary conversation. Later on, in the intermediate grades and beyond, students must adjust to written language that is more precise and tightly organized, more closely reasoned, and more complex in style and content than the language they are likely to hear in ordinary discourse. At all stages of learning to read, therefore, students need experiences that will help them make the necessary adjustments and develop skill in reading comprehension.

Comprehension Instruction

What are the experiences that develop comprehension skill? In general, the classroom activities designed for this purpose are guided reading, question answering, and discussion. Guided reading focuses the student's attention on the pertinent information in a passage; questions help the reader recall and reconstruct that information; and discussion helps him or her to think about and integrate the information. These activities help the student comprehend the individual passage and learn its specific content. At the same time, by "walking" students through the process of comprehension over and over again, these activities show them the nature and organization of connected prose and thus help them develop the ability to understand prose in general.

Other instructional activities related to reading comprehension include direct teaching of the vocabulary items, figures of speech, and background information necessary for understanding a particular selection.

But these activities — all typical prereading activities in a directed reading lesson — are really concerned with concept and vocabulary development, that is, with the skills underlying reading comprehension. Strictly speaking, "comprehension instruction" involves students directly in the process of comprehension by having them read connected prose and respond to it in some way, usually by answering questions. Ideally, the questions teach, albeit indirectly, what it means to understand a selection, how to distinguish between what is important and what is not, how ideas and information are organized and related to each other, and so forth.

Since comprehension instruction proceeds largely by means of questions, the kinds of questions asked take on major significance. The questions must elicit from the reader, in an orderly fashion, the main elements of the text. This shows the student what is important in any given text and develops his or her sense of what is generally important (Sadow, 1982). The questions asked in assessing comprehension should follow the same principle. These, too, must take the student, step by step, through the material. With some exceptions (e.g., questions designed for open-ended discussion or for specific teaching purposes), the questions that are appropriate for teaching comprehension skills are also appropriate for assessing them.

THE ASSESSMENT OF COMPREHENSION

For our purposes, then, from the point of view of educational practice and the instructional model proposed herein, reading comprehension can be defined as the ability to answer appropriate comprehension questions. This ability must, of course, be assessed in terms of the reading task, that is, the type and difficulty level of the materials a student is expected to read. A student who can answer correctly a set of questions that represent fairly the content of those materials is considered to have good comprehension skills.

It is also possible, of course, to test comprehension by "free recall"—by asking the student to retell the story or reproduce the information in his or her own words. The quality of the retelling or reproduction, however, may reflect the student's verbal and expository skills as much as his or her comprehension. Students vary widely in their ability to organize and verbalize information. Like other integrative and language skills, this one depends a great deal on practice. Since questions serve as "cues" or "prompts," much more can usually be remembered about a passage in response to questioning than can be reproduced in free recall. For example, Stein and Glenn (1979) report that in retelling a story young children tended to omit information about the goals and motives of story characters and yet they were able to answer questions about these story elements.

More significantly for our purposes, the tendency to provide additional information in response to questioning is much more pronounced among poor readers than among good readers. Bridge and Tierney (1981) found that of the total number of items of information that were ultimately remembered by a group of low-achieving third-graders, over 40% were given during the probe task which followed free recall. Therefore, while it may be well to give students an opportunity to retell the story in order to assess their ability to do so, a good set of questions will be needed in order to obtain a valid estimate of comprehension skill.

What Are "Good" Questions?

We come now to the heart of the matter. What is a good set of comprehension questions? Of the many questions that may be asked about any given selection of text, which ones will assess fairly the comprehension skill of the student who reads it?

This question has engaged the attention of experts in reading, and in education generally, for a very long time; much has been written about the kinds of questions teachers should ask. In general, teachers are urged to ask a variety of questions, in order to give students the opportunity to respond in a variety of ways to the materials they read. Teachers are also advised, more specifically, to avoid overemphasizing questions that require only memory for directly stated information. They are encouraged, above all, to focus on questions that require high-level thinking, in order to develop high-level cognitive processes. In short, questions have traditionally been approached from the standpoint of the mental processes required to answer them.

A major problem with this approach is that it is difficult to implement. A number of question-classification schemes based on this approach have been developed over the years (e.g., Barrett, 1976; Bloom *et al.,* 1956), but even the simpler ones require distinctions between levels or types of thought that are both difficult to make and "not warranted by the current state of our knowledge about language and cognition [Anderson, 1972, p. 149]." Moreover, questions that appear to elicit high-level thinking because they cannot be answered from directly-stated information may actually be quite trivial. Sanders (1966) points out that "thinking" questions cannot really be derived from insignificant subject matter, and he gives the following examples to illustrate:

> TEXT: This little pig went to market.
> QUESTIONS: Why? Did he go to buy or to be bought? . . . If to buy, what and for whom? Is he an informed buyer, the sort who would study the Buyers' Index and Consumers' Guide? . . . If he is to be sold, what price will he bring? What will be the effect on the market price . . .?
> TEXT: This little pig had roast beef.
> QUESTIONS: Would you consider roast beef proper food for a pig? Which is better, nutritionally speaking, rare or well-done meat? (p. 171).

Sanders's caution is particularly relevant for the field of reading, where the "instructional diet" of simple story materials may provide little "food for thought." That is to say, the stories designed for developing basic reading skills do not always lend themselves to thoughtful discussion, and attempts to use them for this purpose may be unproductive.

Another problem with the mental-process or levels-of-thinking approach to questions is that it does not recognize a distinction between literal questions that pertain to important information and those that pertain to incidental detail. Guszak (1967) alluded to this problem several years ago in his now-classic study of the kinds of questions teachers actually ask. He found that approximately 70% of the questions were of a literal nature, requiring only recognition (locating information in the passage) or recall (answering from memory) of factual information. While this result is frequently cited as evidence that teachers ask too many literal questions, Guszak himself was more critical of the quality of the questions. That is, he did not feel that a 7-out-of-10 proportion of literal questions was necessarily objectionable; he objected, rather, to the fact that many of the questions involved "retrieval of the trivial factual makeup of stories." It appeared to him that students were likely to miss "literal understanding" of story plots, events, and sequences "in their effort to satisfy the trivial fact questions of the teacher [p. 233]." But Guszak recognized, at the same time, that teachers could not employ more appropriate questioning patterns without clearer guidelines.

In sum, the traditional focus on levels of thinking in the design of questions does not effectively guard against trivialization of either nonliteral or literal questions. We believe, therefore, that questions should be approached from the standpoint of their relationship to the text as a whole rather than from the standpoint of the mental processes they elicit. Accordingly, we shall consider questions as either *related* to the text or *beyond* the text, according to whether or not they pertain to the information and ideas set down by the author. We shall also recommend that text-related questions be designed to follow the author's train of thought — that text-related questions as a whole reflect the story as a coherent whole. Beyond-text questions, on the other hand, will be those that take off where the author left off, so to speak. They will go "beyond the lines" and generalize about the author's ideas, extending them to other contexts or relating them to other ideas and issues. In a sense, these questions will relate to the ultimate purposes of reading — the enjoyment and appreciation of literature and the acquisition of knowledge and insight into human affairs. They will consist largely of the types of questions generally categorized and valued as thought provoking.

The rationale for our approach to questions is not just that mental process taxonomies are difficult to work with or that good thinking questions are difficult to derive from simple story materials. It lies also in recent insights into comprehension as a discourse process. These insights (described more fully in a later section) suggest that understanding "what it says" is not a trivial matter. In order to understand the communicative intent of a passage, readers must engage in levels of thought that are as simple or complex as the ideas communicated. They must select, combine, and integrate passage information, including information that is not explicitly stated. This means that text-related questions will generally require both literal and nonliteral (inferential) comprehension and that they must reflect the author's general intent as expressed in the passage as a whole.

In addition, our approach preserves the basic distinction between the ideas of the author (text related) and those of the reader (beyond text), thereby emphasizing that what is written must be understood in its own right before it can be explored in greater depth. The beyond-text questions will stimulate the reader to use the text as a springboard for reflection and conjecture. These questions will also draw on information and ideas that, while peripheral to the text, may be important to the reader.

A good set of questions, then, will consist of two basic parts or distinct types. One part will be text related, in the sense that it will adhere closely to the significant content of the text, including the inferences directly motivated by text coherence. The other will go beyond the text as a communicative entity and explore both its general implications and incidental detail. The first part will assess the student's comprehension of the passage as a whole — of the story told therein or the aspect of human knowledge conveyed — and will be a major factor in determining the suitability of like materials for instruction. The second part will assess the student's ability to use textual detail to broaden his or her knowledge and understanding of physical and social phenomena. The difference between these two parts is illustrated by the following example.

In the opening scene of *Charlotte's Web* (E. B. White, 1952), Fern learns that her father is on his way to the barn, carrying an ax, with the intent of "doing away" with the runt pig that was born the night before. Fern's mother explains that the pig would probably die anyway. Outraged at the "unfairness" of killing the pig "just because it is weak and little," Fern runs after her father and pleads for the pig's life. He gives in to her plea, saying, "I'll let you start it on a bottle, like a baby. Then you'll see what trouble a pig can be [p. 3]." The text-related questions on this passage would establish the facts of the story qua story — who did what, why they did it, and what happened as a result:

1. What is a runt pig? Who is Fern? Where does she live?
2. What was Fern's father going to do?
3. Why was Fern's father going to "do away" with the pig?

4. How did Fern feel when she learned that her father was going to kill the pig?
5. What did Fern do about it?
6. How did her father respond to her?

Notice that the questions follow the sequence of the story and that they are relatively independent of each other. That is, inability to answer (2), for example, does not preclude the possibility of answering (3) and (4). In fact, (3) and (4) give the answer to (2).

The beyond-text questions, on the other hand, might take up the conflict between Fern's point of view and her father's in terms of the more universal conflict between a child's point of view and an adult's. They might also (or alternatively) take up the conflict between the father's point of view as a farmer and as a father. For example:

1. Why did Fern's father "give in" to her plea? (Was he convinced that it would be unjust to kill a runt pig or was he merely being kind to his daughter?)
2. Why would Fern's father believe that it was all right to kill the pig?

It is clear that these questions cannot be answered from a reading of the passage, and it is in this sense that they are beyond the text or reader based. It is also clear that they represent what might be called "literary analysis." If the students have read another story in which there is a similar conflict between young and old or between the dual roles and responsibilities of an individual, the teacher may ask that it be recalled and contrasted with this one. Other beyond-text questions that might be asked include:

3. What was Fern's mother's reaction to the father's intention to kill the pig?
4. Fern's mother said, "It will probably die anyway." Why would that be likely to happen?
5. Fern's father said, "A weakling makes trouble." What is a weakling? In what way would it make trouble?
6. If you were Fern, would you be willing to take care of the pig?

Processes of Comprehension: Integration and Inference

In general, as illustrated above, text-related questions pertain to the communicative intent of a passage. This means that they represent more than a random sample of passage information; connected prose is more than a collection of discrete items of information. Rather, they represent the important statements or elements in a text, the elements that together reconstruct the main story line or the main ideas and related facts. Very simply, text-related questions pertain to the ideas and information without which the passage loses coherence.

The idea of passage coherence, or unity, is of course a familiar one. What is not as familiar, perhaps, is the fact that coherence comes about through the cooperative effort of reader and writer. Some recent investigations into the nature of comprehension make this clear. These investigations indicate that understanding connected prose is both an integrative and an inferential process. It is integrative in the sense that the reader must combine information from one sentence with that of another. For example, in reading the following lines:

(1) Father said, "Happy birthday!" as he handed Jimmy a box. (2) Jimmy opened the box, and (3) there he saw a small brown puppy.

the reader must *integrate* the information in sentences (2) and (3) in order to understand that the puppy was in the box. The reading process is inferential in the sense that the reader must often *infer* the nature of the relationship that obtains between information in two different sentences. In the sample above, the fact that the puppy was in the box must be inferred from the anaphoric referent *there* and from the fact that the puppy must *be* in the box in order to be *seen* there. In addition, the reader can infer from sentence (1) that the puppy is Jimmy's birthday present. Inferences like these are so "natural" that we are seldom aware of them as such. Here is another example:

(1) He placed the big cheese carefully in a wheelbarrow. (2) His wife draped it over with a snowy white linen napkin. (3) And the farmer went down the road, pushing the cheese before him [Schlein, 1966, p. 79].

We understand, although it is not directly stated, that the farmer is not really pushing the *cheese* but pushing the wheelbarrow in which the cheese has been placed. Thus, only with the information in sentence (1) in mind can sentence (3) be correctly interpreted.

In general, the integrative process enables the reader to store information more efficiently (in condensed form), and the inferential process determines the particular way in which information is interrelated (and thus the form in which it can be condensed). In the examples given above, we saw that inferences involved linguistic elements, spatial relations, and cultural knowledge. But inferences may also involve temporal and causal relations, not to mention many others. In fact, in each of the examples, the actions in sentences (1), (2), and (3) are readily understood, through inference, as following each other in close temporal succession. And two sentences occurring together, such as *The boy was scared. This was his first race,* lead equally readily to an inference of causality.

As the examples all show, integrative and inferential processes are by no means unique to written language. Linguistic linkages and spatial, temporal, and causal relations all inhere among statements in ordinary conversation as well as in connected text. And these relations are inferred on much the same basis in both cases — on the basis of general knowledge and previous experiences with the contextual situation. Perhaps it is because these processes are so much a part of the ordinary flow of everyday language that they have so long been taken for granted and only recently become the object of serious study. In any event, like other aspects of spoken language that are important to reading progress (e.g., vocabulary knowledge and knowledge of sentence structure), it is largely through reading that these processes develop; and it is through their development that a student is able to understand more and more "difficult" prose.

The processes of integration and inference are, as was noted, highly dependent on the reader's store of general knowledge and personal experience. There are, however, certain linguistic devices that appear to facilitate the integration of information. A few of these devices are described below. The teacher will find that some familiarity with them is useful in examining instructional materials either to determine their general appropriateness or to pinpoint possible sources of difficulty for students. Comprehension is most likely to break down at those points in a text where these devices have not been used effectively by the reader (or writer).

1.   *Topic Sentences.* A well-known technique for assisting the reader in integrating information involves placing a topic sentence at the beginning of a paragraph. This "points" the reader's attention to the topic of the paragraph and also to certain concepts in his or her knowledge store. The concepts thus activated serve as sources of information for making inferences (to the extent necessary) about how subsequent sentences are related to the first and to each other. For example, consider an opening sentence that reads as follows: "Tom slammed the door as he came out of the house wearing old clothes and carrying a bucket of paint." This points the reader to the idea that someone was or will be painting something (as suggested by the old clothes and, of course, the bucket of paint) and that he may be angry, possibly about having to paint. With these ideas in mind, the next sentence—"The barn was a long way off."—can be understood as (probably) telling what was to be painted. Then, if the paragraph is well structured, subsequent sentences will relate back to the slamming of the door as well as expand on the significance of the location of the barn. Thus, the opening sentence establishes a situational or conceptual context within which each sentence may be related to what has gone before. "Determining

these relationships is part of the integrative process [Carpenter & Just, 1977, p. 218]."

2.   *Pronouns.* Another linguistic device that signals how a sentence is related to the previous discourse is the pronoun. Typically, an author will make repeated references to the same object, event, or idea. The use of a pronoun in such instances alerts the reader to the commonality of reference and thus facilitates (at least for adults) the integration of incoming information with prior information.[1] The pronoun in effect signals that something is related to "old" information, and directs the reader to search his or her memory (or the text) for the previous mention of its referent in order that he or she might integrate the new information with that already given. For example, in the paragraph:

It was a perfect *day* for flying. The air was still and there wasn't a cloud in the sky. He couldn't have asked for a better *one*.

the pronoun *one* facilitates integration of the information in the final sentence with the "old" information about *day*.

3.   *Synonyms and Synonymous Expressions.* Repeated reference to a topic that has already been introduced in discourse may also be made through synonyms. This device is a more difficult one for the reader than the pronoun. Although the antecedent of a pronoun may be ambiguous at times, the pronoun itself always clearly signals that the referent has been mentioned before. A synonym, on the other hand, is not marked as yet another word or expression for something previously mentioned and hence does not instruct the reader to search for its previous mention. If the reader does not recognize, from the referential context, that a word or expression refers to an aforementioned item, the integrative process will be disrupted and there will be some loss in comprehension. For example, notice the word *victims* in the second sentence below.

During the past century nearly one hundred kinds of living creatures have disappeared from the face of the earth. . . . Some of the better known victims have been the European wild ox, . . [Gilbert, 1959, p. 97].

The reader must grasp the fact that the word *victims* is coreferential with "living creatures [that] have disappeared from the face of the earth." This requires an awareness that extinction comes at the hands of others, so that

[1] The unifying effect of pronouns has been demonstrated with adult subjects (Lesgold, 1972b) but not with children; apparently children (ages 8–11) can identify the antecedents of personal pronouns with a high degree of accuracy but they do not derive any advantage from them in remembering information (Lesgold, 1972a).

extinct creatures can be termed "victims." Thus, familiarity with the important facets of a referential situation is often required in order for the reader to recognize coreferents.

4. *Definite Article.* The use of the definite article *the* in a text also marks a distinction between old and new information and thus facilitates comprehension. "*The* implies that the item now mentioned has a unique and specific referent that has previously been established, and therefore cues the listener/reader to match this item with one already in memory [Gourley, 1978, p. 177]." The following pairs of sentences illustrate how dependent we are on this device:

> **1.** Yesterday Beth sold her old Ford to a dealer. Jack bought *the* car [the one Beth sold] today.
>
> **2.** Yesterday Beth sold her old Ford to a dealer. Jack bought *a* car [*not* the one Beth sold] today.

5. *Syntactic Structure.* The structure of a sentence is itself a device by which information may be tagged as new. In general, the information at the end of a sentence is assumed to be the new information. Thus, in the simple active sentence *John loves Mary,* "the fact that John loves someone is interpreted as old information and the identity of that someone is interpreted as new [Carpenter & Just, 1977, p. 232]." Similarly, in the passive counterpart of that sentence (i.e., *Mary is loved by John*), Mary's being loved by someone is marked as old information and the identity of that someone, John, which appears in the last part of the sentence, is the new information being conveyed. When new information is given at the beginning of a sentence, it is often marked as such in the syntactic structure, for example, through "*it* clefts": *It was Mary that John loved; It was John that loved Mary.*

6. *Connective Terms.* The vast majority of words in a language — the nouns, verbs, adjectives, and adverbs, or so-called content words — are *referential* in nature. That is, they refer directly to particular objects, actions, attributes, and qualities. Every language includes, as well, a small set of words that are *relational,* sometimes called "function words." Unlike the linguistic devices described above, which simply signal the *advent* of new information that is related to what has gone before, relational words specify the *way* in which new information is related to the old:

> Causal relations, for instance, are typically marked by causal conjunction (e.g., "since," "because," "due to"). The description of a process may often include such temporal inter-unit links as "first," "next," and "then." Contrastive elaborations may be marked by adversative conjunctions (e.g., "however," "on the other hand"). List-like elaborations are marked by additive conjunctions such as "in addition," "likewise," and "furthermore." Conclusions are typically preceded by temporal conjunctions such as "in conclusion" or "to sum up." Finally,

examples are signaled by the additive conjunctions "for example" and "for instance" [Geva, 1983, p. 385].

Thus, while nouns, verbs, adjectives, and adverbs represent the propositional content of a passage, the relational words express its structure, the connections between propositions.

The linguistic devices described above help the reader relate incoming information to information previously given, and inferential processes play an important role in this aspect of comprehension. There are, however, certain types of inferences required for text coherence that are not directly motivated by linguistic cues. These might be considered "high-level" inferences. High-level inferences require the reader to add information to a text — to make certain connections that are implicit not so much in the language as in the ideation. They are necessitated by the fact that a text does not contain all the information that is needed to fully understand it. Writers — like speakers — must make assumptions about the range of knowledge and social sophistication their readers — or listeners — already possess in order not to burden them with unnecessary detail. Thus, matters of common knowledge or shared cultural values and experiences tend not to be made explicit. This means that there is almost always an implicit as well as an explicit text; understanding the implicit text is what is sometimes referred to as "reading between the lines."

The implicit text, however, does not consist of *all* inferences that *can* be made; it consists of those that must or should be made for purposes of coherence. For example, if we read that "Mike's brother took Mike to a quiet street to teach him to ride his new bike," we may infer that Mike's brother is kind and helpful and that a quiet street in this context is one with little traffic. But these inferences may not be required for text coherence; they may be only incidental, in the same way that certain details found in the explicit text — the color of the bike, perhaps — may be incidental to the story. Only if inferences are connected in some way to what has gone before or what is to come after can they be considered part of the implicit text and necessary for text coherence.

Crothers (1978) has described two general types of inferences the reader must typically make in constructing a coherent text. Both types involve adding information that relates to more than one proposition in the explicit text. In one, the information added is a connective showing how one proposition in the text is related to another. In the other, the information added is itself a proposition linking two other propositions in the text.

1. *Connective Inferences.* These specify the temporal, causal, or other connections between sentences, connections that are frequently left implicit in discourse text. They are equivalent to, and can usually be made explicit by, familiar terms such as *and, but, or, since/because, so/therefore/ that is why, for example, this means,* and *namely.* Note how this type of inference (shown in brackets above the line of actual text) clarifies the information in the following paragraph.

Most people believe that earthworms are of little use except for fish
[for example]
bait. But scientists have found that they are very important. /Earth-
[In this way]
worms eat soil. /They make the soil better by grinding it up as it passes
[For another example]
through their bodies. /The holes that earthworms make as they burrow

in the earth make it easier for the roots of plants to enter the soil.
[For still another example]
/Earthworms use leaves to line their underground homes. These leaves
[Thus]
make the soil richer. /Scientists have found that earthworms are the
[because]
earth's plowmen. /They keep stirring up the soil which helps to raise

better crops.

Additional examples follow:

Ken Baxter, who was 15 years old, wore a costume that was far too
[since]
young for him. /He came as a bunny rabbit.
[therefore]
It was early Monday morning, and /the bank was nearly empty.

2. *Propositional Inferences.* These are "additions of new propositions to the text base [Crothers, 1978, p. 63]." They add the information and ideas that are plausible as "reasons, causes, effects, and the like [p. 63]." In the preceding paragraph on earthworms, it is stated that the leaves the earthworms use to line their underground homes "make the soil richer." Since this information represents an example of how earthworms make the soil better, the propositional inference may be drawn that "richer soil is better soil."

Organization of Information

Beyond the processes of integration and inference, reading also involves the organization of information (both stated and implied) across many sentences — that is, at a more global level, such as that of whole paragraphs or even passages. This type of organization is made possible by what are called internal frameworks or "schemata." Internal to the individual, these schemata are built up over relatively long periods of time out of acquired knowledge, experience, and understanding. But they are more than a simple store of information and ideas. They represent the high-level order an individual has imposed on his or her experiences (including school experiences), and at the same time, they represent the order an individual can *bring* to new experiences. New experiences are "assimilated" into existing schemata, and schemata are always in the process of changing as a result of new experiences. It may be that certain kinds of new knowledge take a long time to acquire because they require the development or rearrangement of whole systems or networks of knowledge.

Schemata are hypothetical constructs that help us understand and explain many of the cognitive behaviors we observe. In terms of reading comprehension, they help us understand why (or how) people remember certain things and forget others, or why certain things are distorted in memory. Since people tend to remember the information in a text that is important or relevant to the central theme, it is assumed that they have available some internal mechanisms for sorting and organizing incoming information. These mechanisms can be thought of as generalized ideas about the high-level organization of information. Thus, we probably have a schema that guides our reading of news stories in the daily newspapers and a different schema for reading editorials, still a different one for mystery stories, for romantic fiction, and so forth.

Educational experiences are surely an important factor in the development of an individual's schemata — in the way an individual comes to organize and understand social and natural phenomena. At present, it is by no means clear how educational practices should be modified, if at all, to facilitate this development. It seems reasonable, however, that the high-level organization of knowledge in a text should be reflected in the questions we ask if these questions are to develop and assess the ability to understand discourse.

Text-related and Beyond-text Questions

The insights discussed above are important for several reasons. They highlight the reading process as a global one, in which the reader is actively engaged in constructing a unified representation of text information, and they heighten our sensitivity to the "connectedness" of written prose. They strongly imply that there can be no substitute for "real" reading experiences, that is, for experiences with a variety of types of discourse text. Another important implication is that materials may be difficult to understand if they require inferences that are beyond the reader's experiential or knowledge base. Finally, these insights provide a rational basis for the design of text-related questions. They help us recognize that while such questions do not pertain to the deepest levels of meaning or the ultimate purposes of reading in the way that beyond-text questions do, they are an important intermediary step.

Recent insights emphasize, further, that text-related questions should pertain to the ideas and information that contribute in some way to the text as a whole, for it is a mistake to confuse comprehension with memory for incidental detail or even for incidental inferences. In fact, these insights suggest that such details are frequently forgotten because they bear so little connection to other textual information and, therefore, are only superficially processed. For example, it may make no difference, in terms of other events in a story, whether a certain incident took place in the morning or afternoon, last week or this week, or whether it was first noticed by one story character or by another. If it does not, the reader has no opportunity to relate these items of information to subsequent events nor any need to relate them to earlier ones. Similarly, in an adventure tale about a series of incidents, if it makes little difference whether the incidents occurred in one order or another, there will be minimal processing of, and little memory for, the sequence of events.

In short, the process of following the main story line or thread of an argument does not tend to reinforce or "activate" nonessential facts, and memory for them is likely to be spotty and idiosyncratic. Such facts may or may not be remembered, but good comprehension of discourse does not imply that they are likely to be. Rather, good comprehension means grasping the vital information in the text and the train of thought (the low-level and high-level inferences) that binds this information together.

If text-related questions involve both "reading the lines" and "reading between the lines," then beyond-text questions may be conceived as "reading beyond the lines." These questions also involve inferential processes, but the inferences are more in the nature of "grand conclusion[s] from a number of explicit and implicit propositions combined [Crothers, 1978, p. 55]." That is, they are not cued by specific linguistic devices nor by any specific inferences that are motivated by text coherence — they do not "connect" specific statements in the text with each other. It is in this sense that beyond-text questions may be said to involve the "deeper" levels of meaning. And as with text-related inferences, the reader must draw on his or her fund of general knowledge to arrive at these deeper meanings.

In the case of story materials, beyond-text questions generally call on the reader to apply his or her knowledge of human events, actions, and feelings to a given situation. For example, in a story about a young boy whose father and brothers are all fishermen, we learn that the thing the boy wanted most was to go fishing with his father. We can understand this desire in terms of boys in general — most boys would think going fishing is fun. But we can also understand it, with reference to this boy in particular, in terms of boys' desires to do what their fathers and older brothers do, to be like them, to feel grown-up, etcetera. In other words, we understand the story character's feelings and appreciate the story more fully because we recognize those feelings as consistent with what we know about little boys in general. Beyond-text questions should assess this application of knowledge.

Another example is provided by Miriam Schlein's (1966) story, "The Big Cheese." In this story a farmer decides to give his finest cheese to the king. Here we recognize the farmer's pride in his work, and it is through knowledge of this type of pride that we understand why the farmer would elect to give his cheese to the king instead of selling it in the open market and allowing "just anyone" to eat it. Also involved, of course, is the special feeling that citizens may have toward their leaders. And parallel to the farmer's pride is the pride shown by a goatherd, who insists that cheese made from goats' milk is better than that made from cows' milk. For this story, too, then, beyond-text questions require an examination of the actions and reactions of story characters from the point of view of their consistency with certain general ideas about human events. As we ask such questions, we help students develop these ideas; and we help them see the relevance of these stories to the "human condition."

It should be noted that a particular question may be either text related or beyond the text, depending on the answer that is expected (or given) (Pearson & Johnson, 1978). A text-related answer can be justified with specific reference to the text. A beyond-text answer is one that is based on insights or logical reasoning that is not clearly implied in the text. Consider the following question and some possible answers concerning "The Big Cheese" (Schlein, 1966).

QUESTION: Why did the goatherd suggest that he and the farmer taste the cheese?
ANSWER A: Because it was lunchtime and he was hungry.
ANSWER B: Because he didn't believe it was the best cheese (because it was not made from goats' milk).
ANSWER C: Because he thought the farmer should be sure it was the best cheese before he gave it to the king.

Answers B and C pertain directly to the goatherd's own statements: "Then how can it be the best cheese ever made? The finest . . . cheeses are always made from goats' milk [p. 80]," and "How can you present the king with a cheese you do not know tastes the best? [p. 81]" So answers B and C are text related and, as such, show good comprehension of the story line. Answer A goes beyond the text, since there is no clear implication in the text that the goatherd's motives are not as he represents them. This answer, then, is ambiguous with respect to the student's comprehension of the text itself. It could represent good insight into the fact that people sometimes have ulterior motives. On the other hand, it could be that the student simply failed to understand the persuasive arguments of the goatherd, as given in the text, and that his or her answer is really a "stab in the dark."

However, beyond-text questions need not be confined to issues involving human goals, desires, and feelings. There is much information of a factual nature to be gained from stories. Teachers' questions should help students "pull" this information out and make it part of their general fund of knowledge — part of the background knowledge they will be able to bring to subsequent stories. For purposes of assessment, these questions may help the teacher evaluate the adequacy of the student's background knowledge in relation to story content. This is important, as it is often a lack of some specific information that leads to misunderstanding of story events. In "The Big Cheese," (Schlein, 1966) for example, students must understand that farmers *sell* their products at a "market" (many city children may think of "markets" only as places where families buy food). They must also grasp the fact that cheese may be made of milk from goats as well as from cows and that in "olden" days a farmer might transport his products by wheelbarrow.

CONSTRUCTING COMPREHENSION QUESTIONS

In general, as explained above, text-related questions recapitulate the main story line or central ideas in a text. Unfortunately, there are no simple prescriptions or rules to follow in constructing these questions, no objective methods for determining that one idea or piece of information is essential or more important than another. Here teachers must rely on their own clear understanding of the text to be used, based on a careful reading, rereading, and analysis of it. One way to proceed, though not necessarily the only way, is as follows.

The teacher should first read the text for an overview of its content and organization, much as would be done for any other material of its kind. On this reading, the teacher will also gain insight into what the passage is like, which parts stand out in memory and which are readily lost. The teacher should then try to construct a set of questions such that the answers will represent a broad outline of its significant content. A second reading of the text will enable the teacher to "fill in" the outline. A third and final reading will suggest some beyond-text questions. These are described more fully below, then illustrated with the questions that would result with a typical passage. Because of their differences in form, content, and purpose, story materials and nonfiction will be treated separately.

Story Materials

On the first reading the teacher should simply follow the story line (i.e., find out who did what, why they did it, and how it all came out). This will form the intuitive base for the group of questions that will reflect the essence of the story and assess story comprehension. Highly relevant to this step are the results of some recent investigations into story structure and story recall.

In general, research has shown, the parts of a story that are remembered best are those which seem to "make up" the story; they are the "structurally important units." What are these "structurally important units"? Basically, they represent the kinds of information commonly found in most stories, and this commonality is probably the reason they tend to be remembered so well. What we call a story is normally made up of certain basic elements, and when people are asked to recall a story, they usually remember something about each of these elements. Apparently, through the experience of reading (or hearing) many stories, people develop a set of expectations about them. These expectations are like "slots," which people fill as they read. A story that conforms to these expectations, and thus permits the reader to find the information for each slot with relative ease, is easier to follow than one that does not. We can say that such a story is well formed (Mandler & Johnson, 1977).

The idea that stories are made up of certain common elements and that these elements are represented in the mature reader's system of knowledge is an important one. It is part of the more general theory of comprehension discussed earlier — the theory that organized systems of knowledge, called schemata, play a central role in discourse comprehension by serving as "advance organizers" for incoming information. It will be recalled that schemata are akin to the background knowledge and experience a reader brings to the reading task; in schema theory, knowledge and experience are further conceptualized as highly organized and abstract. A story schema, it is theorized, represents the reader's generalized knowledge of the elements common to most stories.

A number of investigators in the field of cognitive psychology have attempted to describe the basic elements of a well-formed story. Such descriptions are called "story grammars." These grammars categorize story events in much the same way that traditional grammar categorizes words (nouns, verbs, adjectives, etc.) and sentence parts (subject, predicate, complement, etc.). The grammars that have been developed thus far apply only to very simple stories and are often highly complex, so a detailed study of them would not be useful for our purposes. However, a simplified version of one such grammar (Rumelhart, 1975) is described below in the belief that it may prove useful to teachers in charting the main line of a story and writing questions that pertain to it.

In Rumelhart's (1975) grammar, a story consists of a setting and one or more episodes. The *setting* includes the time and place in which the events occurred, the introduction of the main characters, and any additional information that might be necessary to make the ensuing events understandable. An *episode* consists of *(a)* an initiating event; *(b)* the reaction of the main character to that event; *(c)* an action on the part of the main character that is motivated by his reaction; and *(d)* a consequence that is a direct outcome of the action. The *initiating event* is what sets the story in motion. It may be a sudden change in the external environment (e.g., "Mary heard a strange noise in the kitchen"; "Bob came to Jill with the news that the ice was too thin for skating.") or it may be some internal event (e.g., "Joe remembered that today was Lisa's birthday"; "Bill remembered he hadn't seen Joe in a long time.") In either case, the initiating event sets up a situation to which the main character responds. His response is both internal and external. More specifically, the character's internal *reaction* involves some feeling, thought, desire, or goal ("Joe knew she wanted a gold necklace.") and this in turn motivates him to take some external *action.* The action itself may be simple and direct ("He told his secretary to pick out a gift at Tiffany's."), or it may involve some subsidiary goals, plans, and attempts to carry them out (canceling a luncheon engagement, borrowing money from a friend, etc.). The action is likely to be the most elaborated part of the story. Finally, the action is responsible for (i.e., initiates, causes, or allows) some *consequence,* and that ends the episode. The consequence (or any other part of the episode) may then serve as the initiating event of another episode.

This story grammar, then, indentifies five broad categories of story information — setting, initiating event, internal reaction, external action, and consequence. The amount of detail in each category will naturally vary from story to story, and certain categories may be omitted. Setting information may involve only a simple introduction of the protagonist (e.g., "Jenny was on her way to the library."). This is often the case in stories concerning the routines of daily life. Internal reactions are also sometimes expressed only vaguely, or not at all. A character may simply take some action in response to an external (initiating) event, as in the following example: "Mary heard a loud crash outside. [initiating event] She hurried to the window. [action]" In this example we may infer that the internal reaction was one of curiosity or, perhaps, fear. When, as here, the internal reaction is obvious given the nature of the initiating event, its omission does not interfere with comprehension. The consequence of an action may be self-evident as well (e.g., "He threw the glass across the room [and it broke]."). Finally, there may be no overt initiating event; a story may begin with a desire or goal of the protagonist, for example, "Sara was determined to win the race." In this example, the initiating event (the announcement of the race, perhaps) occurs prior to the beginning of the story and is not mentioned in the story. In addition, the order in which story information is given may deviate from that described above. Setting information may be postponed and introduced in an episode at the point at which it is relevant; or a consequence may be described before its antecedent action: "They couldn't find the ball anywhere. Judy had hit it as hard as she could."

What story grammars do is describe in general terms the basic outline of a simple, well-formed story in Western societies. They suggest that the reader not only expects a story to be about some action or series of actions taken by a main character, but he or she also expects those actions to be purposeful. In other words, an action is expected to have both an antecedent (in the form of some initiating event and/or internal reaction) and a consequence. We believe that this view of stories can serve as a guide in the process of writing questions. If the basic outline of a story typically involves five broad categories of information, then we can think of a story as providing the answers to five categorical or generic questions, somewhat like the following:

[Setting]	1. Where and when did the story take place? Who were the main characters in the story?
[Initiating event]	2. How did it all begin? [What was the predicament of the main character(s)?]
[Action]	3. What did the main character(s) do?
[Internal reaction]	4. Why did he (she, they) do it?
[Consequence]	5. What happened as a result?

These generic questions reflect the idea of a story as a progression of related events — one thing leads to another; that leads to still another, and so on. With these questions in mind, following the initial reading of the story, the teacher should be able to derive a set of questions that reflects the main story line. There may, of course, be more than one question in any category, and some categories may be too sparsely represented in the story — too vague or nonspecific — to be questioned. Thus, the generic questions should make us sensitive to any ambiguities, missing information, or other weaknesses in the story structure.

The derivation of text-related questions based on story structure constitutes the first step in the process of writing questions. For the second step, a second reading of the story will usually be necessary. In this step, the story outline constructed in step 1 will be "rounded out" with important details. With very short stories, all or most of the details may be important for the story line. In fact, the shorter the story, the less likely it is to include "incidental" detail. But, with longer stories, as explained earlier, many details are likely to be forgotten, particularly if they do not carry the story forward.

This process of question construction will be illustrated for the third-grade story, *The Restless Kangaroo,* shown in Figure 5.1. The reader is encouraged to study the story and derive a set of questions that reflect the important content and structure of the story.

A typical set of questions that might result from the first and second steps of question writing is shown in Table 5.1. While the questions derived

Figure 5.1.   Narrative passage.
(From WITH SKIES AND WINGS, LEVEL 9, pp. 207–213. In *Reading 360*, published by Ginn and Company, 1969. Story by Edythe R. Warner; reprinted by permission.)

The Restless Kangaroo

The zoo had a problem. The problem was Tanga who was the mother kangaroo.

She had begun to take her joey, as kangaroo babies are called, out of her pouch in the night. For two mornings Pete, who is the head keeper at the zoo, had found the cold little joey on the dirt floor of the kangaroo pen.

Each time Pete rubbed the joey with a towel until he was warm. Then he tucked him back into Tanga's pouch. And Tanga stood still because she was a gentle kangaroo.

But on the third morning the joey was found on the floor again.

"This is a problem," the zoo director said. "The joey is too young to be out of Tanga's pouch."

"It is a new problem," said Pete. "Tanga has been a good mother. She always kept her other joeys safe until they were older."

"We must find out why she does this now," said the director. "If this goes on the joey might catch a chill. He may even die."

"Tonight I will stand watch at Tanga's pen," said Pete. "Perhaps I can learn why she puts her joey on the floor."

"That is a good idea," said the director.

When night came to the zoo, Pete went to the animal barn where Tanga lived. He sat down on a chair in front of her low gate.

In the next pen the great elk, with its wide antlers, snorted. On the other side of Tanga's pen a zebra stamped its feet and then a deer sneezed.

The llamas and camels and the buffalo gazed over their gates at Pete for a long time. It was plain that they were surprised to see him there at that time of night.

But at last they all became used to him and, one by one, they went to sleep.

And Tanga lay down on her side in her own pen on her clean straw bed and went to sleep also.

The big barn was quiet and dark but for the soft glow of one light up near the roof.

Pete yawned and leaned back in his chair. He had worked hard all day. He was sleepy and it was hard to keep awake. But he did keep awake.

After a while he heard a "scritch-scratch" in the stillness. He stood up and looked into the shadows of Tanga's pen.

Tanga was sound asleep. But something was moving. It was the joey's tiny paw.

It waved back and forth, back and forth, out of the opening of Tanga's

Figure 5.1. (*Continued*)

pouch. Then it dug down into the straw and Pete could hear the same "scritch-scratch" that he had heard before.

When the joey pulled a pawful of straw into her pouch, Tanga kicked her long back feet. But she did not wake up.

Soon the joey pulled another pawful of straw into the pouch. This time Tanga gave a loud sigh.

Without opening her eyes she turned on her back. She lifted the joey with her front paws and dropped him into the straw. Then she turned over on her side and was still again. And she hadn't waked up at all.

The joey scratched around a bit and then he too was still.

"I have found the answer to our problem." Pete whispered to himself. "Tanga's joey is a naughty baby."

He tip-toed into the pen and picked up the shivering joey and tucked him in his jacket. Then he felt inside Tanga's pouch with gentle hands. Besides the straw, he found sharp pebbles from the dirt floor of the pen.

"Poor Tanga!" Pete said. "No wonder you put your joey out in the cold! No kangaroo likes to be scratched by straw and pebbles!"

He cleaned her pouch and Tanga opened her eyes and blinked her long lashes as if she were saying "Thank you."

"There, Tanga," said Pete when he was through. "Go back to sleep. Things will be better from now on."

He took the joey to the zoo office. There he rolled him in a towel and put him in a box to keep warm.

When morning came Pete told the zoo director what happened.

"You see," he said, "when Tanga's joey wakes up he likes to play with the straw and pebbles. Then he takes them into his own pouch-bed. He is a naughty little kangaroo."

The director smiled. "I don't think he is naughty," he said. "He is just a restless little kangaroo. But we will fix it so this will not happen again."

As soon as all the other zoo keepers heard the story about Tanga and her restless kangaroo, they went right to work.

They moved Tanga and her joey away from the animal barn and into a big cage in the zoo's main building. The cage had a smooth floor with no pebbles. And instead of straw for a bed Pete gave Tanga a blanket.

From then on there was no more trouble. When the restless joey awoke at night he pulled and tugged on the blanket until he was tired. Then he went back to sleep.

The zoo's problem was solved. The joey was not found out of Tanga's pouch again until he was old enough to climb in and out by himself — which he did, over and over again, until he finally grew so big that he could no longer fit.

Table 5.1. Questions Based on Narrative Passage[a]

Story structure category	Story structure questions (step 1)	Detail questions (step 2)
Setting	S1. Where did this story take place? S2. Who is Pete? S3. Who is Tanga?	D1. What is a joey? [What is a baby kangaroo called?]
Initiating event/problem	S4. What was the problem that the zoo was having with the kangaroos?	D2. What did Pete do with the joey each time he found him on the floor of the pen?
Internal reaction	S5. Why was that a problem? [Why were the zookeepers worried about the baby kangaroo being out of the mother's pouch during the night?]	
Action	S6. What did Pete, the zookeeper, do to find out about the problem? [Why did Pete stay up all night watching the kangaroo pen?]	
Consequence	S7. What did Pete find out when he watched the kangaroos all night? [What did the joey do in the middle of the night?] S8. Why did Tanga take the joey out of her pouch at night? S9. Why did the joey put the straw in the mother's pouch? S10. What did Pete do to solve the problem for the kangaroos?	D3. What did Pete find when he felt inside the mother kangaroo's pouch? D4. How did the new pen solve the problem? [How was the new pen different from the old one?] D5. What did the joey do in the new pen when he woke up in the middle of the night?

[a] The questions shown in brackets suggest some alternatives in terms of wording and/or emphasis that seem to be equally appropriate.

during step 1 are quite predictable, those written during step 2 result from a less systematic process. There are no hard and fast rules regarding questions of detail; teachers must be guided by their own sense of story cohesiveness.

In examining the questions generated for *The Restless Kangaroo*, it is interesting to note the relationship between step-1 and step-2 questions. That is, there is usually only one correct answer to a step-2 question, whereas step-1 questions give the student more latitude in framing his or her answer. More importantly, step-2 questions are often implicit in one or another step-1 question, so that step-2 questions will often be answered in response to a step-1 question. Thus, step-2 questions often serve as clarifying "probes" where the answer to a step-1 question is incomplete or vague or suggests a slight misunderstanding of the question. For example, in response to question S10 (Table 5.1), one child said, "They put him in a box," suggesting that he did not understand the zoo's final solution to the problem. However, in answering question D4, this child said, "There was no straw to put in the pouch," showing clear understanding of the solution.

The third and final step in the question-writing process is the creation of beyond-text items. As already explained, these deal with the story as an exemplar of something interesting and important about the way people live, work, play, and otherwise conduct their affairs. In searching out ideas for these questions, it is useful to look to each of the five story elements for suggestions. The zookeeper's internal reaction (worry) upon finding the joey on the floor of the cage suggests that he is knowledgeable regarding the care of animals. A good question would be, "From this story, can you tell what a good zookeeper must know or be able to do?" The zookeeper's knowledge and devotion to duty, evident in the action he took to find out about the problem, suggests the following question: "If you were in charge of a zoo, would you hire Pete as a zookeeper? Why (or why not)?"

Expository Materials

Questions concerning expository texts are constructed on the same principle as narrative questions. Only here it is the traditional outline form that guides the procedure. An outline shows the relative importance of text ideas, and ideally, it also specifies how ideas are related to one another. That is, it depicts, in graphic form (the indentation and letter – number system), the superordinate – subordinate structure of passages and expresses, in words, the particular kind of superordinate – subordinate relationship that inheres between each topic and its subtopics. For example, Figure 5.2 gives three possible outlines of an expository passage on trees. Outline 1 shows only the superordinate – subordinate relationships.

There are, however, two different *kinds* of relationship between the subtopics (A, B, C, and D) and the major topic, trees. What are they?

Figure 5.2. Possible outlines of an expository passage on trees.

OUTLINE 1	OUTLINE 2	OUTLINE 3

Main Topic: Trees

A. Deciduous
1. Maple
2. Birch

B. Evergreen
1. Spruce
2. Fir

C. Shade
1. Maple
2. Oak

D. Ornamental
1. Dogwood
2. Hawthorn

Main Topic: Trees

A. Kinds
1. Deciduous
   a. Maple ⎱ Examples
   b. Birch ⎰
2. Evergreen
   a. Spruce ⎱ Examples
   b. Fir ⎰

B. Uses
1. Shade
   a. Maple ⎱ Examples
   b. Oak ⎰
2. Ornamental
   a. Dogwood ⎱ Examples
   b. Hawthorn ⎰

Main Topic: Trees

Kinds ⎰
A. Deciduous
  1. Maple ⎱ Examples
  2. Birch ⎰
B. Evergreen
  1. Spruce ⎱ Examples
  2. Fir ⎰

Uses ⎰
C. Shade
  1. Maple ⎱ Examples
  2. Oak ⎰
D. Ornamental
  1. Dogwood ⎱ Examples
  2. Hawthorn ⎰

Clearly, subtopics A and B are *kinds* of trees whereas C and D are *uses* of trees. A third type of relationship inheres between each set of minor subtopics, i.e., each (1) and (2), and their superordinates, A, B, C, and D: subtopics (1) and (2) are *examples* of their superordinate topics. Thus, the subtopics of an outline are always elaborations of a topic, but there are many different kinds of elaborations. A good outline makes these explicit in some way or other. Two possible ways are shown in outlines 2 and 3 in Figure 5.2.

In addition to the relationships exemplified here — kinds, uses, and examples — subtopics may be related to their topics as causes, effects, functions, parts, characteristics, procedural steps, chronological sequence, etcetera.

The first step, then, in formulating expository questions is the preparation of a complete outline. This is a relatively easy step with well-organized, clearly written passages, such as the one on forest fires in Figure 5.3. The reader should study this passage and develop an outline showing the relationships among the different pieces of information it contains.

Next, the reader should compare the outline developed with that shown in Figure 5.4. Note that there is little, if any, extraneous detail; most of the information in the passage can be subsumed under a few topics.

The next step is to derive questions from the outline using procedures similar to those described for the questions based on narrative selections. Typically, one question may be written to focus on the main topic and one

Figure 5.3.   Expository passage about forest fires.
(From "The Influence of Metacognitive Knowledge of Expository Text Structure on Discourse Recall" by L. M. McGee, in J. A. Niles and L. A. Harris, eds., *New Inquiries in Reading Research and Instruction* [Thirty-first Yearbook of the National Reading Conference. Rochester, N.Y.: National Reading Conference, 1982].)

Forest Fires

An important problem for forest rangers is how to protect forests from being ruined by fire. Each year thousands of trees are destroyed by fire. Careless campers do not put their fires completely out. Cigarettes are left to burn on the dry ground. These small fires in dry forests can burn thousands of trees. One solution to the forest fire problem is to man lookout stations and use helicopters to spot fires. Fires that are spotted right away can be put out before they get too big to handle. Then fires will cause less damage to the forest. A second solution to the problem is to have experts and bulldozers ready to move in quickly to fight the fire. Bulldozers can throw huge amounts of dirt on a fire in a short time. The dirt helps put the fire out quicker. A third solution is to build fire lanes in the forests. Fire lanes are long breaks in the forest where there are no trees. These breaks prevent the fire from spreading and getting too large.

Figure 5.4.   Outline based on expository passage about forest fires.

MAIN TOPIC: How forest rangers protect
forests from fire damage

A.   Causes of fire
   1.   Camp fires
   2.   Cigarettes

B.   Solutions to Problem
   1.   Early detection
      a.   Lookout stations
      b.   Helicopters
   2.   Quick extinction
      a.   Bulldozers — throw dirt on fire
      b.   Experts
   3.   Preventing spread of fires
      a.   Fire lanes

or two questions may be developed to explore each of the subtopics in the outline. The reader should develop questions based on the passage outline and compare them to those shown in Figure 5.5.

Free and Elicited Recall

As an alternative to direct questioning, the teacher might consider an aided recall procedure. The student is instructed to recount everything he or she

Figure 5.5.   Questions based on outline of expository passage about forest fires.

1.   What is the important problem that forest rangers must deal with? (protect trees from fire damage; forest fires)

2.   How do many forest fires get started? (cigarettes and campfires)

3.   How are lookout stations and helicopters used in solving the problem of forest fires? (spot fires in early stages)

4.   How are bulldozers used in fighting fires? (throw dirt on fire)

5.   What are fire lanes? (areas that are bare of trees)

6.   How do fire lanes prevent fire damage to forest? (prevent spread of fires)

*7.   The passage mentioned that "experts" are needed in fighting fires. What sort of thing might experts know that would be helpful in fighting fires? (wind conditions; how and where to approach fires; methods of fighting fires)

*8.   What might be done to prevent fires from getting started in the first place? (punish wrongdoers; supervise campgrounds; educate people)

* Beyond-text question

can remember about the passage. Then the teacher helps the student fill in missing information by asking specific questions about important ideas or events that were not mentioned. This means the teacher must be prepared with a list or outline of the main passage content against which the student's retelling can be checked and evaluated. It would be much the same kind of outline as was recommended for the preliminary step in constructing questions. Open-ended questions (e.g., "Tell me more about _____"; "Explain what you meant by _____") can be used to elicit more information following free recall, or the questions can be more directive. It is important to include this step since several investigations have found that much more information is normally stored than is produced in a free recall task, particularly among poorer readers (e.g., Bridge & Tierney, 1981).

Scoring of aided recall need present no problem if the checklist of information prepared in advance is precise and well ordered. The student is simply given points for each idea or fact recalled, as would be the case with questions. One advantage of this procedure is that it gives the teacher some idea of the student's verbal clarity and fluency. It is more time consuming than direct questioning, however, at least at the point of administration (the preparation phase may take less time), and the added information may be superfluous for a teacher who has many other opportunities to observe students' verbal proficiency.

PROCEDURES

Evaluating Responses

In constructing questions, the teacher quite naturally has specific responses in mind. These should be recorded in parentheses (see Figure 5.5) next to each question for easy reference during testing. Then the teacher can make a quick judgment regarding the quality of the student's response and probe further when that seems appropriate. Often an answer is correct under a slightly different interpretation of the question. For example, in connection with the story of *The Restless Kangaroo,* one of the questions is "What did the zookeeper do to find out about the problem [that the zoo was having with the kangaroos]?" The expected answer is that the zookeeper stood watch over the kangaroos' pen one night while the animals slept. If a child answered, "He gave them a different pen," one must allow for the possibility that the child did not quite catch the words *to find out* and for this reason answered as if the question pertained to what was done *about* the problem. In such a case, it seems reasonable to clarify the question, for example, by saying, "Yes, he did that in the end. But how did he find out what the problem was?"

In other cases, the answer given might relate to an aspect of the story problem that is different from the one the teacher had in mind. In response to the question "What was the problem the zoo was having with the kangaroos?" a student might answer, "The baby kangaroo kept putting straw into the pouch." This is, of course, the "ultimate" or underlying problem in the story; but the initial problem, in terms of the story structure, is that the baby kangaroo was found on the floor of the pen on several occasions. Again, the question should be clarified: "Yes. But they noticed a problem before they found out about that. What was the problem they noticed?" Then, if necessary, further clarification might be given: "What kept happening to the baby kangaroo because it kept putting straw into the pouch?" In general, answers that give information that is correct in terms of the story but slightly oblique in relation to the question should be probed further, either at the time of the initial response or after all the questions have been asked.

Another type of problematic response is one that is too broad or narrow. In the preceding chapter, we saw that Raymond gave too narrow an answer (namely, specific examples in response to the question of what determines the kinds of housing people build), apparently because he did not fully grasp the idea that external conditions can determine what people do. He was given partial credit, however, for recognizing the examples as relevant to the question. An answer that is too broad should also be given partial credit if it represents a reasonable generalization from the evidence.

In addition, we believe it is good practice to give students an opportunity to "sharpen" their answers. For answers that are too narrow, the teacher may ask for a general statement about the specific facts or examples given (e.g., "What does the use of logs from a nearby forest show about the housing people build?"). For answers that are too broad, the teacher should ask for more precise information. Take as an example a passage about the problem of oil spills on the ocean, which discusses the fact that the oil kills animals, birds, and microscopic plant life. A student who says, in response to the question of why oil spills must be prevented, that they "cause pollution" should be asked for some specification of the harmful effects of this pollution.

Administration

A basic principle of instruction in reading is that the reader should be given some general purpose or guiding statement before reading. This principle should be followed in assessing reading as well. We want the assessment to be based on a task that is as much like a "normal" reading situation as possible. Therefore, the teacher should prepare a brief "warm up" or motivating statement to be read to the student before reading. For a selection dealing with the feeding of dogs, for example, the following would be appropriate: "Do you have a dog? What do you feed your dog? Let's read this to find out what a dog should be fed [Betts, 1954, p. 465]."

The questions are asked immediately following the oral (or silent) reading. As the procedure is basically informal, questions can, whenever advisable, be repeated, reworded, and clarified. The teacher must take account of the fact that the questions may be ambiguous, permitting of more than one interpretation, or they may elicit unanticipated (but correct) responses (as discussed above).

Scoring and Interpreting Results

After a student has read and answered questions about a passage, the number of text-related questions answered correctly is determined and a comprehension score computed: the number of questions answered correctly is expressed as a percentage of the total number of questions asked. If this score is at or above 75%, then comprehension is considered adequate; a score that is below 75%, on the other hand, indicates some reading difficulty. Whether the difficulty is considered to be specific to comprehension will depend on the results of the evaluation of word knowledge and print translation skills as described in preceding chapters. If these two aspects of reading are found to be adequate, the reading difficulty can be attributed to the process of comprehension itself. Further diagnosis and instructional implications of this type of difficulty are taken up in the next chapter.

SUMMARY

Assessing comprehension is an important aspect of the diagnostic process. It enables the teacher to estimate the level of materials that are appropriate for instruction and to evaluate the proficiency of a student's print translation skill and the adequacy of his or her word knowledge. Therefore, it is important that the questions be reasonable in the light of what we know about the nature of comprehension. We have argued that the questions should follow, in an orderly fashion, the significant content or communicative intent of a passage. Procedures for constructing such questions were discussed and illustrated with respect to both stories and expository prose. In the next chapter, we will show how a student's performance on a set of comprehension questions should be interpreted in the context of the diagnostic model.

6

Reading Comprehension: Diagnosis and Instruction

An assessment of reading comprehension serves a twofold purpose. It enables the teacher to make an informed decision regarding the level of materials that would be appropriate for instruction, and it alerts the teacher to a student's specific instructional needs. Such an assessment is generally undertaken when there is some question concerning a student's current placement in instructional materials or the type of instructional emphasis that would enable the student to make better progress. For the most part these questions arise when a student is not performing well during daily lessons. But they should also arise when a student is performing extremely well. For instructional materials should be neither so difficult that the student can have little success with them nor so easy as to require little thought or attentional effort. Thus, the student who is always able to answer the teacher's questions may need more challenging materials, while the student who can seldom answer questions correctly may need less demanding ones. Teachers must make every effort to see that instructional materials are optimal from this point of view.

In addition, the teacher must be aware of the area(s) of reading in which a student is relatively weak and, consequently, requires special attention. A student is considered to require special attention in the area of comprehension when his or her performance on a comprehension test is inadequate (below a certain criterion level) *and* the assessment and probe procedures described in preceding chapters indicate that print translation skills and word knowledge are not prime sources of difficulty. That is, a diagnosis of comprehension difficulty is made when poor comprehension cannot be attributed to the areas of reading underlying comprehension.

In this chapter, we consider the instructional level and special needs of students with relative weakness in the area of comprehension. We discuss, first, criteria for establishing whether materials are at an appropriate level

143

of difficulty for use in reading instruction. Then we describe the general types of comprehension problems that students may encounter and a procedure for diagnosing an individual student's major problem. A detailed case study is presented to demonstrate the procedure. Finally, we suggest some instructional techniques for helping students gain proficiency in comprehension.

INSTRUCTIONAL LEVEL

In general, materials are considered suitable for instruction when the student can answer correctly a certain proportion of the questions asked. Unfortunately, there is no firm agreement among reading authorities regarding the exact proportion. Recommendations range from 60 to 75%. Harris and Sipay (1980) suggest that 60% is "marginal." They also note that a 50–60% criterion may be used with students of limited experiential background if "more time than usual will be spent developing the concepts and vocabulary necessary for understanding the stories [p. 185]." Betts (1954), on the other hand, recommends 75% comprehension for oral reading and a substantially higher percentage than that for "silent reading to locate specific information." In the procedures recommended by Betts, however, the oral reading of a passage is *not* the student's first encounter with the text; it is a rereading after silent reading. (Betts is a strong advocate of the principle that silent reading should precede oral reading, although he acknowledges that oral reading at sight provides valuable information regarding word recognition skills.) Nevertheless, we believe that, with well-designed questions, a criterion of 75% is not unreasonable even for a first reading. We also believe, with Harris and Sipay, that this criterion should be applied flexibly. There are certain conditions under which a student who scores below 75% on a diagnostic passage may benefit from instruction in materials at the same level of difficulty as the diagnostic passage. In general, such conditions obtain when a student is relatively strong in word knowledge and, if given an opportunity to reinspect the passage, is able to answer correctly several questions that were initially missed. That is, the student would be proficient in basic language skills but lacking in the ability to interrelate and organize passage information. In addition, the teacher must be in a position to provide instruction that would take account of the student's relative difficulty with this aspect of comprehension.

It was noted earlier that diagnosis is usually undertaken to shed light on difficulties observed during classroom activities in reading. It is, therefore, puzzling when students who have been selected for diagnosis perform well on a diagnostic passage that is at the same level of difficulty as their classroom materials. In such cases, the teacher will want to consider, first of all, whether the reading selection used in the diagnosis is in fact typical of classroom materials. It could be considerably easier in style, structure, and content, even if it came from the same reader level. If the passage appears to be typical, then classroom difficulties could be due to inattention, disinterest, and the like. It must also be recognized that the student has probably put forth a higher level of effort during the diagnosis than can reasonably be expected during daily classroom routines. Still, the diagnostic performance gives evidence of available strength. The teacher should therefore discuss the results of the diagnosis with the student and elicit his or her interpretation or views on the matter. The teacher's expression of interest and concern will undoubtedly be important to the student and may, in and of itself, help the student become more deeply involved in reading activities. Alternatively, the student may have some insights into his or her own difficulty that will be useful to the teacher in planning and implementing classroom activities.

If a student selected for diagnosis scores extremely well in comprehension — 90% or better — the passage should be considered at a level appropriate for independent reading. The teacher may then administer a more difficult passage to determine the student's instructional level; or the student may simply be assigned to more difficult materials on a trial basis.

A 75% level of comprehension, then, indicates that the reader is gathering enough of the important information in a text for reading to be a satisfying and productive experience: the reader is not only successful but has a sense of accomplishment as well. At a much higher level of comprehension, say 90% or above, particularly if the answers to questions are full and unhesitating, the reader is processing information so efficiently that there is little to be gained from the instructional efforts of the teacher; materials that present so little difficulty can be read independently.

On the other hand, when comprehension is below 75% the student is gaining too little of the information in the text for reading to be a comfortable experience under ordinary instructional conditions. It is often possible, however, to adjust instruction to accommodate a student who scores at least 50% in comprehension. A student who scores below 50% is following the text so poorly that even with strong instructional support in the form of extensive prereading discussion and activities, he or she will find reading a frustrating experience. Thus, comprehension scores between 50 and 75% represent borderline situations in which the teacher must consider the nature of the student's problem and decide whether instructional support would increase comprehension to a level that would be acceptable (75% or greater). For example, instructional support focused on the identification and/or meaning of words contained in reading selections may solve enough problems for the student to enable him or her to read with adequate comprehension.

Word recognition proficiency must also be taken into account in determining the instructional level. A student who performs well in comprehension and poorly in word recognition may need to work with easier materials for a time, while he or she develops greater skill in print translation. Easier materials may facilitate progress in this aspect of reading. On the other hand, there may be psychological or social advantages to be derived from working with the higher-level materials that would outweigh the student's difficulty with word recognition. An important consideration in this regard is the type of word recognition difficulty involved. If sight word fluency and accuracy is a major problem in addition to content word difficulties, the easier materials are likely to be the better solution. If, however, identification of unfamiliar content words constitutes the prime difficulty, then the higher-level materials can probably be used. In the latter case, of course, the teacher must plan to provide the student (along with other members of the reading group) with prereading assistance by identifying difficult words. In addition, some provision must be made for the student to receive help with specific word identification skills.

The way in which diagnostic information regarding word knowledge and print translation skill is used in making instructional decisions will be described more fully in the next chapter. In the remaining sections of this chapter, we examine more closely the implications of a specific difficulty in the area of comprehension.

DIAGNOSIS OF
COMPREHENSION DIFFICULTY

It was noted in Chapter 1 that poor comprehension is often related to inadequate print translation skills and/or word knowledge. Sometimes, however, comprehension is poor (below 75%) even though the important words in a passage can be identified and their meanings are reasonably familiar. In such cases, the reading difficulty is considered to be specific to comprehension. In general, this means that the reader fails to see how ideas fit together — how one idea builds on another or is constrained by it. Often it is causal chains that go unrecognized, but other types of relationships give rise to difficulty as well. For instance, the reader might not recognize that one statement is an amplification of another, or that it is a summary of a series of preceding statements, or an example in support of a general statement.

A more precise formulation of the nature of individual problems in comprehension is not yet within diagnostic reach. In the past, it was commonly recommended that teachers attempt to determine which subskills of comprehension were weak in individual cases by analyzing comprehension test performance. It was felt that the types of questions frequently missed would indicate the specific areas of comprehension that were deficient.

However, we believe, with Spache (1976), that this procedure is not really defensible. For one thing, no one passage, or even a series of passages such as is found in a standardized test or informal reading inventory, can provide a sufficient number of questions of each type to yield reliable results. Moreover, even if there were sufficient questions of each type, there is little evidence that the question types represent distinct and independent subskills. Analyses of responses to standardized test items have generally found that the ability (or inability) to answer one type of question tends to be correlated with the ability (or inability) to answer other types (Davis, 1944, 1968; Thorndike, 1973–1974; Thurstone, 1946). That is, there is little tendency for students to show strength (or weakness) in one aspect of comprehension independently of strength (or weakness) in most other aspects.

More recent research tends to corroborate the view that specific difficulties in comprehension cannot be identified through analysis of question types. In a study of sixth-graders, the poorer readers, as expected, answered fewer questions correctly than the good readers; but they were similar to the good readers in that they answered more main idea questions than detail questions (Meyer, 1977). A similar result was observed with good and poor readers at the college level (Marshall & Glock, 1978–1979). With regard to inferences, Bridge and Tierney (1981) found that the proportion of total information recalled that was inferential in nature was the same (approximately 40%) for poor readers as for good readers at the third-grade level. And, among a group of poor comprehenders at the seventh-grade level, Palincsar and Brown (1983) found no tendency for questions about implicit information to be more difficult than questions about explicit information.

At the same time, there is a growing body of evidence, consistent with the view of comprehension presented in the preceding chapter, that poor comprehension revolves around difficulty with the integrative processes involved in understanding discourse. For instance, Marshall and Glock (1978–1979) found that intersentence relationships were a major stumbling block for poor readers at the college level. These relationships may be made explicit through various signaling devices (*however, because, in contrast, instead, in other words, for example, first, second,* etc.) or they may be implicit. Whereas the better readers did equally well under both circumstances, the poor readers suffered a significant reduction in recall of passage information when these relationships were implied rather than directly stated. Moreover, the poorer readers tended to include fewer interpropositional relations in their written recalls. Some further evidence that the absence of signaling devices can be detrimental to poor readers was obtained in a study of ninth-graders (Meyer, Brandt, & Bluth, 1980).

In addition, research indicates that poor readers are generally insensitive to the high-level organization of passage information. That is, in recalling information after reading, poor readers are much less likely than good readers to follow the overall argument or pattern of discourse used by the author. While awareness of textual organization at the discourse level is rarely directly relevant to classroom comprehension tasks, it evidently facilitates the processing of lower-level information, for there is a high correlation between a student's ability to use the top-level structure of text in organizing his or her recall and the total amount of information recalled (Meyer, *et al.*, 1980). In addition, it has been found that instruction in the main types of expository discourse (e.g., main idea–supporting details, problem–solution, comparison–contrast) leads to marked increases in the amount of information students recall (McDonald, 1978; Bartlett, 1978; both cited in *Meyer et al.,* 1980).

Finally, there is considerable evidence that poor readers have difficulty monitoring their mental processes while reading and that they do not make appropriate adjustments when obstacles to comprehension are encountered. For example, poor readers often fail to recognize that something does not make sense or that they do not know the answer to a question. Nor do they regularly reread portions of text in an attempt to gain clarification. In an investigation of the question-answering strategies of good and poor readers in grades 4–10, a passage was used that required the student to look back to the text for the answers to certain questions. It was found that the good readers in grades 6 and 7 (although not in the lower grades) showed some awareness of comprehension difficulty on at least 50% of the questions that required lookbacks. That is, they indicated uncertainty or dissatisfaction with a response by shrugs, grunts, hesitations, and the like, and by such verbal expressions as ". . . I think"; ". . . or something"; and "that's a hard one." By contrast, the poor readers in these grades showed such behaviors on less than 7% of the questions. However, contrary to expectation, the sixth- and seventh-grade good readers did *not* look back to the text with great frequency for the answers to the targeted questions. It was only among the good readers in eighth grade and beyond that this strategy was observed with considerable frequency (79% of the questions that required lookbacks). Thus, while poor readers at all grade levels tend to be unaware when they do not understand or know the answer to a question, even good readers do not employ lookbacks to resolve difficulties until they reach the upper grades (Garner & Reis, 1981).

Given this evidence, we think it useful to view poor comprehension as arising in relation to difficulty with the integration of text information, both at the intersentence level and at higher levels of text structure. Underlying this difficulty are poorly developed strategies for utilizing background knowledge and recognizing failures of comprehension as they occur. Accordingly, we will recommend several instructional techniques for helping students with poor comprehension engage more actively in the reading process. Showing students how to question themselves while reading, how to formulate hypotheses about upcoming information or events, and how to relate incoming information to prior experiences generally leads to improved comprehension. Other techniques to be discussed focus on the development of greater awareness and understanding of the way in which knowledge is organized and conveyed in written discourse.

However, for some students, poorly developed strategies for interacting with text and organizing information represent only part of the problem. Instruction in such strategies can be effective only if students already possess the basic capacity for understanding the ideas and information with which they must interact. Therefore, in order to provide appropriate instruction once it has been determined that a student's difficulty is in comprehension, it is necessary to determine whether the student has this basic capacity. A probe of comprehension is conducted for this purpose. The teacher provides the student with an opportunity to reread relevant portions of the diagnostic passage and answer the questions that were incorrectly answered on the initial administration of the comprehension test. If the student can correct several answers on this second trial, it can be concluded that he or she has the ability to acquire basic text information and can profit from instruction in interactive and organizational strategies. On the other hand, if the student is essentially unable to correct his or her answers, then the difficulty is at the level of acquiring basic text information and instruction in intersentence relationships must be provided. This type of instruction focuses on the anaphoric relations and linguistic devices that interrelate sentence information. It also involves the modeling of certain thought processes or interactive strategies believed to be "second nature" to proficient readers.

Diagnostic Procedures

The diagnosis of comprehension requires the construction of comprehension questions (or a scoring checklist for evaluating a student's retelling), as described in Chapter 5. Once these questions (or the retell task) have been administered following the reading of a passage, the following procedure is used to identify comprehension problems.

1. The number of text-related questions that were correctly answered is determined and expressed as a percentage of the total number of such questions. A retelling score is similarly obtained as a percentage of the total number of elements in the scoring checklist. If this score is 75% or above, comprehension is considered satisfactory and the passage is considered to represent a level of difficulty that is appropriate for instruction

unless word recognition problems dictate otherwise, as explained earlier in this chapter.

2. If the comprehension score is less than 75%, the teacher determines, from the results of the examination of print translation and word knowledge proficiency, whether these areas of reading interfere with comprehension. If so, further diagnosis must focus on these areas. If poor comprehension is *not* attributable to either of these underlying areas then a diagnosis of comprehension difficulty is made. It should be recognized, however, that word knowledge has a subtle, pervasive influence on comprehension and its role in poor comprehension cannot always be singled out. Therefore, students for whom a comprehension difficulty is diagnosed may also have some degree of word knowledge difficulty.

3. If comprehension has been judged to be the main area of reading difficulty, a comprehension probe is conducted. For each question that was answered incorrectly on the comprehension test, the student is directed to reread the portion of the passage in which the answer can be found and given a second opportunity to answer the question. The purpose is to gain insight into the student's thinking and text-processing strategies in order to provide appropriate instruction.

4. When a student can generally correct his or her answers upon rereading the text, it is assumed that the difficulty on the initial trial was relatively superficial — the student is able to grasp basic text information but has difficulty combining that information into coherent units. In some cases, of course, the student will simply have misunderstood the question or failed to link an important piece of information to it. Also, students are sometimes aware of the information that would answer a question correctly but do not give this information because they have little confidence in it or it runs counter to their expectations. In general, a student's ability to answer questions correctly upon rereading the text indicates basic skill in understanding text information. At the same time, the student's inability to answer those same questions correctly on the initial trial, without the motivation and assistance provided during the probe, suggests ineffective strategies for interacting with text and sensing the organization or structure of text information.

5. When students are unable to respond correctly after reexamining the text, the difficulty is considered to be more severe. In such cases instruction should focus on the "flow" and cohesive elements of written discourse, as described later in this chapter.

Thus, the initial administration of the comprehension test provides a measure of the student's general level of comprehension, while the probe enables the teacher to determine the severity of the problem, based on the level of text organization with which the student encounters difficulty.

CASE STUDY APPLICATION

In order to demonstrate the diagnosis and probe of comprehension difficulty, we will look at an individual case in some detail. In the next chapter, we will again focus on comprehension, but we will also give detailed consideration to knowledge of word meaning and print translation skill as well as comprehension. Here, we simply report the final interpretation of the student's performance in these areas.

CASE: PAUL

Paul, a seventh-grader, read a story from his seventh-grade basal reader. This story was about an Eskimo boy, Noni, who was marooned with his dog on an ice island. As there was no wildlife or vegetation on the island, within a few days the two were near starvation. With much anguish, the boy concluded that he must kill the dog for food. The story is shown in Figure 6.1. In order to understand the diagnostic techniques described in what follows, the reader should be familiar with the content and sequence of the story.

Figure 6.1.   Diagnostic reading passage: Paul.
(From NEW WORLDS AHEAD by I. Willis and R. E. Willis, pp. 409–411, published by Harcourt, Brace, and World, 1969. Copyright 1942 by the Crowell-Collier Publishing Co. Reprinted by permission of the author, Hugh B. Cave.)

Two Were Left

On the third night of hunger, Noni thought of the dog. Nothing of flesh and blood lived upon the floating ice island with its towering berg except those two.

In the breakup Noni had lost his sled, his food, his fur, even his knife. He had saved only Nimuk, his devoted husky. And now the two marooned on the ice eyed each other warily—each keeping his distance.

Noni's love for Nimuk was real, very real—as real as the hunger and cold nights and the gnawing pain of his injured leg. But the men of his village killed their dogs when food was scarce, didn't they? And without thinking twice about it.

And Nimuk, he told himself, when hungry enough would seek food. One of us will soon be eating the other, Noni thought. So . . .

He could not kill the dog with his bare hands. Nimuk was powerful and much fresher than he. A weapon, then, was essential.

Removing his mittens, he unstrapped the brace from his leg. When he had hurt his leg a few weeks before, he had made the brace from bits of harness and two thin strips of iron.

(Continued)

Figure 6.1. (*Continued*)

Kneeling now, he stuck one of the iron strips into a crack in the ice and began to rub the other against it with firm, slow strokes.

Nimuk watched him intently, and it seemed to Noni that the dog's eyes glowed more brightly as night came.

He worked on, trying not to remember why. The slab of iron had an edge now. It had begun to take shape. Daylight found his task completed.

Noni pulled the finished knife from the ice and thumbed its edge. The sun's glare, reflected from it, stabbed at his eyes and for a moment blinded him.

Noni steeled himself.

"Here, Nimuk!" he called softly.

The dog watched him suspiciously.

"Come here," Noni called.

Nimuk came closer. Nomi read fear in the animal's gaze. He read hunger and suffering in the dog's labored breathing and awkward, dragging crouch. His heart wept. He hated himself and fought against it.

Closer Nimuk came, wary of his intentions. Now Noni felt a thickening in his throat. He saw the dog's eyes and they were wells of suffering.

Now! Now was the time to strike!

A great sob shook Noni's kneeling body. He cursed the knife. He swayed blindly; flung the weapon far from him. With empty hands outstretched he stumbled toward the dog, and fell.

The dog growled. He warily circled the boy's body. Noni was sick with fear.

In flinging away his knife he had left himself defenseless. He was too weak to crawl after it now. He was at Nimuk's mercy, and Nimuk was hungry.

The dog circled him and was creeping up from behind. Noni heard the rattle of saliva in the savage throat.

He shut his eyes, praying that the attack might be swift. He felt the dog's feet against his leg, the hot rush of Nimuk's breath against his neck. A scream gathered in the boy's throat.

Then he felt the dog's hot tongue licking his face.

Noni's eyes opened, staring, not yet believing. Crying softly, he put out his arm and drew the dog's head down against his own. . . .

The plane came out of the south an hour later. Its pilot, a young man of the coastal patrol, looked down and saw the large, floating ice island with the berg rising from its center. And he saw something flashing.

It was the sun gleaming on something shiny which moved. His curiosity aroused, the pilot banked his ship and descended, circling the ice. Now he saw, in the shadow of the peak of ice, a dark, still shape that appeared to be human. Or were there two shapes?

He set his ship down in a water lane and investigated. There were two shapes, boy and dog. The boy was unconscious but alive. The dog whined feebly but was too weak to move.

The gleaming object which had trapped the pilot's attention was a handmade knife stuck point first into the ice a little distance away and quivering in the wind.

Paul showed excellent print translation skill when he read the story aloud. Further, the word knowledge assessment, shown in Figure 6.2, indicated that he was familiar with the key words in the story (e.g., *marooned, essential, wary, descended, intention*). The questions that Paul's teacher developed to measure his understanding of the story are also shown in the figure, along with his responses. As can be seen, Paul's comprehension score was only 60%. Thus, because his print translation skill and word knowledge were both highly satisfactory, his main difficulty was considered to be in the area of comprehension. The reader should examine the questions that Paul answered incorrectly in order to identify possible reasons for his comprehension failure.

Figure 6.2.   Responses to comprehension and word knowledge questions: Paul.

Comprehension

✓ **1.** Where were Noni and Nimuk marooned? (on an ice island)
   RESPONSE: Ice island.

✓ **2.** How did Noni feel about Nimuk? (loved him very much)
   RESPONSE: Liked him.

✗ **3.** Why did Noni think a weapon was essential? (Nimuk was too powerful to kill with his bare hands)
   RESPONSE: To kill wild animals for food.

✗ **4.** From what did Noni make a weapon? (strips of iron from his brace)
   RESPONSE: Knife.

✓ **5.** Why were they wary of each other? (they were both starving — might kill the other for food)
   RESPONSE: 'Cause one might eat the other.

✓ **6.** Why was Noni unable to attack the dog? (loved him too much)
   RESPONSE: Noni liked the dog; did not want to kill him.

✗ **7.** What did Noni do with the knife? (threw it away — "far from him")
   RESPONSE: Tried to kill Nimuk and left it there.

✗ **8.** When did Noni know that the dog would not attack him? (when he felt the dog licking his face)
   RESPONSE: The dog came closer and closer.

✓ **9.** Who rescued them? (a pilot in a plane)
   RESPONSE: A plane.

✓ **10.** What was quivering in the wind which caught the pilot's attention? (the knife)
   RESPONSE: Knife.

(Continued)

Figure 6.2. (*Continued*)

Word Knowledge

✓ 1. What is a *husky?*
  RESPONSE: An Eskimo sled dog.
✓ 2. What does *marooned* mean?
  RESPONSE: Deserted on an island.
✓ 3. What does *gnawing* mean?
  RESPONSE: A dull pain that doesn't stop.
✓ 4. What does *essential* mean?
  RESPONSE: Necessary.
✓ 5. In the story, it says that Noni "steeled" himself. What does *steeled* mean?
  RESPONSE: Got his nerve up.
✓ 6. What does *wary* mean?
  RESPONSE: Careful-cautious.
✓ 7. What does *descended* mean?
  RESPONSE: Go down.
✓ 8. What does *feebly* mean?
  RESPONSE: Weakly.
✓ 9. What does *quivering* mean?
  RESPONSE: Shaking.
✓ 10. What does *intention* mean?
  RESPONSE: Going to do something.

Comprehension Probe

The first question that Paul missed in the comprehension test was drawn from the following paragraph:

> He could not kill the dog with his bare hands. Nimuk was powerful and much fresher than he. A weapon, then, was essential.

The question was "Why did Noni think a weapon was essential?" Paul had initially answered, "To kill wild animals for food." (The correct answer would refer to the fact that the dog was too powerful to be killed barehanded; partial credit could be given for referring to the need to kill the dog for food.) The probe with regard to this question was as follows:

TEACHER: I'd like you to read this paragraph again and see if you can tell why Noni thought a weapon was essential.
PAUL: (after reading): To kill the dog, for food.
TEACHER: Yes, but why did he need a *weapon?*
PAUL: Can't kill a dog without a weapon, with bare hands.
TEACHER: And why not?
PAUL: It could kill you, too big.

One interpretation of this result is that Paul had initially answered as he did — "to kill wild animals for food" — because he conceived of the question as a generic one — as pertaining to weapons in general, rather than to the story in particular. Another possibility is that he had forgotten — or was never really certain — that there were no wild animals on the ice island. (That information appears in the second sentence of the story, several paragraphs before the one under discussion.) Nevertheless, the fact that he was able to answer the question correctly upon rereading showed that he could, at least, understand the intersentence relationships in the paragraph.

The probe was continued with another question that Paul had initially missed. This related to the part of the story that described how the Eskimo boy made a knife with two strips of metal taken from a brace he was wearing on his wounded knee. The relevant paragraphs read as follows:

> Removing his mittens, he unstrapped the brace from his leg. When he had hurt his leg a few weeks before, he had made the brace from bits of harness and two thin strips of iron.
> Kneeling now, he stuck one of the iron strips into a crack in the ice and began to rub the other against it with firm, slow strokes.
> Nimuk watched him intently, and it seemed to Noni that the dog's eyes glowed more brightly as night came.
> He worked on, trying not to remember why. The slab of iron had an edge now. It had begun to take shape. Daylight found his task completed.

In answer to the question "From what did Noni make a weapon?" Paul had responded, "a knife." After rereading, he responded as follows:

PAUL: Oh. A slab of iron.
TEACHER: And where did he get the iron?
PAUL: His brace for his knee.
TEACHER: Can you explain how he made a knife out of the iron?
PAUL: He rubbed it until it had an edge.
TEACHER: What did he rub it with?
PAUL: Not sure . . . on the ice?

This was a rather difficult sequence of text. It required the reader to visualize a step-by-step procedure, and Paul was evidently unable to do this. Still, upon a second reading he had gleaned the essential idea that the knife was made from a part of the brace.

The third question that Paul missed involved a crucial element of the story. Just as the boy was about to strike the dog, he was overcome with grief and "flung the weapon far from him." Paul evidently understood the boy's reluctance to kill the dog; in answer to the question, "Why was Noni unable to attack the dog?" he had replied, "Noni liked the dog; did not want to kill him." Yet, in answering the next question, "What did Noni do with the knife?," Paul had stated that Noni "tried to kill Nimuk and left it there." Thus, Paul seemed to have two conflicting ideas about a dramatic story event. His teacher explored further by having him reread the following segment:

> Now! Now was the time to strike!
> A great sob shook Noni's kneeling body. He cursed the knife. He swayed blindly; flung the weapon far from him. With empty hands outstretched he stumbled toward the dog, and fell.

Then she asked the question again, "What did Noni do with the knife?"

PAUL: Tried to kill Nimuk. Threw it far.
TEACHER: Did he throw it at the dog?
PAUL: Yeah. But he missed him.

Since the student did not answer correctly on this second trial, the probe then took the form of a detailed analysis of the text.

TEACHER: Show me the part that tells what Noni did; read it aloud.
PAUL: [from passage]: "Flung the weapon far from him."
TEACHER: Yes, I suppose that could mean that he threw it at the dog and missed. But I think it means something else. Do you know how I know?
PAUL: No.
TEACHER: Well, let's look at what happened before that, right after Noni finished making the knife. [The teacher points to the preceding paragraph and the student reads it aloud: "Closer Nimuk came, wary of his intentions. Now Noni felt a thickening in this throat. He saw the dog's eyes and they were wells of suffering."] O.K., so where was Nimuk when Noni threw the knife?
PAUL: [No response.]
TEACHER: [clarifying]: Where was Nimuk in relation to Noni? How close was he?
PAUL: Well, he came closer. . . Oh, he saw the dog's eyes.
TEACHER: Yes, so the dog had to be pretty close to Noni. Do you see now what it means that Noni "flung the weapon far from him"?
PAUL: He wasn't trying to kill the dog?
TEACHER: Right. We have to assume that he wasn't trying to kill the dog— that he changed his mind at the last minute and threw the knife "far from him"—far from himself and the dog.

There was, then, some plausibility to the student's interpretation of the story character's action, at least when that action is taken by itself, out of context. It only becomes implausible that the boy meant to kill the dog when he "flung the weapon far from him" when one takes into account the fact that the dog was in close proximity. Thus, as may have occurred with the first question, the student had failed to keep one fact in mind while considering another. And, as with the first question, the student did seem able to understand the language of the text at both the sentence and intersentence levels.

The fourth and final question that Paul missed involved the next event in the story. After the Eskimo boy threw the knife "far from him," he lay on the ground in fear that the dog would now attack him:

> He shut his eyes, praying that the attack might be swift. He felt the dog's feet against his leg, the hot rush of Nimuk's breath against his neck. A scream gathered in the boy's throat.
> Then he felt the dog's hot tongue licking his face.

In response to the question, "When did the boy know the dog would not attack him?" Paul had answered, "The dog came closer and closer." After rereading, he was able to answer correctly, "When he felt him licking his face."

Taken together, Paul's responses on the probe suggest that his main comprehension difficulty is in integrating story events. He seemed to consider each event an isolated phenomenon. As a result, his grasp of the story line was initially vague and impressionistic. Nevertheless, the fact that he was able to correct three out of four responses indicates that he had the capacity to grasp the basic information in the text. Therefore, Paul's comprehension problem was judged as involving poorly developed strategies for interacting with information and recognizing its overall structure.

Instructional Plans

On the basis of the probe, the teacher decided that the seventh-grade reader from which the story was taken could continue to be used for instruction. To help Paul function more effectively, she planned to use class discussions to emphasize and clarify the process of interrelating story events. She felt that this focus could also benefit other students in Paul's reading group. In addition, she planned to help Paul and a few other students become more conscious of their internal processes while reading by introducing them to the strategies of making predictions and self-questioning. These procedures are discussed in the section that follows.

COMPREHENSION INSTRUCTION

We turn now to instruction in comprehension. How can we improve instruction for students with comprehension difficulties? Some years ago the answer would have been that we must identify areas of specific weakness and strengthen those areas through direct instruction. That is, it was believed that comprehension was made up of a number of subskills and remedial efforts should be directed toward improving one or another of them. Thus, some students might need help in noting and recalling details, while others might need help in following sequences of events or grasping main ideas. As already discussed, this approach is now generally perceived as unduly limited and not entirely consistent with the nature of comprehension. Therefore, we recommend a somewhat different approach.

We recommend three types of instructional procedures for helping students with poor comprehension. The first type emphasizes close reading and scrutiny of relationships at the intersentence and paragraph levels. It is designed to help students with adequate word knowledge who fail to answer comprehension questions after rereading relevant portions of text. The second introduces students to various strategies, such as self-questioning and predicting, which foster an interactive approach to reading. The third type helps students understand the organization of information. The latter two types are appropriate for students who are able to answer questions correctly after rereading relevant parts of a passage. Obviously, students with intersentence processing difficulties may also profit from the development of interactive and organizational strategies, but care must be taken to insure that basic text information is not "over their heads."

Sentence-Level Comprehension

Before discussing the three types of comprehension instruction, let us look briefly at the issue of sentence-level comprehension and instruction. There can be little doubt that knowledge of sentence structure is an important component of the process of comprehension. However, reading authorities generally feel that instruction in formal grammar is not an appropriate means of enhancing students' competence in this aspect of language. Their rationale lies to some extent in the fact that syntactic knowledge is for the most part acquired spontaneously. Children come to school with fairly sophisticated knowledge of the syntactic system of their language. For instance, even kindergarteners understand the difference between active and passive sentences such as *The cat chased the dog* and *The cat was chased by the dog*. They also understand the difference between active and passive forms embedded in cleft sentences; for example, *It was the cat that chased the dog* and *It was the cat that was chased by the dog*. [Gourley & Catlin, 1978].

In addition, young children understand the subtle difference between definite and indefinite articles, recognizing that a definite article is used in referring to something that has already been mentioned whereas an indefinite article is used when there is no antecedent (e.g., *He saw **a** monkey* *there. So he took **the** monkey home;* Maratsos, 1976). Moreover, when asked to state whether they preferred sentences in which causal relations were specified by the connective term *because* (e.g., *We did not sit down, because the benches were wet),* or sentences in which the causal relation was only implied (e.g., *We did not sit down, the benches were wet)* first-graders chose, overwhelmingly, just as adults and older children did, the sentences that included the connective term (Katz & Brent, 1968).

As children get older, they learn to understand increasingly complex language forms as a natural consequence of their reading and other language experiences. Thus, children between the ages of 8 and 11 can identify the antecedents of various types of pronouns (personal, relative, demonstrative, etc.) with a high degree of accuracy (Lesgold, 1974); and they understand implicit causal relations as well as the explicit causal terms *so* and *because* (Pearson, 1974–1975). They also develop competence in certain unusual or exceptional syntactic forms, such as the starred sentences in the following pairs:

> *John told **Bill** to shovel the driveway.*
> * ***John** promised Bill to shovel the driveway.*
> *Sue told **Laura** what to feed the doll.*
> * ***Sue** asked Laura what to feed the doll.*

In these starred sentences the *first* noun phrase is the subject of the verb in the complement clause whereas in the usual case (the unstarred items) it is the *second* noun phrase that is the subject of the complement verb (Chomsky, 1969). In other words, in the first sentence, Bill is the subject of *shovel;* in the second sentence, John is its subject.

It should be pointed out that the high levels of competency reported in the studies cited here were obtained with highly familiar sentence contents. When less familiar materials with a social studies content were used with fourth- and fifth-graders, the level of performance on pronouns and on causal relations signaled by *because* was considerably lower even among good readers (Irwin, 1980; Kameenui & Carnine, 1982). In the final analysis, students' ability to understand complex language structures depends on the conceptual familiarity of the semantic content.

Thus, there is much evidence that sentence structure is learned indirectly — that is, through "exposure" to written and spoken language rather than through direct instruction. There are, however, some few students who need special assistance in developing syntactic competence. Such students are likely to require more individualized attention than can be given on a regular basis in most classrooms. In fact, students who show marked difficulty with sentence-level tasks should probably be referred to other professionals for further evaluation. Therefore, we will not describe specific procedures that focus on the structure of isolated sentences.

Readers interested in learning more about this type of instruction are referred to two procedures that were recently found effective in improving performance on cloze tests (though not on standardized comprehension tests). One, sentence-combining (Froese & Kurushima, 1979; Straw & Schreiner, 1982), engages students in the construction of complex sentences from two or more simple sentences. In the other, a sentence anagram task (Weaver, 1979), students learn to organize words into groups within sentences and then into complete sentences.

Intersentence Comprehension

The three procedures described in what follows are intended for classroom use with students who need help interrelating sentence information. The first, reciprocal teaching/modeling, consists of "walking" students through a passage and making explicit the relationship between the lead sentence and those that follow it. The second focuses on connectives, or "signal" words — the cues that specify how certain ideas are related to others. The final procedure also has a particular focus — this time on anaphoric relations.

Reciprocal Teaching/Modeling. In this procedure, developed by Palincsar and Brown (1983), students and teacher take turns leading a dialogue. The "leader" asks an important question about a small segment of text — no more than a paragraph — and is also responsible for *(a) summarizing* what has been read, *(b) predicting* what might be discussed next, and *(c)* offering *clarification* of anything that seemed confusing. The teacher guides students in these activities by a variety of prompting and modeling techniques (e.g., "Remember that a summary doesn't include a lot of detail"; "What question would a teacher ask?"). The help and participation of other students in the group may also be solicited upon occasion. In addition to prompting the student leader, the teacher provides praise and feedback specific to the student's conduct of the dialogue. A teacher might offer corrective feedback by saying, "That was interesting information. It was information that I would call detail in the passage. Can you find the most important information? (Palincsar & Brown, 1983, p. 14)." Then, at the conclusion of each student-led discussion, the teacher models any portion of the discussion that he or she feels needs improvement (e.g., "I would summarize by saying . . .").

An important element of this instructional procedure is informing students of its self-monitoring purpose: "being able to say in your own words what one has just read, and being able to guess what the questions will be on a test, are sure ways of testing oneself to see if one has understood [p. 14]." The role of self-questioning, predicting, summarizing, and clarifying in enhancing comprehension, and the need for using these strategies during independent reading must also be made explicit. Palincsar and

Brown report that although seventh-grade students had considerable difficulty with the role of dialogue leader during the first few instructional sessions, by the end of 10 sessions they were able to produce questions and summaries of "some sophistication." Therefore, a teacher who wishes to use this procedure should plan to use it regularly for several weeks.

An attractive feature of the reciprocal teaching format is that it emphasizes certain processes of reading while focusing on the *meaning* of segments of text. That is, instruction is provided within the context of "real reading," and it is provided through repeated modeling. This is in sharp contrast to the more traditional "skills" method of helping students with comprehension difficulty. Typically, in the more traditional method, specific aspects of text processing (e.g., sequencing events, recognizing causal relations) are isolated, directly taught through explanation and illustration, and then practiced by students on specially prepared materials and exercises. Students' performance on these materials is then evaluated as correct or incorrect. A major weakness of this method, aside from the isolation of particular aspects of meaning from the holistic process of reading, is that students are not *shown how* to arrive at correct solutions to the problem of meaning. Reciprocal teaching, as we have seen, coordinates students' attention to specific elements of text with a general focus on meaning. Therefore, we believe the method may be adapted to instruction in other features of text, particularly connective terms, as noted below.

Connective Terms. Connective terms specify how ideas are related to one another. Geva (1983) provides a useful four-way classification of these terms. She points out that some of them simply *add* ideas to other ideas (e.g., *and, also, as well,* and *in addition*) whereas others express contrastive or adversative relations (e.g., *but, however,* and *on the other hand*). A third type signals causal relations (*because, so, therefore, as a result, consequently*), and the final type pertains to temporal sequence (*before, after, first, next, then*). The relationships signaled by these terms can, of course, apply to information in any unit of text — to information contained in individual clauses or sentences, in a series of sentences within a paragraph, or in several paragraphs or even larger stretches of text.

Instruction in these relationships must be conducted, quite obviously, in the context of the kinds of situations to which they refer. For example, to show students what specific temporal words mean it is necessary to look at situations that can be temporally sequenced. It is for this reason that reciprocal teaching appears to be a promising format for highlighting connectives and the relationships they signal. A series of sessions could incorporate specific emphasis on these relationships into the procedure; each time a signal word occurred in a passage segment, the dialogue leader would be expected to discuss its informational value. The particular signal words that students should be on the lookout for would be introduced beforehand and displayed in a prominent place for quick reference.

Signal words can also be systematically highlighted during the course of regular basal reader lessons. The teacher simply examines the lesson materials to locate these terms and then plans interesting and appropriate ways to call attention to them during postreading discussion. The purpose is to help students become aware of these terms and attend to them without external guidance.

Anaphoric Relations. Anaphoric relations refer to the way in which certain words can be used as substitutes for words or groups of words that occurred previously in the text. In addition to personal pronouns, anaphoric devices include pronouns that substitute for places *(here, there)* and for things and ideas *(it, this, that)*. One of the more difficult types of anaphora involves the substitution of pro-verbs *(does, can, will)* for previously mentioned verbs or verb phrases: *Mary **skates well.** John **does** too. Mary **does figure eights.** So **can** John.*

An experienced clinician (Daskal, 1983) reports that students with poor comprehension are generally responsive to instruction in anaphora. Not only do they become proficient in identifying the antecedents of anaphoric words, but they learn to attend more closely to the succession or "flow" of ideas in written materials. The procedure she follows begins with oral discussion. The student is simply asked questions that require the identification of pronoun or pro-verb antecedents. For example, given the following text:

> Harry and Josh went to the store to buy hot dogs, potato chips, and soft drinks for the picnic. But *they* were so expensive that the boys didn't have enough money to pay for *them.*

the student would be asked "What was expensive?" or "What couldn't they pay for?" Next, the student learns to draw lines between pronouns and their antecedents. (With nonconsumable materials, a sheet of acetate is clipped to the page of print and the student uses a china marker.) This enables the teacher to monitor the student's accuracy in identifying antecedents, and it helps the student develop awareness of these cohesive text elements. After several weeks of this type of instruction, students automatically relate anaphoric terms to their antecedents.

Interactive Strategies

The procedures described in this and the following section are designed primarily for students who have no difficulty interrelating sentence information but need to develop interactive and monitorial strategies. We view the introduction of background information and concepts as the major task of prereading instruction. Without these, students cannot make bridging inferences, anticipate outcomes, or otherwise engage in an active dialogue with the author. But many students — even those with well-developed knowledge structures — do not spontaneously use their knowledge and experiences to make a text more meaningful. Therefore, instruction that will help students take a more active role in the reading process must be provided.

Several innovative techniques for providing this type of instruction have been developed in recent years. What they do, in essence, is externalize or model some of the thought processes believed to be characteristic of an effective reader. Some model the types of questions such a reader might raise before or during reading. Others demonstrate the necessity of relating what is already known about a topic to the information in a text. While it may be argued that the effective reader does not consciously employ these processes, nonetheless, as devices for teaching the less able reader, they are both practical and sensible. Examples of these techniques follow.

Self-Questioning. According to Singer (1978), a strong proponent of self-questioning, the teacher's questions should not only guide students through their assigned readings but serve as models of the kinds of questions that students should ask themselves. He suggests a gradual reduction of the teacher's role in formulating questions, so that students may learn to direct their own thinking during reading. The procedure is quite simple. The teacher asks a question that will elicit a question in return. For example, after students have read the first paragraph (or sentence) of a selection, the teacher might ask "What would you like to know next?"or "What else would you like to know about _____?" The students formulate their questions and then read to answer these questions. After reading, answers are discussed. This procedure is then followed with each succeeding paragraph (or sentence).

ReQuest Procedure. In Manzo's (1969) ReQuest Procedure, the teacher not only models questions but also provides some feedback on the quality of students' questions by praising those that are good and withholding comment on those that are not. The procedure is one of turn taking, which gives it an attractive gamelike quality. After a sentence is read, first the student asks the teacher questions and then the teacher asks the student questions. All questions must be answered without referring to the passage, though the responder may ask for clarification or rephrasing of the question. (Students are told to try to ask questions that a teacher might ask.) Teacher and students continue in this fashion with succeeding sentences until the teacher feels that enough information has been established for students to make reasonable predictions about the remainder of the story. At that point, predictions are made and students read to verify them.

Postreading Self-Generated Questions. Cohen (1983) has devised a procedure for training students to formulate questions after they have read a story. Students are reminded that a question asks for an answer and that a question ends with a question mark. They are instructed that a good question begins with a question word, can be answered from information in the story, and asks about an important detail in the story. Following this preliminary instruction, which includes practice and feedback on short paragraphs, students read a story. They must then write an answer to the question "What is this story about?" as well as two questions of their own. The questions are then evaluated for conformance to the stated criteria, and the evaluation is discussed with the student. Cohen found that after working on 12 short paragraphs (the preliminary instruction) and 4 stories (the application of instruction), 85% of the children (third-graders) reached 85% mastery on the question-writing task. The trained children also performed significantly better than a control group on a standardized comprehension test. Thus, the experience of formulating literal questions after reading appears to help children understand what they read.

Another study in which students were trained to generate questions after story reading (as well as partway into the story) was conducted by Singer and Donlan (1982). The students were eleventh-graders. They were given a set of generic questions for each of five story grammar categories (e.g., Who is the leading character? What action does the character initiate? What does this leading character appear to be striving for? [p. 173]). These served as examples from which students generated story-specific questions for each story read. The effectiveness of this activity was not immediately evident, but after practicing with four stories, the trained group performed significantly better than a control group on a multiple-choice test. It is interesting to note that the questions the students generated were never evaluated by the teacher; the thrust of instruction was on the structural elements of stories, and writing questions provided the framework within which students worked with those elements.

It is clear that instruction in self-questioning can be as simple as asking, "What would you like to know about _____?" or can be combined with a sophisticated organizational scheme. Moreover, it can be nondirective or it can provide standards of question quality. There seems to be no research on the efficacy of feedback per se; but there is some slight evidence that providing students with training in constructing questions is no more effective than having them generate questions without training (André & Anderson, 1978–79).

Unfortunately, there has been little formal research on the general topic of the efficacy of student-generated questioning. However, giving

students an active role in the learning process is one of the cardinal principles of effective teaching, and having students ask as well as answer questions clearly conforms to this principle. Generating questions could, therefore, on that ground alone, reasonably be a part of every student's
experience.

Using Experiences to Predict Outcomes. A procedure developed
by Hansen (1981a) shows students how their own experiences may be used
in making predictions about story events. The teacher selects three important or difficult ideas from the story to be read and writes two questions for
each idea. The first question focuses on experiences related to the idea; the
second requires children to predict a related story event. Discussion of the
questions is incorporated into prereading activities.

> For example, in one story the isolated idea was that when people are
> embarrassed they break eye contact. In the story, Dick looked at his
> feet when a barber expressed displeasure about Dick's dog. The pre-
> vious experience question was, "What do you do when you feel embar-
> rassed?" After the children volunteered several suggestions (laugh,
> wiggle, get mad), each child wrote his/her own response. Then the
> prediction question was discussed: "In our story, Dick feels embar-
> rassed when the barber asks him if Stanley is his dog. What do you
> think he will do?" (laugh, yell at Stanley, run home). Again, this dis-
> cussion was followed by each student writing down his/her own guess
> [p. 667].

Students who have not had pertinent experiences of their own learn
from hearing about others' experiences; thinking is also stimulated by
hearing others generate hypotheses about story events. Thus, students
begin reading "with a more varied store of knowledge at their disposal [p.
668]," as well as a heightened awareness of the relationship between story
events and their own experiences.

Lookback Strategies. Students must learn to monitor their own
mental processes and make appropriate adjustments where necessary.
Recognizing that something does not make sense and rereading to gain
clarification is an example of this monitoring and adjustment. There is
evidence that poor readers do not regularly employ such a fix-up strategy
when they encounter obstacles to comprehension (Garner & Reis, 1981).
Yet this is a relatively easy strategy to foster, since looking back to the text
to "locate information" is regularly featured in many basal reader series.
The teacher can highlight the important role of lookbacks in reading by
requiring students to reread for information during several successive lessons. At the same time, the teacher should make explicit the purpose and
usefulness of this strategy.

Organizing Information

Recognizing that text information is interrelated is fundamental to comprehension. We have already discussed the role of postreading questions in this connection, arguing that they should recapitulate the orderly progression of events and ideas that make up the story line. But other devices should be used as well. In the following procedures, students participate in the creation of a visual display of interconnecting ideas.

Semantic Webbing.   In this procedure (Cleland, 1981), the teacher provides the high-level organization of text ideas and directs students to read to find the supporting information. After reading, the students contribute ideas while the teacher records them on a chalkboard. Each idea is enclosed in a circle, and lines are drawn to connect the circles as appropriate. Students are permitted to refer to the text to refresh their memories or resolve conflicts.

For example, for a story about triplets, the teacher wrote the name of each triplet in a separate circle and the names of all three in a fourth circle. The four circles radiated from a central circle, the core of the web, which was left blank. The students were directed to "remember important things about each sister [p. 645]." After the story was read (by the teacher in this case, as a listening activity), the children recalled information on how each sister differed from the others as well as on the characteristics they all shared. The core of the web, representing the central idea, was filled in after the four strands had been completed; an appropriate statement of the central idea was arrived at through brainstorming: "sisters who do same and different things [p. 645]." The completed web then served as a springboard for a group discussion of individuality, family relationships, etcetera.

Guided Reading Procedure.   As originally developed by Manzo (1975), this procedure is designed to enhance students' recall of expository materials. It also increases the level of student participation in class and provides challenge as well as variety. The following steps are involved:

1.   A passage of appropriate length is selected. The length is best judged in terms of the reading speed and attention span of the average reader in the group. As a rule of thumb, primary grade students might be expected to read for 3 minutes and to read a 90-word passage in that time (30 words per minute); intermediate grade students might read for 5 minutes at approximately 100 words per minute—a 500-word passage; junior high students might read for 7 minutes at 125 words per minute—a 900-word passage; and high school students could probably read for 10 minutes at 200 words per minute—a 2,000 word passage.

2. The teacher prepares students for the selection by introducing the general topic, relating it to previous classroom instruction as well as to students' personal experiences; and by introducing vocabulary, new concepts, and so on. A general purpose for reading is established, and students are directed to remember as much of the passage as they can.

3. After reading, students tell whatever they remember, and all information is recorded on the chalkboard by the teacher in the order in which it is recalled. (It may be abbreviated in form to save time.) One teacher found that having students write the information in their notebooks while the teacher recorded it on the chalkboard helped sustain students' attention and interest.

4. After students have contributed all the information they can remember, the teacher directs their attention to any inconsistencies, inaccuracies, or inadequacies that may be present. Students are encouraged to consult the text for necessary corrections and additions.

5. The group is then asked to organize the information they have compiled. This may take any form that is familiar to the students — a diagram, an outline, a chronological sequence, or even a semantic web. The teacher guides this process by raising questions, making suggestions, etcetera.

6. The teacher then raises some final questions to help students gain full understanding of the passage.

7. For the final step, a conventional, teacher-made comprehension test is administered. The test items can be of any kind; but they should reflect the ideas and information that were brought out during class discussion. Manzo cautions against omitting this step: "it is important to the overall design because it provides an opportunity for evaluation, feedback, and reinforcement." He also notes that "students . . . come to look forward to these tests as opportunities to show what they have learned — a just reward for effort [p. 291]."

Although Manzo's procedure was originally designed to be used following silent reading of an entire passage, it may also be used as a prereading activity (Bean & Pardi, 1979). In this case, students first survey the passage by reading the title, headings, pictures, charts, introductory and summary paragraphs, etcetera. Then they recall as much as they can, organize their recall, and check it for accuracy and completeness (as in steps 3, 4, and 5 above). They then read the entire passage and take the final comprehension test (step 7). When used as a prereading activity, the procedure demonstrates the value of surveying materials before reading and thus serves to combine the teaching of surveying skills with the teaching of specific content.

Understanding Text Structure. Evidence that understanding text structure plays an important role in comprehension was cited earlier. When ninth-graders were given instruction in the main types of expository discourse (e.g., comparison–contrast, problem–solution, main idea–supporting details), they nearly doubled the amount of information recalled (McDonald, 1978; cited in Meyer *et al.*, 1980). Similar results have been obtained with poor comprehenders in the primary grades (Bartlett, 1978; cited in Meyer *et al.*, 1980). Taylor and Beach (1984) recently showed that training in text structure is helpful to seventh-graders in learning relatively unfamiliar materials (drawn from social studies textbooks). However, Taylor and Beach's instruction did not so much pertain to discourse patterns as to the use of headings and subheadings. The students transferred the headings to their notebooks and organized the information under each heading in terms of main ideas and details. They also made note of relationships between headings where appropriate.

General Instructional Approach

Comprehension instruction generally takes place in the context of a directed reading lesson. In such a lesson students are first prepared for the passage they will read: unfamiliar words are introduced and their meanings explained; the theme or topic of the passage is brought into focus through a discussion of relevant knowledge and personal experiences; and one or more purposes for reading the passage are provided. Then, after reading, a question–answer discussion session provides students with feedback on how well they have understood the passage and (ideally) clarifies any confusions or misunderstandings. As a final step, students are typically introduced to a set of follow-up exercises on which they will work independently, practicing such specific comprehension skills as arranging events in temporal order and noting specific details. This format is featured in most basal reader programs; suggestions for implementing it make up the bulk of teachers' manuals.

As most readers of this text are undoubtedly aware, reading experts have been somewhat critical of basal reader programs. However, most of their criticism has been directed at the quality of the materials rather than the type of comprehension instruction provided. The stories have been criticized as uninteresting or insipid, the characters as simple-minded or culturally stereotyped, and the workbooks as little more than busywork (if not completely inappropriate). Very few objections have been raised against the plan or design of daily lessons. Indeed, the foregrounding of prior knowledge and experience that is the hallmark of these lessons, together with the instruction in vocabulary and related concepts, is entirely consistent with current views of the reading process.

Though basal reader lessons are constructed on sound theoretical principles, they are not without flaws. Not every lesson is true to these principles in every respect. Therefore, one way to improve instruction for students with comprehension problems is to improve the overall quality of the lessons. This is the most important avenue of remediation, at least from a practical standpoint. The procedures described above may be seen as complementary avenues. They introduce students to strategies for assuming a more active role in the reading process and thus for exploiting the background knowledge and personal experiences that will make a text more meaningful. And they show students how text information is interrelated and organized. But they are, at best, complementary to — and not a substitute for — the day-to-day presentations of basal reader lessons.

Reading researchers have been interested in comprehension for a number of years, but it is only recently that they have turned their attention to comprehension instruction as it occurs from day to day in the classroom. Their observations, summarized below, provide fresh insight into the issues with which we must be concerned in conducting reading lessons.

A group of researchers at the University of Pittsburgh Learning Research and Development Center (Beck, McKeown, McCaslin, & Burkes, 1979) has examined in detail the instruction provided in two widely used basal reader programs (the 1976 editions of the Ginn Reading 720 Series and the Houghton Mifflin Reading Series). They found that the prereading activities suggested in the manuals were frequently "problematic" in the sense that they either failed to highlight the central theme of the story or failed to present the background information necessary for understanding it. For instance, in one early first-grade story, there is a picture of a lion with a bandana tied around its head in such a way as to represent the idea of a toothache. The teacher is directed to call attention to the bandana by asking, "What does the lion have tied around its head?" but nothing is said about the purpose for wearing the bandana. Moreover, in the story itself teeth are not mentioned until the third page; before that point only the word *sick* is used to refer to the lion's problem. As *sick* is not normally used in connection with a toothache, students are likely, upon reading the first two pages, to develop an erroneous concept of the story problem. This type of difficulty is common in early reading materials because many of the words needed to convey story ideas (such as *dentist* and *toothache* in the example cited) are beyond the word recognition capabilities of young readers.

Another difficulty associated with the vocabulary restrictions of early reading materials is the use of pronouns where the antecedent is not included in the text but, instead, is suggested by an accompanying picture. Beck *et al.* found that teachers' manuals were not always sensitive to the necessity of clarifying pronoun referents in such cases.

Instances of inadequate background-knowledge development were not confined to beginning materials. In one third-grade story, Pecos Bill ends a drought by lassoing the Little Dipper and tipping it so that the water inside pours out. An understanding of the function of dippers and how the Little Dipper came to be so named are crucial for full comprehension of this story. Yet, prereading discussion of these concepts was not suggested in the teacher's manual — despite the fact that dippers are not familiar objects in today's world and many third-graders may not know that constellations are named after people or objects that they seem to resemble.

Failure to alert teachers to the knowledge that must be developed before students read a passage was found to be even more prevalent in the intermediate grade lessons than in the primary ones. Beck *et al.* relate this to "a trend to reduce the amount of oral preparation for reading in response to a perceived need to provide more reading and less talk in the reading class [1979, p. 57]." This trend is, of course, unfortunate in light of recent evidence that the acquisition of new knowledge depends heavily on existing knowledge frameworks (Pearson, Hansen, & Gordon, 1979).

With regard to the specific purpose for reading that is typically established by the teacher before students read a text, Beck *et al.* found that the suggestions in teachers' manuals could be inappropriate in several different ways. They might direct students to find information that was not actually in the text, they might provide information that was in conflict with the text and they might establish a line of thinking that was not in keeping with the text (e.g., that was too narrow in scope). Poorly formulated purpose-setting questions not only fail to provide the necessary framework for organizing text information, but may actually interfere with comprehension by setting up false expectations. Beck *et al.* suggest that a guided reading activity should not specify information to be gathered but, rather, should activate a central idea that will help a reader "to recognize important story elements as they are encountered and to relate them to each other under some larger design [p. 91]."

It was in the area of postreading questions that the most consistent shortcomings of basal reader instruction were found. The questions reflected no systematic attempt to elicit the explicit and implicit text information that was central to the story. Nor did they follow the progression of ideas or events in the story, either in terms of temporal sequence or in terms of the interrelationship of story ideas. That is, the questions did not build on each other. They therefore could not facilitate the development of a unified conception of the story — what Beck *et al.* call a "story map." Moreover, in the Ginn series, many of the questions tended to be speculative in nature. Although the intent was presumably to develop inferential skills, the speculations were often irrelevant to story events. In the Houghton Mifflin series, the questions did pertain to explicit story information; yet they did not insure that students understood that information in terms of the story. That is, they followed the text so closely that important implicit information was neglected.

In all fairness, it should be pointed out both that basal series are openly committed to the idea of developing background knowledge and setting purposes for reading and that the analysis of the Beck group suggests that they honor these commitments reasonably well. The weaknesses in pre-reading instruction noted above reflect only occasional mishandlings of these activities, and not consistent shortcomings. On the other hand, basal series have tended to follow the more traditional view of questions — namely, that questions should elicit literal, inferential, and evaluative levels of thinking — rather than the text-dependent (story map) view taken by Beck *et al.* So it is not surprising that basal questions did not score well on the criteria by which they were evaluated. Furthermore, questions were evidently used effectively to extend and develop text ideas — having children apply story situations to their own lives, imagining how a story character would act in other circumstances, etcetera.

While prior knowledge and experiences that may be pertinent to a passage are normally brought into focus during prereading instruction, Hansen (1981a) observed that no concurrent attempt is made to integrate these into the reading process. That is, students are not explicitly taught, through explanation and example, to *use* what they know to understand what they read. When Hansen incorporated this type of instruction into a series of 10 basal reader lessons, she found a significant improvement in the literal as well as inferential comprehension of a group of second-graders, all reading at or above grade level (1981b). In a second study with fourth-graders (Hansen & Pearson, 1983), however, the method proved effective only for the poor readers. In a third study (Hansen & Ahlfors, 1982), this time with fifth-graders, there was again little effect on the comprehension of good readers (no poor readers were included in the study). One interpretation of these results is that older children with good reading ability have already learned the appropriateness — indeed, the necessity — of bringing knowledge and experience to bear on written as well as spoken discourse, whereas younger and poorer readers have not yet learned this. We described Hansen's procedure in greater detail earlier along with other useful instructional strategies.

The most serious indictment of instruction in comprehension has come from Durkin (1978–1979, 1981). First, on observing the classroom practices of a large number of teachers, she found a shockingly small proportion of time devoted to comprehension instruction. This may be explained in part by the rather narrow definition of instruction she used in classifying teacher behaviors. For example, she classified question asking as "instruction" only "if what a teacher did with questions and answers were likely to advance children's comprehension abilities [1978–1979, p. 490]." Nor did she classify as instruction preparing students for reading by teaching the meanings of words to be encountered, posing questions, or discussing related experiences. More importantly, however, Durkin noted that these activities were given only cursory attention and that, often as not, the purpose-setting questions raised before reading were not discussed after reading. Durkin also noted that several days often intervened between the time a story was read and the time that children answered questions about it. Finally, Durkin noted that teachers rarely did more than tell children whether their answers were right or wrong. This is unfortunate, since questions are poorly used if some proportion of them are not taken as opportunities for explaining and clarifying text information.

Second, on examining the teacher's manuals of several reading series, Durkin (1981) confirmed the tendency noted by Beck *et al.* (1979) for instruction in prerequisite knowledge to be treated rather scantily. She also found the follow-up component of reading lessons (which the Pittsburgh group had not examined) to be poorly conceived. The directions given to teachers for conducting this instruction were often sketchy, and the relevance of what was taught was not always made clear to students. For example, in one series, first-graders were taught that *and* is a word used to connect two words; then, without further clarification, the children simply read pairs of words connected by *and*. Since follow-up activities occupy a significant share of students' reading time, these criticisms cannot be taken lightly. Regrettably, reading professionals are not entirely clear as to what should be taught in follow-up activities. There are some who question the value of such activities altogether, believing that children learn little from lessons *about* reading compared to what they can learn from reading suitable materials (MacGinitie, 1983).

In sum, basal reader programs guide instruction in ways that are generally consistent with what we know of the reading process. Inadequacies appear here and there in prereading instruction, and postreading questions are particularly vulnerable to criticism because they are generally designed to elicit various levels of thinking rather than a coherent text. But the teacher who is alert to the issues involved can compensate for these deficiencies without too much effort. Knowing the students in his or her class, the teacher is in a fairly good position to identify the concepts that will be unfamiliar to them and provide necessary prereading instruction. The teacher can also make postreading questions more compatible with the story line. And, finally, the teacher can cull follow-up materials and eliminate exercises that seem unnecessary or too difficult. Again, the teacher has knowledge of the students on which to base these judgments. Eliminating certain follow-up activities will allow more time for independent reading if additional teacher-led activities are not feasible.

SUMMARY

We have argued that a diagnosis of difficulty in the area of comprehension can generally be made once it has been determined that print translation skill and word knowledge are not underlying sources of poor comprehension. Once such a diagnosis has been made, it is useful to explore further to identify the nature of the comprehension problem. That is, in order to provide appropriate instruction, it is necessary to determine whether a student's difficulty stems from poorly developed strategies for interacting with text and organizing text information or from the student's inability to understand the information the text contains. A description and case study application of specific procedures for diagnosing and probing the nature of comprehension difficulty was presented. This was followed by recommendations regarding the type of instruction that would be appropriate for each type of comprehension problem. Finally, some general principles for improving basal reader lessons were proposed.

7

Diagnosis Based on
an Instructional Passage

The previous six chapters have introduced ways of thinking about and investigating the development of reading proficiency. Chapter 1 described a model for diagnosis that focuses on the relations among print translation, word knowledge, and discourse comprehension. Chapters 2 and 3 discussed ways to understand and diagnose students' print translation strategies. Chapter 4 focused on the development of word knowledge, and described procedures for assessing students' knowledge of concepts and terms included in their reading materials. Chapters 5 and 6 discussed ways of thinking about reading comprehension and described procedures for developing questions and diagnosing comprehension problems. These various topics and diagnostic procedures were developed in separate chapters because of their complexity. In this chapter, the procedures are combined into a comprehensive diagnosis of reading proficiency in accord with the basic model described in the first chapter.

Although we do not expect teachers to perform a comprehensive diagnosis of the reading strategies of each of their students, conducting intensive case studies is a useful way to consolidate the diagnostic knowledge that was presented in previous chapters and to learn to think about reading development in terms of the diagnostic model. After conducting several case studies, teachers can begin to use the procedures more informally, during the course of daily instruction. The training procedures increase sensitivity to the pattern of oral reading responses and to the demands of comprehension questions as well as the appropriateness of student answers. There will always be students whose reading difficulties are extremely perplexing and for whom it may be useful to undertake an extensive diagnosis. But for most students informal observations during daily instruction over a period of time will suggest ways in which instruction can be more effective.

One of the more important instructional issues confronting teachers is whether the instructional materials being used in the classroom are of appropriate difficulty for their students. Betts (1954) suggested that it is useful to characterize the appropriateness of the match between students and materials in terms of levels (see earlier discussion on page 43). The independent reading level is the highest level at which students can read fluently with good comprehension without instructional assistance. The instructional level is the highest level at which students are able to read with adequate comprehension once they are provided with appropriate instructional support. Finally, the frustration level is that level at which the text is so difficult that even with appropriate support, students may be unable to comprehend. In this last case, faulty comprehension may reflect problems with print processing, word knowledge, or discourse processing. Figure 7.1 presents a graphic representation of the difficulty levels of reading materials.

Reading that is assigned as homework or as independent seatwork should pose almost no print-processing or comprehension problems for students. That is, students should be able to read the material orally with good intonation and phrasing or silently with ease and comprehend the main ideas and important facts. When students have difficulty correctly identifying more than 2 words in every 100, they may well have problems in focusing on the meaning and these problems may hinder them from developing mature reading strategies. Failure to answer more than 1 question in

Figure 7.1.   Betts' levels of reading.
(From E. A. Betts, *Foundations of Reading Instruction*, p. 448. New York: American Book Company, 1954. Reprinted by permission.)

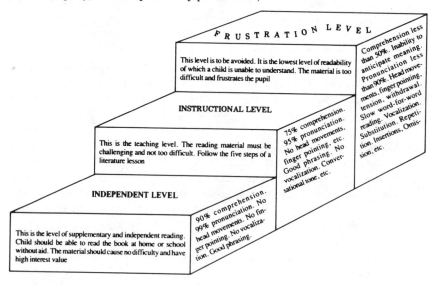

every 10 is another indication that the material is probably too difficult for independent reading. It is important that the questions used in making this assessment be appropriate and nontrivial. There are some disabled readers for whom no reading material is easy and who therefore should not read unless the teacher has prepared them for the passage or provides direct support.

Given the range in reading proficiency in most classes, teachers should have for homework and independent reading assignments materials that represent a comparable range in difficulty. Students can best develop their reading strategies through contextual materials that they can read fluently with good comprehension. Unfortunately, some students never experience the pleasure of problem-free reading and are thereby deprived of appropriate reading practice.

When students read under the direct supervision of their teacher, more problems in print translation and comprehension can be tolerated. As a rule of thumb, if a student is reading aloud, he or she should have difficulty with no more than 1 word in every 20. Comprehension should be good, with at least 3 out of every 4 questions answered correctly.

Teachers need to keep in mind not only the average performance of the group with which they are working but also the performance of individuals in the group. When individual students are missing more than half the questions posed or having difficulty with more than 1 word in every 10, the materials are inappropriate, representing frustration-level work. Instructional support can rarely help a student who is reading frustration-level material enough to permit him or her to perform at acceptable levels of print processing and/or comprehension.

By contrast, students who perform in the borderline region between frustration level and acceptable instructional level may be helped by instruction that has been developed with their particular problems in mind. This borderline region is characterized by an accuracy of 90–94% on oral reading and 50–74% on comprehension questions. The criteria for determining the reading level of materials are summarized in Table 7.1.

Consider the case of Eva, discussed in Chapter 3. Eva's teacher had her read the next story in her basal reader with little instructional support. Her

Table 7.1. Criteria for Determining Reading Levels

	Passage reading	
Level	Oral reading accuracy (%)	Comprehension accuracy (%)
Independent	98–100	90–100
Instructional	95–97	75–89
Borderline	90–94	50–74
Frustration	below 90	below 50

oral reading accuracy score of 91% indicates performance in the borderline range. However, her comprehension was quite good at the instructional level, with 8 out of 10 questions answered correctly. Eva was in the lowest reading group and her teacher wanted her to remain in the group. However, the analysis of her print translation difficulties indicated that her problems were severe. The teacher's alternatives were either to have her receive reading instruction on an individual basis with easier materials or to try to eliminate some of the print-processing problems posed by her current basal reader through increased instructional support.

The teacher decided to try the second alternative, spending more time on word identification and discussion of key story terms prior to reading. After providing such preparation, she listened to the quality of Eva's oral reading and found that it was more fluent than it had been, with less than 5% of the words causing problems. She then proceeded to offer this increased support to Eva's reading group as part of their regular instruction. Other students in the group seemed to profit as well. At the same time, the teacher helped Eva select easy reading material for independent reading. If Eva's comprehension of the story had not been so complete, her teacher might not have found it possible to keep her with the reading group.

For most teachers, the students who cause most concern are those for whom the reading materials are too difficult. When frustration-level reading is indicated, in terms of either oral reading accuracy or level of comprehension, the teacher must find more appropriate materials. If the student's performance is in the borderline region, it may be possible to make the materials accessible through appropriate instruction. Usually, further diagnosis of the student's reading strengths and difficulties must be undertaken in order to pinpoint the nature of the problem and to experiment with instructional support.

In the next section of this chapter, specific procedures for diagnosing reading strengths and difficulties are described. As mentioned earlier, it is important to undertake individual case studies in order to consolidate the diagnostic strategies that were introduced in prior chapters.

DIAGNOSTIC PROCEDURES

In order to judge the appropriateness of instructional materials and the reading development of students, the following steps should be taken. As these steps were described in previous chapters, they are presented in summary form here.

Preparation

The teacher should select from the student's instructional materials a passage that seems to pose some difficulty for the student and that is similar in length to those typically used for instruction. A photocopy or double-spaced typewritten copy should be prepared.

Next, the teacher should study the passage and create a set of word knowledge and comprehension questions according to the procedures described in Chapters 4 and 5. The comprehension questions should be ordered according to the sequence of the story, and typed or written with sufficient space between them to record the student's responses. The word knowledge questions should follow the comprehension questions.

A system such as that described in Chapter 2 should be used to record the student's oral reading responses. The student should also be tape-recorded, so that it is possible to check the time it took the student to read the passage and the accuracy of the handwritten oral reading record.

Administration

The teacher should make sure that the student is comfortable and relaxed. The reason for the diagnosis should be discussed with the student (e.g., to learn more about how to work with him or her on reading). In addition, the procedures to be followed should be described. The student should be told that he or she will be asked to read a passage and answer some questions about it and that next time, his or her reading strategies will be explored more informally. When the student is asked to read the selection aloud, a version of the following directions should be given:

> This is a story in which . . . [theme-related preparatory statement]. Please read this story aloud for me. If you come to a word you don't know, try to figure it out, guess at it, or skip it. I will not be able to help you, so do the best you can. After you finish, I will ask you some questions.

Before the student begins reading, the tape recorder should be tested. The student may wish to record his or her voice and then listen to the replay. The student's oral reading should be recorded on the photocopy or typed version of the story as well as on tape. The tape recorder should be kept running while the comprehension questions are being asked, so that the responses won't be lost if the student proceeds more rapidly than the teacher can write. And, as mentioned, the tape recorder can be used to check the amount of time the student took to read the passage.

Analysis

Performance on the first part of the diagnosis is studied to determine the area(s) of reading that should be probed. If print translation accuracy is below 95%, sight words and/or content words are selected and procedures developed for examining the student's underlying resources for identifying words. If comprehension is below 75%, the teacher should examine the questions that were incorrectly answered and plan questions that may facilitate the probe. At the same time, the influence of word knowledge on comprehension and print translation should be considered and, when appropriate, additional words or phrases should be selected for presentation during the probe.

Probe

During a second session with the student, the teacher administers the probe items according to the procedures summarized in Figure 7.2. If difficulty with print translation is suspected, regardless of the adequacy of comprehension performance, the probe should focus first on content word identification and then on content word meaning. The reason for this order is that presenting the word knowledge items first would invalidate the exploration of word identification. If sight words are also a problem, these should be explored after the content word probe. The student's responses to the print translation probe should be recorded in writing as well as on tape. It is important that complete notes be made since it is often difficult on the basis of a tape recording to reconstruct the questions or word parts to which the student was responding.

Word knowledge items selected for obtaining further evidence regarding background knowledge should be presented next if they were not already presented in exploring print translation. The probe of comprehension is conducted last. In this way, the final probe may be omitted if convincing evidence has already been obtained that print translation and word knowledge are interfering with comprehension.

Interpretation

In analyzing a student's performance on a diagnostic passage, we find it useful to focus first on print translation, then on word knowledge, and finally on comprehension. Then, when we have achieved an understanding of the student's strategies in each of these areas, we examine his or her relative strength in these areas using the model presented in the first chapter.

Print Translation. The evidence concerning a student's print translation strategies comes from two sources: oral reading of contextual materials and identification of isolated words and word parts. Specifically, the first source provides evidence concerning the integrated approach to print that the student has developed; the second yields evidence concerning underlying knowledge about print. Though the two sources of evidence complement each other, the analyses are undertaken separately.

The analysis of contextual reading involves four steps. First, the student's response to the entire passage is examined in order to characterize his or her general proficiency. Analysis then focuses on responses to high-frequency sight words and, subsequently, on responses to content words in

Figure 7.2. Summary of procedures for the probe.

These procedures may be used after the student has read a passage and responded to comprehension questions.

If Student Demonstrates Difficulty Identifying Content Words

1. Select content words that the student missed during the oral reading. Write them on a blank page in list form. For each word, first see if the student can pronounce it without help. If not, use the procedures described in Chapter 3: See if the student can divide the word into syllables and pronounce them. If not, see if the student can pronounce just the first syllable (cover the remainder of the word with a finger). If not, see if the student knows the sound corresponding to the first consonant or consonant cluster, then the vowel and final consonant(s). For syllables that lend themselves to visual analogy, test to see if the student can think of a word that ends the same and on that basis identify the syllable; if not, provide such a word and see if the student can use it to identify the syllable. Test a sample of consonants, consonant clusters, vowels, word endings, and word families. Continue with successive words on the list as long as the procedure yields new information and the student is responsive.

2. Ask the student to define the words missed, using the procedures described in Chapter 4.

If Student Demonstrates Difficulty with Sight Words:

1. Select sight words that the student misread during oral reading. Write them on a blank page in list form. See if the student can pronounce each word. Note whether the response is immediate or delayed. Continue the probe only as long as it yields new information and the student is able to respond attentively.

If Student Demonstrates Inadequate Comprehension:

1. Probe the student's knowledge of word meanings and/or concepts that may be interfering with comprehension, as described in Chapter 4. If word knowledge is adequate, probe comprehension further as described in the next two steps.

2. Note those questions that were answered incorrectly. Have the student reread the portion of the passage on which the question is based and reask the question. Continue this procedure for the remaining incorrectly answered questions.

3. If a question is not answered correctly after rereading, explore further using the informal interview technique illustrated in Chapter 6. Note intersentence and sentence-level problems of the text that may interfere with comprehension, and use informal procedures to explore these areas.

order to determine how the student identified words that were unfamiliar. Finally, the student's reading integration and fluency are assessed. The results of this four-step analysis should be recorded on the oral reading analysis form.

The analysis of performance on isolated words — the probe — may focus on sight words, content words, or both. The probe of sight words should reveal whether they are recognized on sight when other problems involved in contextual reading are removed. The probe of content words provides answers to the following questions: Can the student divide multi-syllabic words into syllables? Can the student identify simple syllables and more complex syllables (those containing blends, digraphs)? Can the student identify word endings (-*ing*, -*es*, -*ed*, . . .)? Does the student know vowel pronunciations and markers? Can the student blend letter sounds?

The results obtained from the oral reading analysis and the probe are then consolidated on the oral reading analysis form in order to answer the following questions:

1. Is the passage of appropriate difficulty in terms of the student's print translation skills and instructional needs?
2. What is the student's strength in rapid sight-word recognition?
3. What resources does the student possess for identifying unknown words?
4. Are the student's print-processing skills integrated and fluent?
5. What, if any, aspect of print translation skills should be the focus of instruction?

In answering these and subsequent questions the teacher should note any supporting evidence.

Word Knowledge.   Informal questioning and discussion can be used to ascertain whether the student has the background experiences that are needed to understand the passage. But word knowledge questions and probes will be needed to assess the student's knowledge of the specific words that pertain to these experiences. They also provide evidence on whether the student is able to select the particular meaning of a word that is appropriate to the sense of the passage. This evidence concerning word knowledge should answer three questions:

1. Does the student have command of the concepts used in the passage?
2. Is this knowledge explicit and clear (definitions) or implicit and somewhat vague (sentence use)?
3. Can the student use context to select the appropriate word meaning?

Comprehension. The interpretation should begin with the evidence concerning the student's ability to respond correctly to text-related comprehension questions. In completing the comprehension – word knowledge summary form, answers to the following questions are sought:

1. Did the student understand the essential information contained in the passage and the import of the message? Is the passage at an appropriate level for the student for instructional purposes?
2. If not, what are the student's strengths and weaknesses in comprehension?
3. Is the problem mainly in the area of comprehension, or do difficulties with print translation or word knowledge underlie and account for comprehension difficulties?
4. On the basis of the comprehension probe, what, if any, instruction in comprehension is needed?

Summary/Integration. First, conclusions about the student's print translation, word knowledge, and comprehension should be summarized. Then, it should be determined whether word knowledge or print translation difficulties interfere with comprehension. Finally, the student's major strengths and difficulties in reading should be discussed.

Instructional Plan

On the basis of the summary and final integration of diagnostic information, the following questions can be answered:

1. Is the instructional material of appropriate difficulty for this student under ordinary conditions? Would certain forms of instructional intervention help the student to cope with the material?
2. What forms of instruction will help this student further refine his or her reading strategies?

Recommendations for instruction should follow directly from the final summary – integration of results and should be listed in order of priority.

It is extremely important that the diagnosis and recommendations be discussed with the student. It is also important to ascertain how the student feels about the recommendations. The instruction can only be successful to the extent that the student becomes a part of the planning and implementation.

CASE STUDY APPLICATION

The two case studies described in the remaining sections of this chapter demonstrate how these procedures can be applied. A teacher using this form of diagnosis may wish to prepare the student for reading the passage in the manner he or she normally follows in the classroom, rather than, as we have suggested, to have the student read with only a brief introduction.

CASE 1: SHARON

Sharon is 12 years old and in seventh grade. She has difficulty in reading and is in a remedial reading class. She works hard and is very cooperative in school. She is a shy student with very little experience outside of her lower-class neighborhood. Her mother is dead, and she lives with an older sister who is her guardian and other sisters and brothers. She does not have many interests —"just likes to stay home and watch TV or play outside

Figure 7.3.   Diagnostic reading passage: Sharon.
(From ADVENTURE TRAIL, Diagnostic Reading Workbook, Grade 4, by E. M. Johnson, p. 46. In *New Diagnostic Reading Series*. Columbus, Ohio: Charles E. Merrill Publishing Co., 1969. Reprinted by permission.)

Bringing Light to the Blind

Only about one-fourth of the blind people in our country can read. They read Braille (brāl). As you know, Braille is a way of printing by raised dots. The blind run their fingers over the raised dots.

Did you ever shut your eyes and run your fingers over a page of Braille printing? All the little raised dots seemed to run together. Even if you knew the Braille alphabet, your fingers could not pick out each separate dot. But the boys and girls who cannot see read stories in Braille. Their fingers are trained to be their eyes.

A Frenchman, Louis Braille, made it possible for those who cannot see, to read. When he was a small boy, he used to play around his father's harness shop. One day, he was trying to punch holes in a piece of leather with a big awl. The tool slipped and hurt Louis' eye. Before long, he became blind.

When Louis was ten years old, he was sent to a school for the blind in Paris. There he began to study music and learned to play the organ. He became a very fine musician.

Louis did not just want to become famous. He wanted to help all those who could not see. So he set to work to find an alphabet which could be read with the fingers. Today that system of writing is known as Braille.

Some books and magazines are printed in Braille for boys and girls. "My Weekly Reader Number Four" is one of them. Every week, the American Printing House for the Blind prints Braille copies of this newspaper.

There are even books that "talk." The books are like phonograph records that talk to the blind. When a blind person wants to read, he turns a key and then listens. It is as if someone were reading a book aloud to him. Our Government sends the talking books free to blind people in all parts of our country.

with her younger sister." Her teacher noticed that she often had difficulty comprehending assigned materials and decided to learn more about her reading strategies.

Preparation

Sharon's teacher selected a passage that she thought might be of interest to her. It was entitled "Bringing Light to the Blind" and was taken from a high fourth-grade reading workbook called *Adventure Trail* (Charles E. Merrill). The teacher's first step was to study the passage in order to derive comprehension and word knowledge questions. The reader should examine the passage shown in Figure 7.3 and try to develop appropriate comprehension and word knowledge questions.

Before proceeding, the reader should compare his or her questions with those developed by the teacher. Figure 7.4 shows the teacher's comprehension and word knowledge questions and the responses that she expected. The first six comprehension questions involve text-related comprehension, while question 7 encourages the student to generalize beyond the text.

Figure 7.4.   Comprehension and word knowledge questions: Sharon.

Comprehension

1. How do blind people read? (They run their fingers over raised dots, or by Braille.)

2. What do blind people train to be their eyes? (fingers)

3. How did Louis Braille become blind? (He was hit in the eye with a tool [awl] while punching holes in leather in his father's harness shop.)

4. When Louis Braille was at school, what did he study? (music; playing the organ)

5. What did Louis Braille do for the blind? (made it possible for blind people to read by inventing an alphabet which could be read with the fingers, etc.)

6. What are books that "talk"? (like records that talk to the blind)

*7. Do you think that Louis Braille was a brave person? Why?

* Beyond-text question

Word Knowledge

1. What is *Braille*? (printing by small raised dots that can be read by touch)

2. What is an *awl*? (a tool for punching holes)

3. What does *raised* mean? (higher; above)

4. What is a *system*? (a method)

Administration

Sharon was quite relaxed when she read the passage orally and responded to the prepared questions. The record of her oral reading is shown in Figure 7.5. The reader should study the pattern of her responses in order to determine whether she has difficulty in any area of print translation.

Following the oral reading, Sharon was asked to retell as much of the selection as she could remember. Here is what she said: ". . . about blind

Figure 7.5.   Record of oral reading: Sharon.
(From ADVENTURE TRAIL, Diagnostic Reading Workbook, Grade 4, by E. M. Johnson, p. 46. In *New Diagnostic Reading Series*. Columbus, Ohio: Charles E. Merrill Publishing Co., 1969. Reprinted by permission.)

Bringing Light to the Blind

Only about one-fourth of the blind people in our country can read. They

read Braille (brāl). As you know, Braille is a way of printing by raised dots.

The blind run their fingers over the raised dots.

Did you ever shut your eyes and run your fingers over a page of Braille

printing? All the little raised dots seemed to run together. Even if you knew

the Braille alphabet, your fingers could not pick out each separate dot. But

the boys and girls who cannot see read stories in Braille. Their fingers are

trained to be their eyes.

A Frenchman, Louis Braille, made it possible for those who cannot see,

to read. When he was a small boy, he used to play around his father's harness

shop. One day, he was trying to punch holes in a piece of leather with a big

awl. The tool slipped and hurt Louis' eye. Before long, he became blind.

When Louis was ten years old, he was sent to a school for the blind in

Paris. There he began to study music and learned to play the organ. He

became a very fine musician.

Louis did not just want to become famous. He wanted to help all those

who could not see. So he set to work to find an alphabet which could be read

with the fingers. Today that system of writing is known as Braille.

Skipped entire line in passage

Figure 7.5.   (*Continued*)

Some books and magazines are printed in ~~Braille~~ ^Braley^ for boys and girls. "My   ✗ O

Weekly Reader Number Four" is one of them. Every week, the American⃝ |

Printing House for the Blind prints ~~Braille~~ ^Braley^ copies of this newspaper.   ✗O

There are even books that "talk," ⃝The⃝ books are like phonograph   ✗ |

records that talk⃝to⃝the⃝ blind. When a blind person wants⃝to read, he turns⃝a   ✗ |

key and then listens. It is as if someone were reading a book aloud to him. Our

Government sends ⃝the⃝ talking books free to blind people in all parts of ~~our~~ ^a^   ✗ |

country.

*Dialect-based miscues occurring more than twice were not counted.

---

people . . . reading and stuff. About this boy . . . he was doing something and something hurt his eye. That's all I remember." Because her
retelling was so incomplete, it was necessary to administer the questions
that had been prepared. Her responses are shown in Figure 7.6. The
reader should study her answers in order to decide whether she is experiencing difficulty with word knowledge and/or comprehension.

**Figure 7.6.   Responses to comprehension and word knowledge
questions: Sharon.**

Retelling

> . . . about blind people . . . reading and stuff. About this boy — he
> was doing something and something hurt his eye. That's all I re-
> member.

Comprehension

✓ **1.** How do blind people read? (They run their fingers over raised dots, or
by Braille.)
RESPONSE: They read from Brā-ley.

✓ **2.** What do blind people train to be their eyes? (fingers)
RESPONSE: They use their hands, don't they?

½ **3.** How did Louis Braille become blind? (He was hit in the eye with a tool
(awl) while punching holes in leather in his father's harness shop.)
RESPONSE: He was doing something and he knocked something over
and it made him blind. [Q.: What hit him in the eye?] That
harness stuff.

(*Continued*)

Figure 7.6. (*Continued*)

✓ **4.** When Louis Braille was at school, what did he study? (music; playing the organ)
RESPONSE: Music.

✗ **5.** What did Louis Braille do for the blind? (made it possible for blind people to read by inventing an alphabet which could be read with the fingers, etc.)
RESPONSE: He helped them learn to read and put up this thing about blind.

✗ **6.** What are books that "talk"? (like records that talk to the blind)
RESPONSE: Don't know.

✗ ***7.** Do you think that Louis Braille was a brave person? Why?
RESPONSE: Yes, he was brave. He helped people that were blind to read and write.

* Beyond-text question

Word Knowledge

✗ **1.** What is *Braille?* (printing by small raised dots that can be read by touch)
RESPONSE: Like a thing that goes through a line or something. [Q.: can you explain that?] Well . . . not sure.

✗ **2.** What is an *awl?* (a tool for punching holes)
RESPONSE: Don't know.

✓ **3.** What does *raised* mean? (higher; above)
RESPONSE: You raise it . . . raise it up.

✗ **4.** What is a *system?* (a method)
RESPONSE: Don't know.

Analysis

On the basis of Sharon's oral reading of the passage and her responses to the comprehension questions, it was decided that the probe should focus on two areas: exploration of her content word errors, in order to better assess her word identification skill, and assessment of her word knowledge in areas pertinent to the passage.

Probe

The results from the oral reading analysis and probe are summarized on the oral reading analysis form in Figure 7.7. The probe indicates that Sharon has good knowledge of basic phonics concepts but has difficulty applying this knowledge during contextual reading.

The summary of Sharon's comprehension performance and the results from the word knowledge probe are presented on the comprehension–word knowledge summary in Figure 7.8. Because her

Figure 7.7. Analysis of oral reading responses: Sharon.

ORAL READING ANALYSIS

Name _Sharon_ Grade _7_ Date _2/84_

Book/Page _Adventure Trail_ Level _4th Grade_

A. DIFFICULTY

_20_ / _329_   _94_ % Correct   Level: Independent Instructional   (Borderline) Frustration

B. WORD LEARNING: Sight Word Errors

Printed Word	Oral Response	Probe	Evaluation
is	it	✓	Immediate and correct
our	a	✓	recognition of sight words.
② the	[omitted]	✓	Sight words are probably
② a	[inserted]	✓	not a problem with easier
could	[inserted]	✓	materials.
[a line]	[omitted]		

C. WORD IDENTIFICATION: Content Word Errors

Printed Word	Oral Response	Probe	Difficulty	Evaluation
② Braille	Brā/ Brăly /Brăley Brāley	✓	no major problems	Consonants ⎤ good
page	paget	✓		Blends/Digraphs ⎬ knowledge
known	knows	✓		Vowels ⎰ of phonics.
sent	seen ©	✓		Vowel Digraphs ⎱ Application may
seemed	seems	✓		Markers ⎰ be more of a problem
learned	learning	✓		Affixes —Has knowledge
separate	sē per ©	✓		Syllables —Good knowledge
began	begin	✓		Comments: Well-developed
became	become	✓		word identification skill;
system	simple	✓		need to check application
American	America	✓		during easier
				contextual reading

D. INTEGRATION – FLUENCY

Integration: _Errors are generally not contextually appropriate;_ _infrequent correction of errors; highly dependent on graphic cues._

Fluency: Rate _329_ / _6.1_ = _54_ wpm Evaluation _Slow, even for a fourth grader._

Phrasing _Choppy- does not read with appropriate phrasing_

Figure 7.8.   Summary of responses to comprehension and word knowledge questions: Sharon.

COMPREHENSION – WORD	Name _Sharon_ Grade _7_ Date _2/84_
KNOWLEDGE SUMMARY	Book/Page _Adventure Trail_ Level _High 4th_

COMPREHENSION

_3½ / 6_   _58_ % Correct

Level: Independent   Instructional
(Borderline)   Frustration

A. RETELLING: Complete   Main Idea   Partial   (Inadequate)

Comments: _She had a difficult time expressing herself – limited vocabulary, problems with sentence structure._

B. TEXT-RELATED COMPREHENSION

Item #	Response	Probe (Comments)	Item #	Response	Probe (Comments)
1	✓		6	NR*	
2	✓	(Mentioned "hands" not fingers)			
3	½				
4	✓				
5	X				

* NR = no response

C. BEYOND-TEXT GENERALIZATION

Item #	Response	Probe (Comments)	Item #	Response	Probe (Comments)
7	X				

WORD KNOWLEDGE

_1½ / 6_   _25_ % Correct

Item Tested	Response	Comments	Item Tested	Response	Comments
Braille	X				
awl	X				
raised	✓	Knows verb form			
system	X				
separate dot (P)*	½				
harness (P)	X				

* P indicates a probe item

EVALUATION

A. COMPREHENSION: _Vague understanding of ideas in passage. Her comprehension is inadequate – the materials are inappropriate._

B. WORD KNOWLEDGE: _Very limited word knowledge – even unable to use words in a sentence._

word knowledge was so limited, there was no point in probing her comprehension skills further.

Before reading the interpretations made by the teacher, the reader should think for a moment about Sharon's reading. What are Sharon's strengths and difficulties?

Interpretation

Print Translation. Sight words do not seem to be a problem for Sharon and she possesses good phonics and structural skills. It is difficult to know whether her failure to apply these skills during contextual reading occurred because of the large number of unfamiliar words in the passage or because the general meaning of the passage was difficult for her to grasp. Most of the substitutions that did not make sense occurred in sentences that were too technical for her. While it is clear that Sharon's reading of this passage was neither integrated nor fluent, the number of problems posed may simply have overwhelmed her. It will be important to have Sharon read an easier passage with fewer unfamiliar words in order to have a more valid test of her integration and fluency.

Some affixed words and verb forms posed problems for Sharon. Dialect substitutions where the final *s* was either omitted or inserted were eliminated from consideration. But Sharon's problem seems to extend beyond that of pluralization and possession to other affixes. Her oral language differs in certain respects from standard English; further, at times she appears to be overcorrecting for dialect. It is important to determine the extent to which Sharon's problems with affixes arise from dialect influence as opposed to lack of knowledge. The probe results suggest that she understands affixes but during difficult oral reading becomes confused about their pronunciation.

Word Knowledge. Sharon's vocabulary and understanding of words seems to be quite limited for a seventh-grader. She does not know some words typically known by students her age *(harness, system, volume)* and has vague or limited concepts of others *(separate, raised)*. The possibility that she is in command of more knowledge than she is able to express was not supported by the probe, but further observation of her word knowledge should be undertaken.

Comprehension. The results from the retelling and the text-related questions are consistent, and they reveal that Sharon had difficulty understanding this selection. Even when her responses were correct or partially correct, they indicated serious limitations. She seemed to have particular difficulty describing major concepts explained in the passage. The main underlying problem seemed to be her failure to understand the technical concepts (raised dots, awl) necessary for understanding the central concepts (Braille) and events (the eye injury). However, print-processing problems may have also interfered with her understanding of *books that "talk"*

Summary/Integration. The analysis shows that Sharon's sight recognition and her phonics and structural skills are strong even though she sometimes fails to apply this knowledge during contextual reading. Given the difficulty of the passage for her, it was not possible to evaluate her reading integration (use of context) and her fluency. On this fourth-grade selection, she showed poorly integrated strategies and extremely slow reading.

Sharon's main problem is that her word knowledge is extremely limited. It is assumed that poor reading comprehension is a direct reflection of her limited word knowledge.

Instructional Plan

Materials. High fourth-grade level material is too difficult for Sharon unless the reading is preceded by extensive instructional support focused on the development of word meanings. Sharon should be reading from easier material (level to be determined) to enable her to attend to meaning, use context, and increase her reading rate.

Instructional Priorities. The major focus of instructional support should be on the development of Sharon's vocabulary and her reading integration and fluency. This instruction can be provided in a group that includes other students with similar problems.

1. Before Sharon reads a selection, the teacher should identify concepts that may be unfamiliar and encourage Sharon to speculate about their meaning and relationship to the theme of the selection. Unfamiliar or partially known concepts should be explained. Because the goal of vocabulary development is the improvement of comprehension, thorough discussion should follow the reading of each selection in order to develop comprehension and establish its importance.

Other procedures can also be used to expand Sharon's word knowledge. For example, stories should be read to her (along with other students) and new concepts should be discussed with suggestions for their use in alternative contexts. Sharon may also profit from working with another student or synonym, antonym, and root word – affix activities.

2. To improve Sharon's reading rate, integration, and fluency, she should be given short selections that are easy for her. She should be encouraged to concentrate on gaining meaning from everything she reads.

CASE 2: PATRICIA

Patricia is in ninth grade. Like 80% of her freshman class, she is in a double-period basic English class for students reading on a second-to-fifth-grade level. On this year's California Achievement Test, she scored a grade equivalent of 5.2 on vocabulary and 3.2 on comprehension. In contrast to many other students in her class, Patricia attends regularly and does all the assigned work. She understands and enjoys the mysteries that she reads on her own but has difficulty with most of her school reading. Because Patricia's teacher is able to spend some extra time with her, she decided to undertake a more systematic diagnosis of her reading strategies in order to determine which should be the areas of instructional focus.

In the testing situation, Patricia was relaxed, friendly, and eager to proceed. She was asked to read a fifth-grade level passage, entitled "Rescue in a Burning Building." The record of Patricia's oral reading is shown in Figure 7.9.

She was then asked to retell the selection and to respond to the questions that the teacher had prepared. Patricia's responses to the comprehension and word knowledge questions are shown in Figure 7.10. The reader should study the records in Figures 7.9 and 7.10 to decide what should be probed further.

Figure 7.9. Record of oral reading: Patricia.
(From *Real Stories,* Book 1, pp. 200–202, Milton Katz, Michael Chakeres, and Murray Bromberg, eds., New York: Globe Book, 1969. [Originally published in *Newsday;* reprinted by permission of the publisher, Newsday, Inc., Melville, N.Y.])

Rescue in a Burning Building   6̲

NEW YORK, June 17 — A fireman rescued a 76 year old woman from a

burning apartment building yesterday by tossing her off a fire escape. The

woman, Mrs. Mary Rogers, landed safely in the arms of another fireman |

waiting on the roof of an adjoining building. |

Fireman Edward Lane had risked his life to reach the woman, who was
                             fired
trapped in her smoke-filled top floor apartment in the five-story building. |

The fire was blazing out of control as Lane carried the almost unconscious

woman onto a fire escape.

(*Continued*)

Figure 7.9. (*Continued*)

As flames threatened them, Lane tried without success to first climb to

the roof and then to go below the height of the flames. He could not do ~~so~~ ^such |

while carrying the dead weight of the helpless 115-pound woman.

Then he saw another fireman, Mike Mays, ~~motioning~~ ^motion ^motering to him with his |

arms held out. Mays was on the roof of the next building, which was level

with the fire escape. A space of only four feet separated the two buildings, but ×○

there was a fifty-foot drop to the ground. Lane tried to pass Mrs. Rogers over

to Mays, but the gap was too wide.

Then the two men decided that the only chance to save the woman was

to try something very dangerous. Lane reached back and threw Mrs. Rogers

across the space between the buildings. For a moment the woman was not

supported above the ground. Then Mays caught her by the neck and

shoulders, and pulled her safely onto the roof. Mrs. Rogers was uninjured.

Lane then climbed to the roof of the burning building, went down an-

other fire escape and back to fighting the fire. ⓒ |

Figure 7.10. Responses to comprehension and word knowledge questions: Patricia.

Retelling

RESPONSE: It was a fire. He had to get this lady out of the building. They had to use the fire escape to get the lady out of the building.

Comprehension

✓ 1. Where did Fireman Lane find the woman? (in her smoke-filled apartment, on the top floor of the building)
   RESPONSE: In the building, in the house (house means apartment).

✓ 2. How serious was the fire? (It was blazing, out of control)
   RESPONSE: Real serious.

✗ 3. Why couldn't Fireman Lane carry the woman up or down the fire escape? (She was too heavy in her unconscious state —"dead weight.")
   RESPONSE: Because it was too hard. [Q.: Explain how.] Just too hard.

4. Where was the other fireman, Mike Mays? (on the roof of the next building, level with the fire escape)
   RESPONSE: Trying to get the fire out.
5. Why couldn't Fireman Lane pass the woman to the other fireman? (The gap between buildings was too wide — four feet.)
   RESPONSE: (Could not answer.)
6. What did Fireman Lane finally do with the woman? (threw her across the space between the two buildings; Mays caught her)
   RESPONSE: (Could not answer.)
*7. Why do you think the woman was "almost unconscious"?
   RESPONSE: Because of the smoke.

* Beyond-text question

Word Knowledge

1. What does *risked* mean, as in "He risked his life"?
   RESPONSE: Took a chance.
2. What does *unconscious* mean?
   RESPONSE: Knocked out.
3. What does *tossing* mean?
   RESPONSE: You throw it.
4. What does *adjoining* mean?
   RESPONSE: Like you join a club.

Analysis and Probe

On the basis of Patricia's responses to the passage and the comprehension and word knowledge questions, it was decided that the probe should further examine her comprehension responses and her word knowledge. In addition, the teacher decided to have Patricia respond to several of the content words that she had had difficulty pronouncing in order to confirm that print translation was not an area of difficulty. When probed, Patricia responded quickly and accurately to words such as *adjoining, escape,* and *motioning.* Thus, no further analysis was made of her oral reading responses.

Comprehension and word knowledge responses and the results of the probe are given in the comprehension – word knowledge summary form shown in Figure 7.11.

Before learning how the teacher made sense of the evidence, the reader should make some tentative interpretations. In what area or areas is Patricia experiencing major difficulty? What are the implications of this diagnosis for Patricia's instruction?

Figure 7.11. Summary of responses to comprehension and word knowledge questions: Patricia.

COMPREHENSION – WORD
KNOWLEDGE SUMMARY

Name *Patricia* Grade *9* Date *11/82*
Book/Page *Real Stories* Level *5th gr.*
200 – 202

COMPREHENSION

2 / 6 *33* % Correct

Level: Independent Instructional
Borderline (Frustration)

A. RETELLING: Complete Main Idea Partial (Inadequate)
Comments: *Incomplete and inaccurate retelling; she had only the barest*

B. TEXT-RELATED COMPREHENSION *understanding of story*

Item #	Response	Probe (Comments)	Item #	Response	Probe (Comments)
1	✓		6	X	
2	✓				
3	X				
4	X				
5	X				

C. BEYOND-TEXT GENERALIZATION

Item #	Response	Probe (Comments)	Item #	Response	Probe (Comments)
7	✓	*possesses some background knowledge about fires.*			

WORD KNOWLEDGE

6 / 8 *75* % Correct

Item Tested	Response	Comments	Item Tested	Response	Comments
risked	✓		motioning (P)	✓	
unconscious	✓		gap (P)	X	
tossing	✓				
adjoining	X				
blazing (P) *	✓				
dead weight (P)	✓				

* P indicates a probe item.
EVALUATION

A. COMPREHENSION: *Does not seem to understand the situation – e.g., where the second fireman was and what the problem was. May need to work on visualizing situations. Dense prose and expository materials may be particularly difficult for her.*

B. WORD KNOWLEDGE: *Some concepts are unknown, but generally she shows good strength in word knowledge.*

Interpretation

Print Translation. Patricia seems to have almost no problems with sight word recognition and word identification. Most of her errors on content words involved word endings (*-ed, -ing, -s*). Examination of the passage shows that typically she does pronounce these endings. In fact, she often pronounces endings that she drops during oral conversation. When words were presented in isolation during the probe, she pronounced the affixes according to standard English. Thus, it is clear that she possesses knowledge about word endings. Print processing does not appear to be a problem area that interferes with comprehension. Nevertheless, her reading rate is slower than the average range for fifth-graders, so some improvement in integration and fluency may be needed. It is difficult to evaluate her use of context since her word attack skills are strong but comprehension is low.

Word Knowledge. Patricia knew three-quarters of the vocabulary items tested. The two she missed, while not key words, would definitely have aided her comprehension. They also indicate that Patricia probably does not know many words typically known by ninth-graders. Verbal knowledge is a possible area of weakness that may contribute to Patricia's comprehension difficulties. Nevertheless, as also suggested by the results from the standardized reading test, her comprehension is lower than might be expected on the basis of her vocabulary knowledge.

Comprehension. Patricia's retelling (incomplete and inaccurate) showed that she had only the barest understanding of the situation in the story. Her answers to the factual questions (two correct out of six) support this. Even her two correct answers were not specific. In the probe, where she had an opportunity to reread most of the text orally and silently, she still did not grasp the point of the story. She reread the key paragraph many times before she comprehended it.

Summary/Integration. Patricia's main area of reading difficulty lies in comprehension. Since she could not answer the questions upon rereading, her problem appears to be at the sentence and intersentence level. Her word knowledge is relatively strong and does not seem to account for the comprehension difficulty. Print processing represents an area of strength, although work may be needed to improve integration and fluency.

Instructional Plan

Materials. While the currently used fifth-grade-level material is appropriate for instructional purposes with respect to print-processing demands, it represents frustration level (below 50%) with respect to comprehension. Given the test results, instruction should begin with

Instructional Priorities. Instruction should focus directly on the development of basic text-processing strategies, particularly those that are useful for expository materials. Key terms should be discussed as needed.

1. Patricia's comprehension may be improved through individual work. Instructional materials (on a third- or fourth-grade level) that ask specific questions about information presented and provide corrective feedback should be used. At least once a week Patricia's teacher should review her work with her. At this time, the teacher may wish to engage in reciprocal teaching of comprehension strategies (as described on page 160). Patricia should then be encouraged to concentrate on comprehending what she reads, paraphrasing sentences to herself, and interacting with the text as described in Chapter 6. Work on anaphora and connectives is also appropriate.

2. Students with comprehension problems similar to Patricia's should be brought together into a group. The group should learn to speculate on the basis of titles, headings, and initial paragraphs what a selection may be about. Discussion should follow each main segment of the article, to check the accuracy of group predictions. For both expository and narrative selections, the group should be given help in organizing information as described in Chapter 6.

3. Patricia should be encouraged to read on her own and to expand her reading interests. She could be given mysteries or exciting biographies that are slightly harder than the ones she presently reads. Her integration and fluency should be checked on these high-interest materials.

SUMMARY

We have shown, through detailed presentation of two case studies, how the procedures introduced in preceding chapters may be used to diagnose reading problems and modify instruction in accordance with students' needs. While the process of acquiring expertise in using these procedures may be time consuming, it leads to deeper understanding of the various facets of reading and provides the teacher with a framework for making sense of students' successes and failures and for refining instructional approaches.

8

Diagnosis with
a Series of Passages

The diagnostic procedures outlined in the preceding chapter are useful for evaluating a student's ability to profit from classroom materials. However, when these materials are inappropriate, the diagnosis does not provide information as to what level materials would be appropriate. A teacher with a range of reading materials can construct an inventory of passages representing different levels of reading difficulty. Then, when a student has difficulty with the materials used by the class or the reading group, the teacher has available other materials with which to assess his or her reading proficiency.

The term "informal reading inventory" (IRI) refers to a testing procedure in which reading comprehension and oral reading accuracy are assessed on more than one passage. The student reads a series of passages that range in difficulty, and comprehension questions are asked after each passage has been read. The results provide an "inventory" of reading levels; they indicate, in other words, the student's independent reading level, instructional level, and frustration level.

When introduced by Emmett A. Betts (1954) many years ago, the reading inventory was indeed "informal." The passages used were selected by teachers from graded materials available in the classroom, and the criteria determining whether a student "passed" or "failed" a given passage were simply based on what Betts and others considered reasonable. Since then, a number of inventory-type tests have been developed and published commercially. These instruments, to be described further in the next chapter, not only provide the test passages and comprehension questions but also specify the criteria for passage success.

We believe that both the teacher-constructed and the standardized informal reading inventories are useful tools for classroom teachers. The advantage of the teacher-constructed inventory lies in its direct relationship to the materials being used in a classroom (see Fuchs, Fuchs, & Deno, 1982, for further discussion of teacher-constructed inventories). That is, when a teacher learns that a student can profitably read a particular selection, he or she also knows exactly the materials to be used for instruction and has a basis for selecting other appropriate materials. The published instruments, however, have the advantage of professional expertise in the selection of graded passages, the development of comprehension questions, and the choice of criteria for acceptable performance.

In this chapter, we focus on teacher-constructed informal inventories and we describe procedures for the construction, administration, and interpretation of a series of graded passages. In Chapter 9, we examine ways in which published informal inventories with several passages per grade level may be used.

INVENTORY CONSTRUCTION

Passage Selection

The first task in creating an informal reading inventory is to select appropriate passages that correspond to classroom materials. An inventory should be limited to passages within a content area; thus, separate inventories should be constructed for each content area of concern. For the reading content area, the inventory may consist of selections drawn from the various levels of materials being used in the class. By contrast, in social studies and science, where single texts are being used for instruction, the inventory may include a selection from the text and also selections from other available materials that range in difficulty.

Most instructional materials have a grade level assigned by the publishers. If the grade designation is not discussed in the teacher's manual, it may be possible to obtain such information from the librarian or other services that grade materials.

Alternatively, the difficulty level or readability of a passage may be assessed using a formula that considers such features as the length of words, the abstractness of words, the complexity of sentences, and the length of sentences. Formulas that are commonly used include the Spache formula (Spache, 1953) for primary grade reading materials, and the Dale–Chall formula (Dale & Chall, 1948) for materials for fourth grade and beyond.

The Fry Readability Chart (Fry, 1968, 1972), shown in Figure 8.1, is particularly useful as an easy way of obtaining a readability estimate. It is based strictly on the length of words and sentences in the passage. Although this method is insensitive to some conditions that make reading difficult, the two criteria it uses *are* usually themselves indicative of passage difficulty. That is, usually passages with longer words contain more

Figure 8.1.   Fry Readability Chart. From Edward Fry, "A Readability Formula That Saves Time," *Journal of Reading,* 1968, *11,* pp. 513–516.

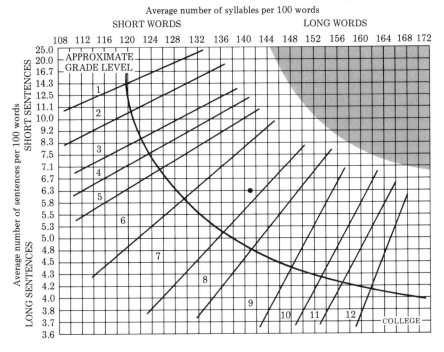

Average number of syllables per 100 words

SHORT WORDS   LONG WORDS

Directions: Randomly select three 100-word passages from a book or an article. Plot average number of syllables and average number of sentences per 100 words on graph to determine the grade level of the material. Choose more passages per book if great variability is observed and conclude that the book has uneven readability. Few books will fall in gray area but when they do grade level scores are invalid.

Example:

	Syllables	Sentences
1st hundred words	124	6.6
2nd hundred words	141	5.5
3rd hundred words	158	6.8
Average	141	6.3

Readability 7th grade (See dot plotted on graph)

complex ideas than those with shorter words, and usually passages with longer sentences discuss more complicated relationships than those with shorter sentences.

There are, of course, exceptions to these generalizations. For example, readability estimates are not very accurate in assessing the difficulty of poetry. Further, some textbook materials have been rewritten with shorter words and shorter sentences, so that they appear easier, but the complexity of the ideas remains the same. However, at the present time, no better way exists for assessing the difficulty of materials. In order to avoid problems, estimates of readability provided by publishers or by a formula should be coupled with the judgment of teachers. When a passage is rated as relatively easy but seems complex to the teacher, it should probably not be included in the inventory.

Passages should be selected from materials representing each grade level or half-grade level in the classroom. Generally, four or five passages will represent a range in difficulty that encompasses most students in the class. As discussed in Chapter 3, passages should be about the same length as those that students typically read at any one time in the classroom. Generally, passages from primary-grade materials should be from 50 to 100 words in length and those for higher grade levels from 100 to 200 words or more. It is not clear that it is useful to select passages corresponding to the preprimer and primer levels of difficulty, but if such passages are included, they should be short, from 25 to about 60 words in length.

Word Knowledge and Comprehension Questions

Each of the passages should be studied in order to derive appropriate text-based comprehension questions as described in Chapter 5. At least 5, and preferably 10 questions, should be written to follow each passage. Shorter passages (primary level) typically lend themselves to fewer questions than do more advanced and longer selections. The important consideration is that none of the questions pertain to trivial information. In addition, at least one beyond-text question should be formulated in order to assess this kind of thinking.

The passage's key vocabulary and central concepts should then be identified so that the student's word knowledge may be assessed. Three to eight word knowledge questions should be written, using the procedures described in Chapter 4.

Test Materials

Both the passages and the questions must be prepared for use. Clear photocopies should be made of the text passages. These should then be mounted on cardboard or laminated, sequenced in order of difficulty (with the easiest passage first), and bound in a loose-leaf notebook.

The questions for each passage should be sequenced and typed, allowing space for the student's responses to be recorded. Photocopies of the questions and of each of the passages should also be prepared so that the student's comprehension and oral reading responses can be recorded according to the procedures described earlier.

Criteria for Assessing Performance

As discussed in Chapter 7, 75% success is the level of comprehension generally suggested for the instructional level; 90% comprehension is recommended for the independent level. Oral reading accuracy should be at least 95% for the instructional level and 98% for the independent reading level (see Table 7.1, page 177).

Both oral reading accuracy and comprehension are considered in determining the student's instructional reading level. Classroom materials should be on a level the student can read with 75% or better comprehension and 95% or better accuracy. However, if the student scores in the borderline range, it may be possible through appropriate instruction to bring his or her reading performance into an acceptable range, as described in previous chapters.

ADMINISTRATION

The teacher decides what passage a student should start with, on the basis of prior informal experiences with the student or information from previous teachers. If the teacher wishes to assess the student's print translation skills, he or she should have the student read the passage aloud and should record any errors made, using the procedures described in Chapter 2. However, there are situations in which a teacher may prefer to have a student read the passage silently.

When the student finishes the passage, the teacher may first ask him or her to retell the story and then, if necessary, proceed to the comprehension questions. With students who have great difficulty retelling a passage, this step will become excessively time consuming and usually will not yield accurate evidence regarding comprehension. In such cases, after one or two retellings, the teacher should simply omit this step. At the other extreme are the fluent "retellers," whose responses are so complete that most comprehension questions will not need to be asked. For such students, it is an efficient strategy to continue the retellings.

The student's oral reading and comprehension performance determines the level of the next passage to be read. If the student scores at frustration level in either oral reading accuracy or comprehension, the next easier passage should be administered. If, by contrast, the student scores above the frustration level in both oral reading accuracy and comprehension, the teacher should ask the student to read the next-most-difficult passage. Increasingly difficult passages may be administered until the student's comprehension score falls below 50% or the oral reading accuracy below 90%. Once the frustration level has been established, the student should be asked to read increasingly easier passages until a high level of *both* comprehension (near 90% comprehension, or no more than 1 text-based comprehension error when there are fewer than 10 questions) *and* oral reading accuracy (near 98%, or no more than 1 error for every 50 words) are demonstrated.

INTERPRETATION OF RESULTS

The interpretation of the informal reading inventory is a two-stage process. First, judgments are made about the level of materials appropriate for reading instruction and independent reading. Then, the evidence concerning print translation, word knowledge, and reading comprehension is examined in order to determine relative strengths and weaknesses. Recommendations concerning the appropriateness of alternative materials are based on the first analysis and those regarding instructional priorities on the second.

Levels of Materials

Instructional Reading Levels. One major use of the teacher-constructed informal reading inventory is to determine reading group placement. The inventory provides evidence about word attack strategies, the development of reading rate and fluency, the need for word knowledge reinforcement, and the development of comprehension strategies. A teacher may use this evidence in either of two ways. He or she may use it to assign students to reading groups based on the level of materials to be used. The instruction provided to such groups must be sufficiently broad to meet the needs of all group members. As these needs will be varied, some instructional activities will probably focus on word identification, others on reading fluency, others on the development of background and word knowledge, and still others on the development of comprehension strategies.

Alternatively, the teacher may establish groups based on the specific reading strengths and difficulties of students. For example, a third-grade teacher may have two groups needing help with reading comprehension, one of which reads second-grade-level material and the other of which reads beginning third-grade-level material. Further, there may be other flexible groups for which the teacher provides special help with word knowledge, reading rate, and word identification strategies.

Although flexible, skill-based grouping is recommended in many reading methods textbooks, research shows that in actuality teachers tend to use relatively stable all-purpose groups based on the contextual reading level or the skill development level of students. Accordingly, we describe procedures for using informal reading evidence to assign students to essentially stable, multipurpose instructional groups.

We believe that the decision as to which group is most appropriate for a student should be based on a joint consideration of the student's comprehension and oral reading proficiency. Some of the factors involved can be illustrated by means of an example.

Peter was placed in a fourth-grade classroom just before Thanksgiving. Because no records were available on his reading achievement and past performance, the teacher decided to have him read passages from the informal inventory that she had developed. She had already grouped her students into four reading groups: an accelerated group reading fifth- and sixth-grade-level materials, a large group reading at grade level, a fairly small group reading from third-grade-level materials, and two students reading at the second-grade level.

Peter was first asked to read the third-grade selection. Although he made several oral reading errors, his comprehension was excellent. Thus, the teacher had him read the fourth-grade selection. He made many oral reading errors and showed signs of frustration, despite which his comprehension was quite good. Because of the signs of frustration he had shown, his teacher did not ask him to read the fifth-grade-level passage. Rather, she went next to the second-grade passage, which he read fluently with good comprehension. Peter's performance on the inventory is summarized in Table 8.1.

The reader should study the evidence in Table 8.1 and determine the group to which Peter should be assigned. Should he be assigned to the group reading the fourth-grade-level material because of his adequate comprehension at this level? Should he be instructed with the students reading the second-grade-level material because both his oral reading and comprehension are strong at this level? Or should he be grouped with the students reading the third-grade-level material even though his oral reading accuracy is in the borderline range?

His teacher made her decision in the following way. Whereas Peter showed relative strength in word knowledge and comprehension, he is experiencing difficulty with print translation. Thus, she believed that his instruction should be geared to the level that would support the further development of his word identification skills. While second-grade materials (his independent level) are appropriate to help him consolidate his sight recognition and develop fluency and the integration of skills, they do not pose enough word identification problems to help him develop his skill with multisyllabic words. Accordingly, the teacher chose to group him with students reading from the third-grade-level materials. A further considera-

Table 8.1. Summary of Performance on an IRI: Peter

Mode	Grade level	Oral reading		Text-based comprehension (%)	Beyond-text comprehension	Word knowledge
		Accuracy (%)	Rate (wpm)			
Oral reading	2	99	120	100	1/1	3/3
Oral reading	3	93	90	100	1/1	3/3
Oral reading	4	89	81	75	1/1	3/3

tion was that he was not the only member of that group who needed help with the identification of multisyllabic words.

To summarize, placement of a student into a reading group should be based on the identification of his or her instructional reading level. The decision involves two steps. First, the area of the student's greatest need is identified. Second, the level of material that poses some challenge for the student in that area and yet does not frustrate him or her should be identified. This level represents the student's instructional level.

Independent Reading Level. The student's independent reading level is the level of material that he or she can read with pleasure and profit without the support provided in "directed reading lessons." It is the level at which the student can recognize and identify words with few errors and read with proper intonation and fluency. It is also the level at which the student can concentrate on meaning without instructional support. In Peter's case, this level is that of second-grade materials, as with such materials Peter is able to use good print-processing strategies *and* to realize a high level of comprehension.

Areas of Reading Difficulty

The informal reading inventory provides more conclusive evidence about a student's reading strengths and difficulties than does assessment with a single passage. Although with a single passage it is possible to identify areas of relative strength and difficulty, the graded series allows us to specify how much weaker or stronger the development of a student's reading skill is in some areas than others. The series of passages provides more comprehensive evidence on how a student's reading strategies vary in response to the difficulty of the materials. Passages on which few errors are made are useful in identifying the student's independent reading level, but they do not provide much evidence about the difficulties the student is encountering. By contrast, passages that fall into the instructional range and sometimes those in the borderline range yield evidence that is useful in specifying the nature of the reading problems.

Despite this difference in comprehensiveness, the diagnosis of reading with a series of passages proceeds in much the same fashion as it does for a single passage. The procedures summarized in Chapter 7 for identifying areas of reading strength and difficulty should be followed (see pp. 179–183). As discussed below it will be important to consider the questions about print translation, word knowledge, and comprehension that were posed in earlier chapters. The oral reading analysis and the comprehension–word knowledge forms may also be useful in summarizing the evidence in areas in which the student is experiencing difficulty.

Print Translation. If the student's major reading problem is in the area of print translation, a detailed analysis of his or her oral reading of one or two passages at the instructional or borderline levels will reveal the general nature of the difficulty. Further probe of the student's print skills may be needed to obtain more specific information. Thus, in Peter's case, because print translation represented an area of major difficulty for him, his teacher not only analyzed his oral reading responses to the third-grade-level passage but also explored some of his responses using probe techniques.

Word Knowledge. When key words are carefully selected, they provide useful information about the student's general knowledge. Typically, the words from successive passages represent tasks of increasing difficulty. The level at which the student knows less than half of the key words is usually the level at which the demands of the reading task have become too great. When fewer words are missed, it is possible that instruction that includes prior discussion of important background concepts may make the materials accessible to the student. Often teachers need to experiment with the prior development of concepts in order to learn whether such instruction is effective with a particular student. In Peter's case, word knowledge is probably not an area of difficulty: he missed none of the words at the fourth-grade level, and this is above the level at which he will begin his reading instruction.

Comprehension. Analysis should again focus on those passages where the student scores in the instructional or borderline range. If the student's major problem is in the area of comprehension it may be useful to examine his or her comprehension strategies further, using the probe procedures described in Chapter 6. However, in Peter's case, because comprehension is an area of strength, no further analysis is needed.

CASE STUDY APPLICATION

The remainder of this chapter is devoted to three case studies. The first two are "minicases" which show how information from a graded series of passages may be interpreted using the general model presented in Chapter 1. The third case is more comprehensive, discussing each of the six stages of the diagnosis (preparation, administration, analysis, probe, interpretation, and instructional plan) in some detail.

CASE 1: JACOB

Jacob's teacher initially became aware that he might have some sort of reading problem when he failed the first social studies test that she gave his class. His poor performance caught her by surprise because he had always been an active participant in the eighth-grade social studies class discussions and because he seemed to enjoy reading aloud portions of the text to the class. When she asked him about the test results after class, he said that he hadn't been doing his homework assignments because they didn't make sense to him. She then asked him if he would be willing to meet with her after school so that she could see what he does when he reads the text and could try to make some suggestions to help him. He said, "It probably wouldn't hurt." When they met, she had him read a passage from the text followed by two easier selections, one from a seventh-grade text and one from a sixth-grade text. Because she already knew that he was proficient at reading aloud, and because his difficulty was apparently with reading homework assignments, she had him read the passages silently and then asked him to respond to the questions that she had prepared.

Jacob's performance on these graded passages is summarized in Table 8.2. As can be seen, he does indeed have difficulty understanding the eighth-grade textbook and because he does not comprehend some of the text information, he also had difficulty responding to the beyond-text generalization question. His good performance on the word knowledge questions indicates that his comprehension difficulties do not arise from a deficit in background knowledge, but rather are in synthesizing and shading the meanings of words to form a coherent understanding of a topic.

When she asked him to read the seventh-grade-level passage, he still experienced some difficulty; his comprehension was in the borderline region. Again his knowledge of word meanings was strong and this time he was able to answer the beyond-text generalization question.

Finally, on the sixth grade passage, he had difficulty with only one comprehension question and it was one that the teacher did not consider to be of major significance. He mentioned that in this passage the discussion was easy to understand whereas in the other passages he had "gotten lost."

Jacob's teacher decided that it might be interesting to test his comprehension when he read aloud. She had him read another selection from the eighth-grade text. His oral reading was fluent with good intonation, similar to what it had been in class. When she asked the comprehension ques-

Table 8.2.   Summary of Performance on an IRI: Jacob

Mode	Grade level	Text-based comprehension (%)	Beyond-text comprehension	Word knowledge
Silent reading	6	88	1/1	3/3
Silent reading	7	63	1/1	3/3
Silent reading	8	50	0/1	3/3
Oral reading	8	100	1/1	3/3

tions, in sharp contrast with his earlier performance following silent reading, he answered all correctly.

Jacob explained that he could always understand things better when he read them out loud. He mentioned that prior to this year, his mother usually helped him with his homework. He would read the assignment aloud and then they would discuss it. This year his mother has a new job, and she doesn't have time to help him.

Given this information, what conclusions can be drawn about the nature of Jacob's reading problem? How should his instruction be modified to help him improve his reading comprehension?

Interpretation

The informal testing results confirm Jacob's well-developed print translation skills and his good knowledge of word meanings. It is clear that his major problem is in the area of comprehension and is specific in nature, having to do with silent but not oral reading. During silent reading, Jacob has considerable difficulty organizing the ideas of a passage. He apparently has not developed strategies for monitoring and directing his comprehension when he reads silently. That he is capable of doing so is indicated by his excellent comprehension when he reads aloud. Probably years of reading aloud to the neglect of silent reading practice account for the discrepancy between what he is capable of comprehending and what he actually does comprehend during silent reading.

Instructional Recommendations

Materials. The results from the informal inventory of Jacob's silent reading indicate that the class material is too difficult for him to read silently with good comprehension and too difficult for him to use to develop the monitoring strategies that he needs to learn. The sixth-grade-level material is easy for him. He is able to comprehend it without using any special monitorial procedures.

The seventh-grade-level material may be too difficult; Jacob's performance was in the borderline range. Nevertheless, this level would seem to be most appropriate. The teacher has identified readings in the seventh-grade text that correspond to those being read by most of the class. The content is similar, but the concepts are presented in somewhat less complex sentences.

Instruction. Jacob's awareness that he was not understanding the homework assignments represents a real strength. His teacher has told him that he will read the seventh-grade material for a little while and that when his silent reading strategies are better developed, he can return to the regular class material. She has told him that it is important to learn to read the materials silently and also to be aware of whether or not he is understanding. When he doesn't understand, he should reread the passage.

The teacher has also decided to provide more formal instruction on comprehension strategies because she suspects that there are others in the class who are having difficulty with their homework assignments. Thus, she has decided to present, each Monday, one strategy that students may use to improve their reading comprehension and study efficiency. (See Chapter 6 for further description of such instructional procedures.) She plans to model the technique and then to have students try it out in class. In order to encourage its application during homework, she will also discuss how successful students were in applying the previous week's study tip. Privately, she will encourage Jacob to try out each of the approaches presented and to develop a set of strategies that best suit him.

CASE 2: MARIE

Marie had been in the top reading group until the middle of fourth grade when her teacher noted that she was having considerable difficulty with some of the comprehension skill sheets. In fifth grade, her current teacher worries about her lack of participation in class discussions. She reads with the middle group and is more active in this setting; she particularly enjoys reading aloud. Several times, however, her teacher was surprised that she was unable to answer a fairly obvious question.

Marie's teacher decided to meet with her alone, during a class period, and have her read a selection from the book being read by her group. Because she had difficulty with many of the comprehension questions, her teacher also had her read a selection from the next-easier book. When it was clear that even this material posed problems for Marie, her teacher asked her to read a selection from the third-grade book. The results from this inventory are shown in Table 8.3.

Table 8.3. Summary of Performance on an IRI: Marie

Mode	Grade level	Oral reading Accuracy (%)	Rate (wpm)	Text-based comprehension (%)	Beyond-text comprehension	Word knowledge
Oral reading	3	100	136	75	0/1	2/3
Oral reading	4	98	125	63	0/1	1/3
Oral reading	5	99	132	38	0/1	0/3

Interpretation

The reader should consider the results shown in the table in terms of the diagnostic model presented in Chapter 1. Is Marie's comprehension at an acceptable level for her to profit from the fifth-grade materials that her reading group is presently reading? Is comprehension a major area of difficulty? Are underlying problems in the areas of print translation and word knowledge implicated?

The answers to these three questions should be: no, perhaps, and yes. Even though Marie demonstrates fluent and almost flawless oral reading, she is not able to understand her present reading book as indicated by frustration-level performance on the text-based comprehension questions and her failure to answer the beyond-text question.

When neither print translation nor word knowledge interferes with comprehension, then it is possible to conclude that a student has a major problem in the area of comprehension itself. However, since Marie's knowledge of key word meanings is poor for the fifth-grade selection and uneven for the fourth- and third-grade selections, poorly developed word knowledge is implicated in her difficulty comprehending. But it is still possible that she has problems in comprehension that are not accounted for by her limited knowledge of word meanings. Further probes of her comprehension strategies, similar to those described in Chapter 6, might be undertaken to explore this possibility.

Instruction

With respect to instruction, two questions need to be answered. First, what level of material should Marie be reading? Second, what sort of instruction will be most effective in helping her to develop her reading proficiency?

Materials. The answer to the first question is complicated by the fact that all reading groups in this class read from the same basal series. Many times the decision to move a student into a lower group means that the student may have to reread stories encountered earlier. What has to be considered is whether the selections were processed in an appropriate fashion the first time around. Although Marie had previously read the third- and fourth-grade-level passages included in the inventory, the results indicate that she is not able to reread them with a high level of comprehension. Moreover, on both the fourth- and fifth-grade selections she encountered a number of words that were unfamiliar. Because of the limited number of words tested, the results are not definitive. But they do indicate a consistent pattern, which should be tested through further observation.

In any case, because Marie's word knowledge was the area in greatest need of development, materials were selected that required her to develop her vocabulary further but that did not completely overwhelm her. Marie's teacher asked her to read with the group reading from the fourth-grade basal. She made the change after she shared the results from the diagnosis with Marie and discussed the ways in which she could best improve her reading.

Instruction. To change Marie's reading group and the level of material she was reading without also changing the nature of the instruction to meet her special needs would accomplish little. Students who fail to develop word concepts spontaneously through reading need special instruction to help them become sensitive to the meanings of words and the ways in which context governs word meaning. Marie was not the only student in the most slowly paced group who needed instructional reinforcement to support conceptual development.

Before reading each story, the teacher identified the words that were centrally connected to the theme of the story. Techniques described in Chapter 4 were used to make the meaning of the words more vivid. After students read and discussed the story, they turned again to the key terms, seeing if they could remember where they occurred in the story and how the context determined their meanings. The teacher also encouraged students to make cards, which they could review for occasional quizzes. Students who found the words in new contexts were given special praise.

In addition to conducting this group-based instruction, the teacher met with Marie individually to describe other ways in which she could expand her vocabulary. She emphasized the importance of becoming aware of unfamiliar words encountered during reading, conversation, or television viewing. Marie began recording such words in a notebook and asking her parents, older siblings, and friends what they meant. When necessary, she would look the words up in the dictionary and, if she still felt confused, would consult her teacher.

CASE 3: JOHN

John, a third-grader, was in the middle reading group, using Level 9 of the Macmillan Reading Series. However, his teacher noticed that he seemed to be under considerable pressure, so she decided to work with him individually to understand more about the problems he was experiencing.

She had him read passages that she had selected from the Macmillan program. In designing the informal series of passages, she selected a portion of a story from each of the basal readers that she used. This included the readers for Levels 8 – 12. For each of the five passages, she constructed a set of text-based comprehension questions and word meaning questions. She did not construct beyond-text questions, because she felt that the portions of the stories that she used in the inventory were too brief to support such questions.

During the work with the informal inventory, John concentrated hard on his reading. The first passage he read was one that he had not yet come to in his reader. His teacher introduced the passage by saying that this was a story about Tommy and his father during their summer vacation. John's oral reading is shown in Figure 8.2. The reader should examine the record in order to determine whether the Level 9 passage is too difficult and to try to characterize the problems that John is experiencing when he deals with print.

Figure 8.2. Record of oral reading, Level 9: John.
(From "The Boy Who Couldn't Swim" by Lee C. Deighton. In SHINING BRIDGES, Second Reader, Level 9, *The Macmillan Reading Program*, Albert J. Harris and Mae Knight Clark, Sr. Authors. Copyright © 1974 Macmillan Publishing Co., Inc. Reprinted by permission.)

The Boy Who Couldn't Swim

23

"Tomorrow I'll ~~learn~~ [leave] to swim," Tommy said one night at ~~supper~~ [soup] time. "I   2

am ~~really~~ [ready] going to do (it) this time."   2

His father looked at him clos~~ely~~ [closly]. "Tommy," he said. "I think it's too late   1

for you to ~~learn~~ [leave] to swim now. The summer is almost over. In two weeks we'll   1

be saying goodby to the country."

Tommy ~~stared~~ [started] at his father. "Too late?" he cried. "Oh, Dad, I didn't   1

mean to ~~break~~ [start] my ~~word~~ [work]." ~~Tears~~ [Trair] came into Tommy's eyes.   3

"I know you ~~didn't~~ [do] mean to ~~break~~ [bring] your ~~word,~~ [work home] said Father. "Tommy, do   4

I see ~~dirt~~ [drink] (on your hands? Why don't you go and wash) up. ~~Then~~ [of them] you'll feel   4

better."   skipped line ↗

Tommy ~~hurried~~ [hurry] to his room. His father hadn't ~~sent~~ [seen] him out because of   2

© [different] the ~~dirt~~ on his hands. He had sent him out because Tommy was about to cry   1

and ~~wanted~~ [wait] to do it alone. Tommy's father was a very understanding man.   1

He, too, had found it ~~hard~~ [had] to learn to swim.   1

After John read the passage, his teacher asked six comprehension questions and three word meaning questions. The reader should study the questions and John's responses, both shown in Figure 8.3, in order to draw conclusions about his comprehension and knowledge of key terms.

Figure 8.3.   Responses to comprehension and word knowledge questions, Level 9: John.

Comprehension

✓**1.**   What did Tommy say that he would learn to do?
   RESPONSE: Swim.

✓**2.**   Why did his father say that it was too late to learn to swim?
   RESPONSE: Summer was almost over.

✗ **3.**   What was going to happen in two weeks?
   RESPONSE: Wasn't washing his hands.

✓**4.**   How did Tommy feel about it's being too late for him to learn to swim?
   RESPONSE: Sad.

✗ **5.**   Why did Tommy's father send him out of the room?
   RESPONSE: 'Cause his father went, he was crying.

✗ **6.**   What happened when Tommy's father learned to swim?
   RESPONSE: He liked it.

Word Knowledge

✓ **1.**   In the story it says, "I know you didn't mean to break your word." What does "break your word" mean?
   RESPONSE: To not keep a promise.

✓ **2.**   In the story it says that Tommy's father was an "understanding man." What does this mean?
   RESPONSE: That he was sympathetic.

✓ **3.**   What does *stared* mean?
   RESPONSE: That he looked real hard.

On the basis of the evidence, John's teacher tentatively concluded that the Level 9 passage was too difficult for John, mainly because of the print problems that it posed for him. His comprehension was poor mainly because he was not able to read some of the words in the passage. However, his responses to the word meaning questions suggest that he possesses the background knowledge necessary to comprehend this passage.

The next question that the teacher explored was whether the material being read by her low group would be more appropriate for John. Thus, she had him read a portion of a story from Level 8 about a boy named Danny who is building an airplane. Figure 8.4 shows the record of his oral reading of this passage. The reader should examine the record and draw conclusions about his reading strategies. The question of what he can do with material at this level that he could not with more difficult material should also be considered.

Figure 8.4.   Record of oral reading, Level 8: John.
(From "What Did Danny Do?" by Mae Knight Clark. In ENCHANTED GATES, Second Reader, Level 8, *The Macmillan Reading Program*, Albert J. Harris and Mae Knight Clark, Sr. Authors. Copyright © 1974 Macmillan Publishing Co., Inc. Reprinted by permission.)

What Did Danny Do?

$\frac{9}{1}$

© why
"Mother," said Danny, "~~will~~ you give me two dollars?" |

"Why do you want two dollars?" his mother asked.

"I want to finish my airplane," answered Danny. "I'll have to hurry. I

part from② plane
             for ① plane
want it finished for the school fair. I must have a ~~pint of red~~ paint and some   4

other things. Then I can finish it."
                                        © can
"Oh, Danny!" said his mother. "I do want to help you, but I ~~can't~~ give |

you two dollars now."

"Saturday?" asked Danny.
        © might
"No," she said. "It ~~may~~ be a long time before I can give it to you." |
                                        © wouldn't
Danny didn't say anything more. He knew that his mother ~~would~~ help |

him if she could.

Danny went to look at his airplane. He liked the way it looked. He had

worked very hard on it.
                                © might
"If I can just finish it in time!" he said to himself. "I ~~may~~ get the prize. I |

told my teacher I would have it ready. I must think of some way to get two

dollars myself. It's just ten days until the fair."

There are two important differences. Whereas on the Level 9 passage he made many errors (14%), on the Level 8 passage he had difficulty with considerably fewer words (5%). Whereas on the Level 9 passage he was

Figure 8.5.   Responses to comprehension and word knowledge question, Level 8: John.

Comprehension

✓ **1.** How much money did Danny want his mother to give to him?
RESPONSE: $2.00.

✓ **2.** Why did he want two dollars?
RESPONSE: To get parts for the plane

✓ **3.** What did Danny's mother say about giving him the two dollars?
RESPONSE: She couldn't do it.

✓ **4.** What might Danny get if he finished it in time for the fair?
RESPONSE: A prize.

✓ **5.** What was Danny going to do in order to finish the airplane?
RESPONSE: To get it hisself.

Word Knowledge

✓ **1.** What does "finish" mean?
RESPONSE: To get something done.

✓ **2.** What is a "prize"?
RESPONSE: Like a present that you win.

✓ **3.** What is a "fair"?
RESPONSE: Like there are booths, with games and food . . . and, well, you just have fun.

---

able to self-correct only one miscue, on the Level 8 passage he self-corrected five miscues. This suggests that John is developing effective reading strategies which he is able to make good use of when the material is not too difficult.

Consistent with his better oral reading, his comprehension was perfect. Further, as shown in Figure 8.5, he again had no difficulty with the word meaning questions.

In order to confirm her impression that John would be a good reader once his problems with print were solved, his teacher administered the passages from Levels 10, 11, and 12 as listening tasks. As shown in the summary in Table 8.4, John demonstrated perfect text-based comprehension on each of these passages.

Interpretation

The results from the inventory show that John's major problem is in the area of print translation. The evidence also shows that his knowledge of words and his comprehension strategies are well developed. Problems observed with reading comprehension are a direct reflection of the difficulty that he is experiencing with print.

Table 8.4.   Summary of Performance on an IRI: John

Mode	Level	Oral reading accuracy (%)	Text-based comprehension (%)	Word knowledge
Oral reading	9	86	50	3/3
Oral reading	8	95	100	3/3
Listening	10		100	3/3
Listening	11		100	3/3
Listening	12		100	2/3

Comparisons of his print strategies on Level 8 and 9 materials show that John is experiencing problems with sight words as well as content words. For example, on the Level 8 passage most of his miscues were on sight words. The fact that he was able to subsequently correct these errors indicates that he knows these basic sight words but that they have not yet been consolidated through extensive reading experience. On the more difficult passage, fewer basic sight word errors were made, possibly because he directed his full attention toward reading the print. In any case, John needs practice to help him consolidate his basic sight vocabulary.

John is also experiencing difficulty recognizing unfamiliar content words. Since many of his responses to unknown words are correct in the initial portion and sometimes in the final portion, he may be using a sight word substitution strategy similar to that used by Eva in Chapter 3. Further probe of his knowledge of letter–sound associations, however, revealed that he does know consonants, consonant blends, and short and long vowel sounds. He still has trouble with the *r* and *w* controlled vowel sounds and the vowel digraphs.

John's tendency to overlook the endings of words may be part of a more general reading strategy in which he attends mainly to the initial portions of words. This problem may be solved as John develops more systematic procedures for perceiving words.

Instructional Plan

Materials.   The level of material that would be appropriate for John to read directly determines the reading group with which he will receive instruction. His current placement is inappropriate, because the materials being read are at his frustration level. He should therefore be placed in the more slowly paced group, which reads from the Level 8 basal. Because John has previously read from this book, it is extremely important to use the results from the informal inventory to explain to him why he needs to be reading somewhat easier material than his current group is reading and to show him that his strategies are much more effective on the Level 8 materials. For this same reason it is also important to find other beginning second-grade materials on which he can refine his print-processing strategies. John should be told about the results from the listening comprehension tasks, which show that he is a capable student with good comprehension skills.

It is also extremely important to encourage John to do extensive reading of first-grade-level materials. This reading will help to consolidate and expand his sight vocabulary. Appropriate material in the form of easy and high-interest children's books can be obtained from the library. Further, the teacher should build her own library and include such materials.

Instruction.   Reading skill instruction for students in the Level 8 reading group has followed the recommendations in the teacher's manual. However, the teacher has noted that to learn the concepts being developed, students in the group need more practice than the basal program typically provides. Thus, she has decided to develop her own instructional sequence in word identification. She will begin by reviewing the vowel digraphs and r- and w-controlled vowel sounds. She will then focus on the pronunciation of complex one-syllable words (e.g., *tears, learn, dirt, hard*) by considering first the initial consonant or consonant blend pronunciation and then the pronunciation of the ending. Finally, she will work on the identification of two- and three-syllable words, as a way of developing systematic left-to-right word analysis. Throughout this instructional sequence the teacher will introduce procedures encouraging students to apply their new knowledge as they read contextual materials.

Since students other than John also need to work on developing their word knowledge and comprehension, relevant activities will be included in the directed reading lessons. John's strength in these areas should lead to his active participation in the group and contribute to the learning of his classmates.

As mentioned earlier, it is extremely important that John read materials that are at his independent level in order to develop appropriate reading strategies and consolidate his sight vocabulary. Other students in the group will profit from similar reading. Therefore, a group project may be used to encourage reading. For example, the group might "win" a field trip or some other pleasurable activity (e.g., a popcorn treat for the class) once they have read a specified number of pages. Through independent reading, each student would contribute his or her share of pages.

SUMMARY

This chapter has described procedures that teachers may follow in developing an informal reading inventory. How the inventory is used will depend on what questions the teacher has about a particular student. The inventory is particularly useful in determining the level of reading materials that is most appropriate for students new to the class. In addition, it can be used when a teacher wants more systematic evidence about a student's reading, to reconsider his or her group placement and/or to develop more appropriate instruction.

9

Diagnosis with Standardized IRIs

There are a number of informal reading inventories that have been commercially developed and published. These standardized inventories are comprehensive in that they usually include two or more equivalent passages (plus comprehension questions) per grade level and range from first grade to junior or senior high in difficulty. In addition, they often include a series of graded word lists for determining the appropriate level at which to begin testing and a manual describing procedures for test administration and interpretation. Some inventories also provide a series of tests for assessing word identification skills. Table 9.1 briefly characterizes some of the published IRIs (see Richek, List, & Lerner, 1983, for a detailed discussion).

As mentioned, one of the useful features of IRIs is that they specify the criteria for passage success. These criteria are based on the actual performance of representative samples of students at various grade levels. For each passage there is an indication of the number of oral reading errors allowable and the number of comprehension questions that must be answered correctly. As with teacher-prepared inventories, the comprehension and oral reading accuracy a student obtains on a passage serves as the basis for determining subsequent passages to be read.

ADMINISTRATION

The following describes the general method for administering a standardized IRI. First, the word recognition test is administered and scored according to the instructions in the test manual. This provides the basis for determining the level of the first passage to be read orally by the student. The student then reads progressively more difficult passages aloud until his or her performance falls below the oral reading accuracy and comprehension criterion levels. Next, the student begins reading silently a passage

Table 9.1. Selected List of Published IRIs

Inventory (publisher and date)	Word lists grade range	Passages grade range	Number of forms
Analytical Reading Inventory Charles E. Merrill, 1981	P–6	1–9	3
Bader Reading and Language Inventory Macmillan, 1983	PP–12	PP–12	3
Basic Reading Inventory Kendall/Hunt, 1978	PP–8	PP–8	3
Contemporary Classroom Inventory Gorsuch, Scarisbrick, 1980	PP–8	PP–8	3
Diagnostic Reading Scales CTB/McGraw-Hill, 1972	1–6	P–8	2
Ekwall Reading Inventory Allyn and Bacon, 1979	PP–9	PP–9	4
Informal Reading Assessment Rand McNally, 1980	PP–12	PP–12	4
Informal Reading Assessment Tests Houghton Mifflin, 1980	PP–8	PP–12	4
Standard Reading Inventory Klamath, 1966	PP–7	PP–7	2
Sucher-Allred Reading Placement Inventory Economy, 1973	PP–9	PP–9	2

at the instructional level established through oral reading. He or she then reads progressively more difficult passages, until comprehension falls below the criterion level. For silent reading, it is also important to establish the independent reading level; thus, the student must also read progressively easier passages until he or she achieves 90% comprehension or higher. On some tests, this standard may be unrealistic, since if there are nine questions or fewer, it means that no questions can be missed. Finally, beginning one level above the student's instructional level established during oral or silent reading, the teacher reads progressively more difficult passages aloud to the student until the student's comprehension falls below the specified criterion. Figure 9.1 summarizes these steps in administering an IRI and the general considerations for starting and discontinuing of each task.

The administration of the IRI allows the teacher to identify the level of material that can be read easily by the student at his independent level, the levels that may be appropriate for alternative instructional purposes, and the levels that are too difficult for the student. Testing usually continues until each of these levels has been established. There may be times, however, when a teacher wishes to use the IRI to answer a more limited

Figure 9.1. Criteria for administering informal reading inventory tasks.

Word Lists
Begin with the easiest list.
Discontinue when the student scores below 75% correct on the untimed administration.

Oral Reading Task
Begin with a passage at the highest level where the student achieved 90% correct on the flash administration of the Word Lists.
Discontinue when the instructional and frustration levels are established.

Silent Reading Task
Begin with a passage at the highest level where the student met the criteria for instructional level in oral reading accuracy and comprehension on the Oral Reading Task.
Discontinue when the independent, instructional, and frustration levels are established.

Listening Task
Begin with a passage one level above the highest level where the student met the criterion for instructional level in comprehension on the Oral Reading or the Silent Reading Task.
Discontinue when the frustration level is established.

---

question (e.g., to determine a student's independent level of silent reading or instructional level for print processing). Obviously, in such cases, the procedures described here for the systematic use of the IRI would not be followed. Only the relevant portion of the IRI would be used. This is important, as diagnostic work should never blindly follow an established set of procedures. Although it is necessary to be familiar with the procedures involved in a comprehensive approach, it is equally necessary to know when to follow only a portion of these procedures.

CASE STUDY APPLICATION: CHUCK

To illustrate the comprehensive procedures, we will consider the case of Chuck, a fourth-grader, tested with the Ekwall Reading Inventory (Allyn & Bacon, 1979). Chuck was first administered the preprimary-level word recognition list. Words were exposed for a half-second interval (flash), and if not recognized, they were shown in an untimed fashion. As shown in Table 9.2, Chuck quickly recognized all words on the preprimer list, but he failed to recognize one word (out of ten) on the primer list. He was able to identify that one when it was presented without the pressure of time. Administration of the lists continued until the fifth-grade list, on which Chuck's untimed score fell below 75%.

Second, Chuck was asked to read a passage aloud and answer comprehension questions. The passage selected was at the highest level at which Chuck recognized 90% of the flashed words, the first-grade level. Chuck's oral reading and comprehension on the first-grade passage were good, and he was then asked to read the second-, the third-, and finally the fourth-grade passage. Oral reading was discontinued after the fourth-grade passage because both his oral reading accuracy and comprehension dropped below the test criteria.

Third, Chuck's silent reading comprehension was assessed by having him read a passage at the third-grade level, his instructional level on the oral reading task. His comprehension of this passage fell below the criterion. Thus, easier passages were administered. Testing proceeded down to the first-grade passage in order to establish Chuck's independent level for silent reading comprehension.

Finally, the passages were administered as a listening test. That is, the teacher read the passage aloud to Chuck and then asked him to answer comprehension questions. Testing began at the fourth-grade level, the level where Chuck's oral reading comprehension fell below the instructional level. Because he demonstrated adequate listening comprehension (75%) on the fourth-grade passage, the fifth-grade passage was administered. Since his comprehension was not acceptable at this level (50%), the listening task was discontinued.

Table 9.2. Summary of Performance on an IRI: Chuck

INFORMAL READING INVENTORY SUMMARY

Test _Ekwall R. I._ Child _Chuck_ Age _9_ Grade _4_ Date _1/82_

Level	Recognition test		Informal reading inventory					
			Oral reading task			Silent reading		
	Flash (%)	Untimed (%)	Accuracy (%)	Comprehension (%)	Rate (wpm)	Comprehension (%)	Rate (wpm)	Listening comprehension (%)
Preprimer	100	100						
Primer	90	100						
First	90	100	97	100	95	100	105	
Second	80	90	95	100	81	85	84	
Third	80	90	95	75	73	50	87	
Fourth	40	80	89	50	62			75
Fifth	—	60						50
Sixth								
Seventh								
Eighth								
Ninth								

These procedures work well for younger disabled readers and older disabled readers suspected of having print translation problems. However, for some older readers for whom silent reading proficiency is of particular concern, it is useful to test silent reading comprehension first and to sample oral reading second in order to obtain a more valid measure of silent comprehension. For most readers the complete IRI can be administered at one time; but for younger readers, the silent reading tests when administered last may not be valid because of fatigue. Therefore, it is advisable to break the testing into two sessions if fatigue is noted.

Procedures for Administering the Word Lists

The word lists measure the instantaneous sight vocabulary of the student (flash presentation) and his or her word identification skills (untimed presentation). In Chapter 2, procedures were described for assessing the "basic" sight vocabulary of students through oral reading analysis. While the primary and first-grade word lists provide a similar measure of basic sight vocabulary, the subsequent lists show how well students are incorporating other words into their store of words that are quickly recognized. Proficient readers are in command of a large store of sight words, and students during the elementary grades expand their set of sight words beyond the basic set to include most other words that they encounter frequently during contextual reading. Flash performance on the more advanced word lists shows whether the development of this larger sight vocabulary is grade appropriate.

The procedures for flash administration consist of using two rectangular cards, one placed just above the word to be flashed and the other covering the word. When the student is ready, the teacher quickly moves the bottom card down exposing the word. After a half second exposure, the top card is moved down to cover the word. Correct responses are marked on the student record form with a check (✓) whereas incorrect responses are recorded phonetically. When the student fails to respond, this is recorded as "NR" (no response), "DK" (don't know) or as "x".

Words that are not recognized during the flash presentation are re-exposed immediately, with no time limitation, in order to see if the student can identify the word. The probe procedures described in Chapter 3 for determining the knowledge a student possesses about phonics and structural analysis can be used with words incorrectly read on an IRI as well as on a diagnostic passage.

Procedures for Administering the
Oral Reading Task

The first passage the student reads is determined by his or her performance on the word lists. If the student's performance on this first passage is at or above the prescribed criteria, he or she reads progressively more difficult passages until performance falls below the criteria. If, on the other hand, his or her performance falls below the criterion for either accuracy or comprehension, this level represents the borderline or frustration level. In this case, the student reads increasingly easier passages until his or her instructional level is established (acceptable comprehension and oral reading accuracy).

As the student reads each passage aloud, the teacher records any errors made, using the procedures described in Chapter 2. A count should be made of the number of errors. When the student finishes reading a passage, the comprehension questions are asked, answers are recorded, and a comprehension score is determined. On occasion the teacher may wish to assess comprehension by having the student retell the passage prior to asking the comprehension questions, as described in Chapter 5.

Procedures for Administering the Silent Reading Task

Following the oral reading task, the student is asked to read certain passages silently. The point of this task is to determine whether the student is at least as proficient in silent reading as he or she is in oral reading. Although many normal readers are able to read with greater comprehension when they read silently than when they read aloud, this is not the case with most disabled readers. Therefore, the first silent reading passage administered is at the *same* level of difficulty as the one the student was able to read orally with good comprehension (the instructional level). After the student reads the passage silently, the comprehension questions are asked and answers are recorded and scored. If the student's comprehension is below the criterion, successively easier passages are administered until the student achieves adequate comprehension when reading silently. On the other hand, if the student's comprehension score on the first silent reading passage is at or above the criterion, progressively more difficult passages are administered until the frustration level is established. It is also particularly important during silent reading assessment to establish the level at which comprehension is extremely high (around 90%) for independent reading.

Procedures for Administering the Listening Task

The listening task measures a student's comprehension and underlying verbal knowledge when print translation difficulties (if any) are eliminated. As a rule, a listening task is administered only with passages that are more difficult than those the student is able to comprehend through his or her own reading. It is unnecessary to administer as a listening task passages that represent a level of difficulty the student can read and understand through reading.

Thus the listening task usually begins with a passage one step higher in difficulty than the most difficult passage the student was able to read orally or silently with adequate comprehension. The passage is read aloud to the student, the comprehension questions asked, and the student's answers recorded and scored. If the student's comprehension score is below the criterion, the listening task is discontinued. The reason for discontinuing at this point is that under normal circumstances the next lower level passages will have been read by the student with adequate comprehension during oral or silent reading. If the student's listening comprehension score on the first passage is adequate, the next higher level passage is read to him or her, the questions asked, and the answers recorded and scored. Progressively more difficult passages are read until comprehension falls below the criterion. The listening task is then discontinued.

If the particular IRI materials being used provide only two passages at each level of difficulty, it may happen that both passages at the level that would be appropriate for the listening task have already been administered, one for oral reading and the other for silent reading. In this case, the listening task should proceed to the next higher level.

INTERPRETATION OF RESULTS

For the teacher-constructed series of graded passages, consisting usually of a single passage per level, the interpretation was similar to that for diagnoses made with individual reading passages. In contrast, the standardized inventories allow for a variety of comparisons, which provide a comprehensive basis for understanding a student's reading strengths and difficulty. For example, in addition to comparing a student's performance from level to level, as was possible with the teacher-constructed inventory, it is now possible to compare oral and silent comprehension and reading rates. The student's identification of isolated words on the graded lists can be compared with his or her print processing during oral reading. Further, a student's level of word knowledge as estimated from the vocabulary questions following each passage can be compared with his or her listening comprehension. This variety of comparisons is complicated, but it does increase the precision of the diagnosis. As discussed earlier, such a comprehensive diagnosis should be unnecessary for most students in a class. Occasionally, however, there is a particularly perplexing problem that requires a comprehensive reading inventory.

Like teacher-constructed inventories, comprehensive IRIs are interpreted in two stages. First, judgments are made about the level of materials appropriate for reading instruction and independent reading. Then the evidence concerning print translation, word knowledge, and comprehension is examined in order to determine relative strengths and weaknesses. Recommendations concerning the appropriateness of alternative materials are based on the first analysis; the establishment of instructional priorities is based on the second.

Level of Materials

Instructional Reading Level. The level of instructional materials selected depends on the nature of instruction. For example, the level of material that is sufficiently challenging to foster the further development of word identification skills may be higher than the level of materials appropriate for the development of silent comprehension strategies. The instructional level for word identification is based on oral reading accuracy, whereas the selection of instructional material for group-based comprehension instruction is based on oral reading comprehension. For instruction that emphasizes the monitoring of silent reading comprehension, material selection is based on silent reading comprehension.

Independent Reading Level. The silent reading task determines the highest level of materials the student can read silently with good comprehension. This will normally be the student's independent reading level. It represents the level at which the student can recognize and identify words without pronouncing them aloud and at which he or she can concentrate on meaning without instructional support.

Areas of Reading Difficulty

Print Translation. As previously mentioned, the listening task provides a measure of the strength of the student's comprehension skills unconfounded by his or her ability to process print. In general, if a student can, through listening, understand materials that are too difficult for him or her to read, we may infer that print translation difficulty interfered with reading comprehension. A detailed analysis of oral reading of one or two passages at the instructional or borderline level (as outlined in Chapter 3) should confirm this inference and reveal the specific nature of the difficulty and appropriate instructional emphasis. Evidence from the word lists (flash and untimed), the oral reading, and the reading rate scores (silent versus oral) should all be considered in drawing conclusions about a student's print-processing skill.

Word Knowledge. Information about a student's word knowledge comes from two sources. First, specific questions about vocabulary and phrases provide information on whether the student understands the key terms of a passage. Word knowledge performance on any of the three tasks (oral reading, silent reading, listening) that were administered at any one level should be combined to determine the percentage of terms correctly defined or described at that level. Second, the listening comprehension score reflects a student's underlying word knowledge. A high score indicates good verbal development, whereas a low score is ambiguous since it may reflect limited word knowledge, poor discourse comprehension strategies, or both.

Comprehension. Evaluation of reading comprehension begins with a comparison of oral versus silent reading comprehension. If silent reading comprehension is a grade or more lower this indicates that the student has not yet internalized strategies to monitor comprehension during silent reading. That is, the student is able to comprehend but, because of limited practice or for some other reason, has not learned to attend to meaning without the added support of pronouncing words aloud. Once a reader becomes proficient, it is not unusual for silent comprehension to exceed oral comprehension; a discrepancy in this direction is not viewed as a problem.

Next, the highest level of reading comprehension (oral or silent) should be compared with listening comprehension. A discrepancy here indicates the existence of print-processing problems. At the same time, the higher listening comprehension score suggests that once the print problems are solved, comprehension will be similar to listening comprehension.

Finally, an analysis should be made of the student's responses to the reading comprehension questions. When it is determined that the student's major problem is in comprehension, further probe should be made of his or her strategies, using the procedures described in Chapter 6.

CASE STUDY APPLICATIONS

The two cases described in the remaining sections of this chapter show how diagnosis using an informal reading inventory can be undertaken. The first case provides an overview of the diagnostic thinking involved in the interpretation of the inventory. The second case goes into much greater detail, presenting passage-by-passage evidence from an informal reading inventory.

CASE 1: SARA

Sara is in the middle reading group in a second-grade class. The basal program being used in her class is the Houghton Mifflin series, and her group currently reads from the second-grade reader. Her teacher decided to take a closer look at her reading because of her poor comprehension of stories in the reading group in contrast to her relatively good performance on seatwork assignments. She decided to administer the Basic Reading

Table 9.3. Summary of Performance on the
Word Recognition Tests: Sara

Level	Recognition test	
	Flash (%)	Untimed (%)
Preprimer	95	100
Primer	95	95
First	80	90
Second	70	95
Third	55	70
Fourth		
Fifth		
Sixth		
Seventh		
Eighth		
Ninth		

Inventory by Johns (Kendall/Hunt Publishing Co., 1978) to gain a better understanding of Sara's reading strategies. The word lists and the oral reading passages were administered on the first day, and the silent reading and listening passages on the second day. Sara worked hard and was involved in these reading activities.

The results from the administration of the word lists are shown in Table 9.3. The reader should study these results to determine what level passage should be administered first as an oral reading task.

Administration of the oral reading passage should begin at the highest level at which the student obtained at least 90% correct on the flash administration of the word lists. Thus, for Sara, oral reading should begin on the primer-level passage. When given this passage she made only 1 oral reading error and got all the comprehension questions correct. She was then given the first-grade passage. On this she made four oral reading errors on the 100-word passage; and she missed 2½ out of 10 passage questions. Given these results, what should the teacher do next? Should testing be discontinued or proceed to the next higher level?

According to the scoring guide of the test, up to 5 oral reading errors and up to 2½ comprehension errors represent the instructional level. Thus, oral reading should continue at the next higher level. On the second-grade passage, Sara made 8 oral reading errors (8% of the words) and missed 6 of the 10 questions. Because the comprehension score shows that the second-grade passage is in the frustration range for Sara, oral reading was discontinued.

When Sara's teacher worked with her again on the next day, she had her read the passages silently. Given Sara's performance the previous day, on what level should her teacher have her begin reading?

Sara's teacher had her read at the highest level where she last demonstrated instruction-level oral reading and comprehension. This was the first-grade level. She read this passage and knew the answers to all of the passage questions. Given this performance, what passage should Sara be asked to read next?

Her teacher had her read the next more difficult passage, which was at the second-grade level. On this passage she read with good comprehension, missing only 1 of 10 questions. Consequently, her teacher asked her to read the third-grade-level passage. On this passage she knew the answers to only 3 of 10 questions. Since this performance indicated the material was at the frustration level, her teacher discontinued the silent reading, and, instead, had her listen to a passage. On what level should the listening task begin?

The administration of the listening task should begin at the level above the highest level successfully comprehended when the child read either orally or silently. For Sara, this means the third-grade level. (Since Sara could comprehend at the second-grade level when reading silently, there was no need to test listening comprehension at that level or below.) When her teacher read the third-grade passage aloud, Sara missed only 1 question. Thus, the teacher proceeded to the next more difficult passage. On the fourth-grade passage, Sara missed only 3 of 10 questions. Therefore, her teacher read the fifth-grade passage to her. On this passage she was able to answer only 4 of the 10 comprehension questions. The results from the inventory are summarized in Table 9.4.

Scores in the vocabulary column are based on answers to passage questions. Since for each passage there were two questions about word meaning, it was possible to tabulate the total number of correct answers on these questions at each level. For example, on the second-grade level, the word knowledge percentage was based on the results from the passage read orally and that read silently. On the third-grade level, it was based on the passage read silently and the one read to Sara by her teacher.

Given these results, what tentative conclusions can be drawn about the nature of Sara's reading difficulty? Further, given these conclusions, what level material should Sara be reading and should she remain in her current reading group? It is not our intention here to undertake a complete diagnosis, but rather to show how the evidence contained in the summary form may be used to draw some tentative conclusions and focus further diagnositic efforts.

Tentative Instructional Conclusions

Areas of Reading Difficulty.   The diagnosis of Sara's reading is complicated in several ways. Because her reading profile does not conform to

Table 9.4. Summary of Performance on an IRI: Sara

INFORMAL READING INVENTORY SUMMARY

Test _J. Johns' BRI_   Child _Sara_   Age _8_   Grade _2_   Date _12/83_

Level	Recognition test		Informal reading inventory					Listening comprehension (%)	Vocabulary	
	Flash (%)	Untimed (%)	Oral reading task			Silent reading			N	%
			Accuracy (%)	Comprehension (%)	Rate (wpm)	Comprehension (%)	Rate (wpm)			
Preprimer	95	100								
Primer	95	95	99	100	111				2/2	100
First	80	90	96	75	91	100	100		4/4	100
Second	70	95	92	40	67	90	77		3/4	75
Third	55	65				30	71	90	4/4	100
Fourth								70	1/2	50
Fifth								40	0/2	0
Sixth										
Seventh										
Eighth										
Ninth										

typical patterns, it is important to come to terms with the nature of her reading strengths and difficulties before specifying the levels of materials that she should read.

With respect to reading comprehension, Sara's silent reading comprehension is better than her oral comprehension by one grade level. It is not unusual for silent reading to be better than oral reading comprehension when a reader is proficient. But other evidence from the word lists and the oral reading accuracy indicates that Sara is not a proficient reader. For example, on second-grade-level materials, where her silent reading comprehension was good, she is in the borderline region for oral reading accuracy, and the flash presentation of second-grade words indicates some problems with sight recognition. The discrepancy between oral and silent comprehension would seem to indicate that Sara can compensate for poorly developed print skills when she reads silently. But when faced with the additional demands of oral reading, she is not able to process print accurately and also comprehend at the same time.

Sara's listening comprehension shows that she possesses the necessary background knowledge to understand third- and even fourth-grade-level material. The word knowledge evidence confirms her strength in this area, at least through the third-grade level. We can conclude that Sara's difficulty in oral reading comprehension is not a reflection of poorly developed word knowledge.

It is in the area of print translation that Sara's difficulties appear to lie. The results for the word lists, for example, indicate that she had difficulty with immediate recognition of some first-grade-level words. While a single error (95%) may occur by chance, the 4 errors (80%) on the first-grade-level list suggest that some first-grade words are not familiar to her. Even when given more time, Sara was able to correct only 2 of the 4 errors. She had even more difficulty with the flash administration of the second-grade list, although here she was able to correct all but one of her errors with time. Her performance on the third-grade list is at the frustration level.

In addition to her problems reading isolated words, Sara made 4 errors on the first-grade passage and 8 on the second-grade passage (each 100 words in length), and her reading rate diminished from a relatively fast rate on the first-grade passage to a slow-average rate on the second-grade passage.

These results point to print processing as the area in need of further study. Sara's teacher should analyze the errors that she made on the second-grade passage and probe some of her responses to the passage and word lists. We can tentatively conclude, given the discrepancy between her flash and untimed scores on both the first- and second-grade lists, that she possesses knowledge about word identification but has not done enough easy reading to consolidate this knowledge and expand her sight vocabulary. Because of this lack of experience, she is able to read orally with a high degree of accuracy only when she focuses mainly on print and somewhat superficially on meaning. And as materials become more difficult (second grade), she is no longer able to avoid errors. When reading silently, primary focus on meaning and probably less stringent monitoring of print allows her to comprehend second-grade material. But this strategy is no longer functional at the third-grade level, where she encounters many more print problems. Thus, on the basis of the evidence, we conclude that Sara's major problem is in the area of print translation. Further, we speculate that the problem pertains to the consolidation and application of her existing knowledge about print as well as to the development of new knowledge about word identification.

Levels of Materials. If taken alone, Sara's silent reading comprehension might suggest that her independent reading should be at the second-grade level. However, her difficulty processing print at this level suggests that it might not be the appropriate place to begin if Sara is to develop good reading strategies. Indeed, even first-grade-level material may pose print problems that require her undivided attention. The level of material that appears to pose no print translation or comprehension problems is the primer level. Although she may soon progress to first-grade-level materials, at the present time primer is her independent reading level and the level that will be effective in helping her consolidate good reading strategies.

To determine Sara's instructional level, we focus on the area of her greatest need and then ask what level material would best serve to develop this area. We have tentatively concluded that Sara's main reading problem involves print translation. Not only does she need to consolidate and expand her sight vocabulary through extensive reading at her independent reading level (primer and then first grade), but she also needs to further develop her word identification strategies. Whereas first-grade materials may be appropriate for instructional purposes, second-grade materials may be too difficult. Following further study of her print-processing strategies (oral reading analysis for the second-grade passage and probe of responses), the teacher should examine her response to second-grade-level materials when instruction is specially designed to prepare her for the reading. If Sara shows better print strategies with instructional preparation, it is appropriate to keep her with her present reading group, which is working with second-grade material, and to offer appropriate instructional support that will further develop Sara's word identification skills and permit her to focus on comprehension.

Sara's performance on the third-grade-level passage indicates that this is her frustration level. Even though she is able to understand materials at this level when they are read to her, her print-processing problems are so great that she cannot comprehend them when reading.

CASE 2: JAMES

James is a freshman in high school and is in an intensive reading program. He is ranked 31st among 50 disabled readers. He was referred to the class on the basis of teacher recommendations and diagnostic reading test results. On the most recent standardized reading test, he scored a grade equivalent of 5.3 in comprehension and 6.8 in vocabulary. These scores reflect an average gain of 2.5 grade equivalents over the prior year's test. This achievement is a result of his desire to improve his reading so that he might go to college. Because of his extremely high motivation, his teacher asked him if he would like to have an inventory made of his reading skills so that she could better advise him as to how he might improve his reading even further. He agreed that this would be of interest to him.

During the testing with the Analytical Reading Inventory by Woods and Moe (Charles E. Merrill, 1981), James was pleasant and responsive. Between passages he talked about the books he likes to read, the movies he has seen, and one of his favorite authors, Edgar Allan Poe.

Administration

First, James read all of the word recognition lists. He achieved 90% accuracy on flash administration at the fifth-grade level but 95% at the sixth-grade level (the highest level list). He then read the sixth-grade passage orally, followed by the passages for grades seven through nine. Next, he read the seventh-grade passage silently. This level was selected because it corresponded to the highest oral reading passage where his comprehension score was at the instructional level. Because of his low comprehension on this passage, he next read the sixth-, and then the fifth-grade passages silently. Finally, he was administered the eighth-grade listening passage, on which he correctly answered 7 out of 8 questions. Although James scored 81% on the next higher passage (grade nine), the testing was discontinued because there are no higher level passages on this IRI. The IRI records from James's performance are shown in Appendix C.

Analysis and Probe

The first step in the analysis is to examine the test records and to score them (see Appendix C). On the word lists it is necessary to determine the percent of words correctly recognized for the flash and the untimed administrations.

The next step is to score the passages. It is useful to keep the passages in the order in which they were administered and to identify them as "oral," "silent," or "listening." For orally read passages, the number of errors should be recorded line by line and then the total determined. The total number of errors in relation to the total number of words read and the percentage of errors are then recorded following the passage. On the sixth-grade passage (see Appendix C, page 251), James made 3% errors and thus read with 97% accuracy. In this example, it would also be important to note that the problems were concentrated in the first three sentences, with few occurring thereafter.

Next, the comprehension questions must be scored, using the expected answers as a guide. When ambiguous responses occur, it is important to ask the student to "explain further" during the administration of the test so that credit may be given if the information has been comprehended. The total number of questions answered correctly out of the total asked and the corresponding percentage figure should be recorded on the passage next to the number of oral reading errors. For example, as shown for the Level 6 passage, James correctly answered 8 out of 8 questions, for 100% comprehension.

Finally, the student's rate of reading needs to be determined. For example, James read the Level 6 passage in 1 minute and 36 seconds, which is equivalent to 96 seconds or 1.6 minutes (96 divided by 60). Because the passage is 192 words in length, 192 is divided by 1.6 to yield a reading rate of 120 words per minute. This information should be recorded next to the comprehension percentage score.

After all the orally read passages have been scored, comprehension and rate scores are determined for the silently read passages. These scores are also recorded following the passage. The comprehension of the passages administered as listening tasks should then be scored and recorded. The final step is to transfer all accuracy percentages, comprehension percentages, and reading rates to the summary sheet, as shown in Table 9.5.

Once the results have been summarized, the next step is to consider each area of James's reading to determine whether any of his responses should be probed further. The results pertaining to oral reading accuracy, reading rate, and isolated word recognition accuracy suggest that James is experiencing some difficulty with word identification. The Level 7 passage was selected for further analysis, and further probe was undertaken to explore his recognition of sight words and content words presented in isolation.

The comparison of oral reading comprehension with silent reading comprehension suggests a problem in silent reading. As James is able to comprehend, but not without the support of oral reinforcement, the interactive and monitorial strategies described in Chapter 6 represent appropriate instructional approaches.

The results from the listening task suggest that James's word knowledge is sufficiently well developed for the comprehension of ninth-grade material. However, the vocabulary-related comprehension questions suggest otherwise. These results, summarized in Table 9.5, show that

Table 9.5. Summary of Performance on an IRI: James

INFORMAL READING INVENTORY SUMMARY

Test _Woods-Moe_ Child _James_ Age _14_ Grade _9_ Date _3/83_

Level	Recognition test		Informal reading inventory					Listening comprehension (%)	Vocabulary (%)
	Flash (%)	Untimed (%)	Oral reading task			Silent reading			
			Accuracy (%)	Comprehension (%)	Rate (wpm)	Comprehension (%)	Rate (wpm)		
Primer	100	100							
First	100	100							
Second	100	100							
Third	95	100							
Fourth	95	100							
Fifth	90	100				100	109		100
Sixth	95	100	97	100	120	81	97		100
Seventh	95		95	88	105	56	111		25
Eighth	92		92	63	91			88	50
Ninth	93		93	25	87			81	25

many terms from the seventh-grade level on up are unknown to him. Thus, the probe of the Level 7 content words needs to focus on word meaning as well as recognition.

The analysis of miscues made on the seventh-grade-level passage and the probe based on this analysis are shown in Figure 9.2. The results show that James's knowledge of sight words and word identification is strong but that his application of this knowledge is inconsistent. Further exploration of his knowledge of word meaning revealed inconsistent understanding of vocabulary items (for example, he knew the meanings of such words as *terrifying, miserable, wretched,* and *vaguely* but he did not know the meaning of *independent* and *belligerent*).

Interpretation

Print Translation. The analysis and probe based on the seventh-grade passage reveal that James possesses considerable knowledge about phonic and structural analysis and that his basic sight vocabulary is well developed. Whether the larger stock of sight words that he recognizes instantaneously is grade appropriate cannot be determined from the evidence because lists beyond the sixth-grade level are not included in the text. But the fact that he experienced some difficulty with the flash presentation beginning at the third-grade level suggests that his broader sight recognition vocabulary is not as large as it should be. Indeed, some of the difficulty he experienced during passage reading may have been based on the unfamiliarity of many words that are typically recognized by students his age.

Though James is able to apply his knowledge about print effectively when he is not under the time pressure of contextual oral reading or flash presentation, he does not do so easily when he *is* under pressure. If he were more proficient reading silently than orally, these difficulties might be attributed to nervousness and be overlooked. However, because his comprehension is less adequate during silent than oral reading, we can infer that his silent print-processing strategies are no more efficient, and probably less efficient, than his oral reading strategies.

The probe indicates that James does not need special instruction to learn about print but, rather, needs considerable practice with easy materials in order to consolidate and apply what he already knows. His slow reading rate reflects his current difficulty in application and should improve once he does more reading; if reading rate does not improve spontaneously, then it may need to be the focus of special instructional intervention.

However, James's print translation difficulties may not simply be a function of too little practice. Recently, James has seen several eye doctors because of blurred vision. The conclusion from the examination is that the blurred vision stems from eye strain and that James must learn to relax

Figure 9.2. Analysis of oral reading responses, Level 7: James.

ORAL READING ANALYSIS

Name _James_ Grade _9_ Date _3/83_

Book/Page _IRI Woods Moe_ Level _7_

A. DIFFICULTY

_13_ / _262_   _95_ % Correct

Level: Independent (Instructional)
Borderline Frustration

B. WORD LEARNING: Sight Word Errors

Printed Word	Oral Response	Probe	Evaluation
run	return	✓	_Sight words are known when_
did	had ©	✓	_presented in isolation. Given the_
had	[omitted]	✓	_number of such errors, James_
from	[omitted]	✓	_should be encouraged to do_
a	[omitted] ©	✓	_more easy reading to_
the	[insertion]	✓	_consolidate his sight_
			recognition

C. WORD IDENTIFICATION: Content Word Errors

Printed Word	Oral Response	Probe	Difficulty	Evaluation
turn	to ©	✓	vowel-ending	Consonants ___ ⎞ Ability to
friend	friends	✓	ending	Blends/Digraphs ⎟ correct
				Vowels ___ ⎟ miscues
terrifying	terrific ©	✓	⎫ Imprecise	Vowel Digraphs ⎟ indicates strong
miserable	miserably ©	✓	⎪ readings	Markers ___ ⎟ knowledge of
wretched	wretcher ©	✓	⎬ (particularly in	Affixes ___ ⎟ phonics and
picnic	band ©	✓	⎪ word endings)	Syllables ⎠ structural analysis.
vaguely	vă/vā-galy ©	✓	⎭ that are corrected.	Comments: _Systematic_
				syllable by syllable word
				attack - but slowness of
				process indicates little
				reading practice.

D. INTEGRATION–FLUENCY

Integration: _Good use of content - both graphic cues and context serve as a basis for correction._

Fluency: Rate _262_ / _2.5_ = _105_ wpm Evaluation _Below norms for seventh grade_

Phrasing _Many repetitions and pauses for word ident. and perhaps comprehe._

while reading. Glasses were not recommended. The eye strain may actually be the result of his difficulty in reading print fluently rather than the cause; but, in any case, James's visual difficulties should be kept in mind.

Word Knowledge. James's listening comprehension is good at the ninth-grade level (81% comprehension). This passage about Pygmies develops a topic with which James is unfamiliar and contains many difficult words (e.g., *equatorial, Itiru Forest, Zaire, contagious, blasphemy*). It would seem that when James is not faced with the task of print translation, he may be better able to compensate for not knowing the meaning of some key terms. His listening comprehension is better than might be expected on the basis of his knowledge of specific terms.

Comprehension. James's retelling of selected passages is comprehensive: he reported the sequence of events accurately and related many details. While his comprehension following oral reading is adequate through the seventh-grade level and borderline at the eighth-grade level, his silent reading comprehension is near frustration on the seventh-grade level. These results indicate that he will have considerable difficulty reading grade-appropriate (i.e., ninth-grade) materials, particularly when he is reading silently. Within the area of comprehension, silent reading should be the focus of instruction.

Summary and Integration. On the basis of the listening test results, James should be able to read ninth-grade-level materials with comprehension. Currently, however, he experiences comprehension problems with eighth-grade materials and even seventh-grade material that he reads silently. Two separate problems contribute to his reading comprehension difficulties. First, his print-processing strategies are not adequately developed and, thus, he reads slowly with many repetitions and corrections of miscues. Second, his knowledge of key terms is limited. While he is able to compensate for this limited knowledge when materials are read to him, when he is faced with print-processing problems as well, his comprehension fails. The fact that comprehension failure is more severe under silent reading conditions suggests that in addition to developing his vocabulary and refining his print-processing strategies, he must learn to monitor comprehension during silent reading.

Instructional Plan

Materials. Materials above the seventh-grade level yielded borderline or poor comprehension results on the IRI. With instructional preparation (discussion of the meaning and pronunciation of key vocabulary), James should be able to comprehend course materials that he reads at the seventh-grade level and perhaps at the eighth-grade level when topics are familiar.

Special reading instruction should focus on three areas: consolidation of print-processing skill, development of vocabulary, and development of silent reading comprehension. For the first, the material should be easy for James when he reads silently. Thus, fifth- (and somewhat later, sixth-) grade materials should be used. The selections should be about topics of high interest to James. Vocabulary development may be undertaken along with content area instruction and should reinforce the concepts being presented in his course materials. Silent reading of short passages followed by comprehension questions should begin on sixth-grade-level material and, as rapidly as comprehension warrants, proceed to seventh- and then eighth-grade-level passages.

Instructional Priorities. James's content area teachers should be advised that James will have difficulty reading materials independently above the sixth-grade level, but that if appropriate instructional support is provided, including the discussion of the meaning and pronunciation of key terms, James can cope with seventh- and perhaps even eighth-grade-level materials.

James also needs help in improving his vocabulary. He should be taught how to prepare vocabulary cards for words from his courses that are unfamiliar and how to review and use these words orally. If possible, he should be paired with another student who could profit from vocabulary instruction so that they can discuss words together.

For James, the development of print-processing skills will be a major priority. James needs to learn to apply his good knowledge efficiently and to enlarge the set of words that he recognizes instantaneously. His fluency can best be developed by extensive reading of easy and highly interesting materials. These materials should initially be at the fifth-grade level although James may soon progress to more difficult material. In conjunction with this reading, James should be taught a system for recording and evaluating his reading rate. Charts should be kept of the number of pages read to provide a tangible record of his accomplishments.

Finally, James should be taught study strategies, such as those described in Chapter 6, for monitoring his comprehension during silent reading. It is important that the passages for this purpose be limited to several pages at most and be followed by comprehension questions so that James can have immediate feedback on the effectiveness of his comprehension strategies.

SUMMARY

The standardized informal reading inventory has many advantages over a diagnosis based on oral reading of a single passage. It allows for the comparison of silent and oral reading and for an assessment of fluency and word recognition proficiency at various levels of difficulty. These comparisons make it possible to determine more precisely the level of materials that a student should read under various conditions. Perhaps its greatest strength lies in the assessment of listening comprehension, which allows a more definitive conclusion to be drawn regarding the influence of word recognition on a student's comprehension. However, many of these comparisons are available to the classroom teacher on a more informal basis. For instance, the teacher will note that many students have greater difficulty with silent than oral reading. What is important is that the teacher understand the significance of these comparisons in relation to the kinds of problems students encounter in becoming proficient readers.

CONCLUSION

Learning to diagnose the reading problems of students is not a simple process. This is because the process of learning to read is itself extremely complex, and there are important differences from one stage of reading development to another. We believe that a teacher must understand the nature of this development in order to be an effective diagnostician. This means having an overview of the reading process and a thorough understanding of its component processes. Instead of providing a simple "cookbook" solution to problems, we have in this book attempted to build, step by step, a conceptual framework for viewing the component processes of reading development: print translation, word knowledge, and discourse comprehension.

But it is not enough to understand how the three components work as separate entities. The teacher must also learn to understand how they go together to form a balanced and smoothly operating system — and to recognize when imbalances occur that interfere with effective reading development.

One way in which we attempted to show the nature of these imbalances was through detailed case studies. We carefully selected the cases to reflect major types of problems that students encounter as they attempt to establish a balance among the component processes of reading.

Just as we believe that students are active problem-solvers responding to the demands of their instructional materials, so we believe also that teachers must become active problem-solvers as they learn to diagnose reading problems. To this end, we focused on developing the observational skills that are necessary for gathering evidence about reading, and the interpretive skills that are necessary for making sense of the evidence. In our presentation of the case studies, we have encouraged the reader to assume an active role, by interspersing into the text various activities, both procedural (generating questions, selecting key words) and interpretive (drawing conclusions about the component reading processes, deriving instructional recommendations).

But skill in diagnosis can be acquired only if the teacher goes beyond this book, carrying out projects that build on the concepts and skills presented. This book will have been used most effectively if such projects were undertaken while it was being read. And this is just the beginning. The development of diagnostic skill is in many ways similar to the development of reading skill. Just as students need to undertake much contextual reading, so must teachers continue to study the reading problems of their students in order to consolidate their diagnostic strategies.

Finally, it must be emphasized once again that the purpose of diagnosis is to create instruction that is responsive to the needs of students. If this last step is omitted, the diagnosis is an idle exercise. There are two prerequisites to effective instructional planning. One is to understand the strengths and difficulties of a student well enough so that instruction is "on the mark." In this book we have been attempting to provide the basis for such an understanding. The second — more difficult, perhaps, to convey in a book — is to create instruction that captures the interest and energy of students and leads them to assume an active role. Accordingly, many of the instructional procedures we have described are designed to create active learners. As in the development of diagnostic skill, teachers will become more expert in providing high-quality instruction through experimentation with these and other procedures.

Dolch Basic Sight Vocabulary[1]

a ____	but ____	fly ____
about ____	buy ____	for ____
after ____	by ____	found ____
again ____	call ____	four ____
all ____	came ____	from ____
always ____	can ____	full ____
am ____	carry ____	funny ____
an ____	clean ____	gave ____
and ____	cold ____	get ____
any ____	come ____	give ____
are ____	could ____	go ____
around ____	cut ____	goes ____
as ____	did ____	going ____
ask ____	do ____	good ____
at ____	does ____	got ____
ate ____	done ____	green ____
away ____	don't ____	grow ____
be ____	down ____	had ____
because ____	draw ____	has ____
been ____	drink ____	have ____
before ____	eat ____	he ____
best ____	eight ____	help ____
better ____	every ____	her ____
big ____	fall ____	here ____
black ____	far ____	him ____
blue ____	fast ____	his ____
both ____	find ____	hold ____
bring ____	first ____	hot ____
brown ____	five ____	how ____

[1] *Source:* E. W. Dolch, Basic Sight Vocabulary, *Elementary School Journal,* 1936, *36,* 456–560. Published by The University of Chicago Press. Copyright © 1936 by the University of Chicago. All rights reserved.

hurt	out	these
I	over	they
if	own	think
in	pick	this
into	play	those
is	please	three
it	pretty	to
its	pull	today
jump	put	together
just	ran	too
keep	read	try
kind	red	two
know	ride	under
laugh	right	up
let	round	upon
light	run	us
like	said	use
little	saw	very
live	say	walk
long	see	want
look	seven	warm
made	shall	was
make	she	wash
many	show	we
may	sing	well
me	sit	went
much	six	were
must	sleep	what
my	small	when
myself	so	where
never	some	which
new	soon	white
no	start	who
not	stop	why
now	take	will
of	tell	wish
off	ten	with
old	thank	work
on	that	would
once	the	write
one	their	yellow
only	them	yes
open	then	you
or	there	your
our		

Blachowicz Informal Phonics Survey[1]

This informal survey gives subtests for many sound–symbol correspondence patterns. It is rarely useful or advisable to give the *whole* test to any student. It should be used after an oral reading diagnostic test to pinpoint those areas that look like possible weaknesses.

Since the test utilizes nonsense syllables, some mispronunciations will be artifacts of the test. Often a child will try to make a nonsense syllable into a real word. All conclusions from this test should be verified in real reading situations. For example, if you think a student has done badly on *bl*-, you might want him or her to read a paragraph containing words like *blue, blend, blood*, and so forth. Never lose sight of the fact that phonics used in context is the important tool.

GENERAL GUIDELINES

1. The subtests get harder. For very young children, start at subtest 1. For most students, subtest 3 is a good starting point.

2. For subtests 3 and up, always write down what the student says when he or she mispronounces a stimulus item. This is essential for final analysis.

3. Stop whenever the student shows signs of distress. If you want to give other subtests, do them another day.

4. Always tell the students what you are doing and why. Be sure to tell them that THESE ARE NOT REAL WORDS and that they are not expected to know them all.

5. Give praise and encouragement whenever you can. Start a child on an easy subtest to give success. If a student flounders, you can go back to an easier subtest to end with success.

[1] *Source:* Blachowicz, Camille L. Z. *Blachowicz Informal Phonics Survey.* (Unpublished assessment device.) Evanston, Illinois: National College of Education, 1980. Reprinted by permission.

6. Try to modify the materials to make them more usable. You might want to cut and mount the subtests for the student's copy. This makes the order less obvious.

7. A most effective use of the materials is to turn it into a board game. Place the stimulus items on index cards and have the student draw cards and move spaces for each one correctly pronounced. You can put different subtests on different colored cards for easy use and sorting.

ANALYSIS

1. Look for patterns.

2. Test your conclusions with real reading materials.

3. Try and break down the task into its parts when conclusions don't add up. For example, if the student could recognize *up*, knows the consonant sound associated with *t*, but could not pronounce *tup*, perhaps he or she cannot blend sounds.

4. Keep a record of your findings to check out in the real-life reading situation. Remember, testing is always artificial.

TEST ITEMS

1. *Naming upper and lower case letters.* Circle those not known when pointed to.

a	S	q	I	R	h	k
s	J	d	A	f	O	U
l	w	z	Q	v	X	B
n	H	T	b	e	G	P
V	N	j	y	K	w	f
F	r	Z	x	L	m	O
E	o	C	D	P	g	A
i	M	t	u	c	Y	d
S	j					

2. *Sound values of isolated consonants.* Point to each letter and ask the child to tell you what sound "this letter makes" or to give you a word that starts with this letter. Circle those not known.

b	c	k	j	g	t	v	d	m	h	r
p	z	l	f	n	s	u	w	y	qu	

3. *Short vowel phonograms blended with initial consonants.* Check to see if the student knows the following simple sight word phonograms: *up, it, am,* and *on.* (If they are not known, try to train the student to recognize them, or choose phonograms the child does know.) Point to each item and have the child pronounce it. If an item is mispronounced, write the mispronunciation above it for later analysis.

mup   zam   tup   sam   con   rit   gam   kon

dup   vit   hon   quam   bup   pon   wup   jam

nit   fup   lam   yup

4. *Consonant blends plus short vowel phonograms.* This and all subsequent tests follow the same procedure as test 3. Have the child pronounce each item, and write in any mispronounced words.

brup   scon   plit   skam   slup   twit   dron

gram   swis   spup   fron   blit   snam   glup

clam   trit   flon   smam   slup   cron   prit   glup

5. *Consonant digraphs plus short vowel phonograms.*

chup   shon   thup   whit   pham   shup   whon

chon   thon

6. *VCe̸ pattern plus initial consonants.*

dake   mime   fole   tule   mede   tate   fope

dute   dite   sede

7. *Long vowel digraphs.*

leat   mied   boad   tay   ley   moe   teef

buel   moes   lail   bie   toat   meep   tay

lue   bain   leam

8. R-*controlled vowels.*

mer   tir   hur   dir   fer   dar   mor   tur

sar   dor   bur

9. *Ending-blend phonograms.*

selt	mext	basp	mick	dunch	mulk	tand
goft	sunch	mimp	kent	munk	jung	dulf
baft	dilk	nolt	satch	fodge	hink	disp
folt	namp	dist	gelf	mond	bant	ting
dast	holf	fask	rept	felp	nold	hent

10. *Ending-digraph phonograms.*

tath fash nich baph dith sosh tach ruph

11. *Alternate sounds of c and g.*

gap gity cot came gend cend git cim

12. *Three-letter blends.*

splan	chrin	thrup	schon	strat	scrup
squit	spron	chris	thrat	scris	spron
strup	splup	squis	schan	shrat	

13. *Diphthongs.*

dow doy dound doint doy doud doil fown

14. *Silent letters.*

talf	tamb	demn	falm	knop	wrid	gnap
knop	ghat	wrod	gnom	phot	pnip	psin

15. *Multisyllabic words.* Show division points in responses with slash marks.

buffle	hotrat	rewant	sunting	fendle
inserg	unpottle	rembat	rebark	bullingable
minkfall	refizwissing	wenkerfil	mendle	submarkable
raction	bunded	madsion		

Complete Records of Performance on an IRI[1]: James

Analytical Reading Inventory, Word Lists

Level 3	Flash	Untimed	Level 4	Flash	Untimed
1. beginning	✓		1. worm	✓	
2. thankful	✓		2. afford	afforded	✓
3. written	✓		3. player	✓	
4. reason	✓		4. scientific	✓	
5. bent	✓		5. meek	✓	
6. patient	✓		6. rodeo	✓	
7. manage	✓		7. festival	✓	
8. arithmetic	✓		8. hillside	✓	
9. burst	✓		9. coward	✓	
10. bush	✓		10. boom	✓	
11. gingerbread	✓		11. booth	✓	
12. tremble	treb—	✓	12. freeze	✓	
13. planet	✓		13. protest	✓	
14. struggle	✓		14. nervous	✓	
15. museum	✓		15. sparrow	✓	
16. grin	✓		16. level	✓	
17. ill	✓		17. underground	✓	
18. alarm	✓		18. oxen	✓	
19. cool	✓		19. eighty	✓	
20. engine	ing-✓		20. shouldn't	✓	

Number correct _95_ _100_   Number correct _95_ _100_

[1] *Source: Analytical Reading Inventory, Second Edition,* by M. L. Woods & A. J. Moe. Columbus, Ohio: Charles E. Merrill, 1981. Word Lists and Questions reprinted by permission of Charles E. Merrill Publishing Co. Passages reprinted by permission of original sources.

Level 5	Flash	Untimed	Level 6	Flash	Untimed
1. abandon	✓		1. seventeen	✓	
2. zigzag	✓		2. annoy	✓	
3. terrific	✓		3. dwindle	_dind –_	✓
4. terrify	✓		4. rival	✓	
5. plantation	✓		5. hesitation	✓	
6. loaf	✓		6. navigator	✓	
7. hike	✓		7. gorge	✓	
8. relative	✓		8. burglar	✓	
9. available	✓		9. construction	✓	
10. grief	✓		10. exploration	✓	
11. physical	✓		11. technical	✓	
12. commander	_Commanded_	✓	12. spice	✓	
13. error	✓		13. spike	✓	
14. woodcutter	✓		14. prevail	_pre_ ✓	
15. submarine	✓		15. memorial	✓	
16. ignore	✓		16. initiation	✓	
17. disappointed	✓		17. undergrowth	✓	
18. wrestle	✓		18. ladle	_lădle_ ✓	
19. vehicle	_vick_	✓	19. walnut	✓	
20. international	_in -ter_		20. tributary	_tri — ✓_	

Number correct	90	100	Number correct	95	100

Analytical Reading Inventory, Form A
Level 6 (192 words   12 sent.)

Dr. Charles Drew overcame many obstacles to become a remarkable black American surgeon. Dr. Drew, who died in an auto crash at the age of forty-six, lived a life of dedication and kindness. The following information was derived from a book entitled, *Black Pioneers of Science and Invention,* by Louis Haber.

"Thousands of people are dying on the battlefields from loss of blood," *5*

said Dr. Charles Drew. "I must give ⓒ my time to solving the problems of blood /

trans fer ←

~~transfusion.~~" /

ⓒ physics

~~Physicians~~ had studied blood transfusion for years. However, they had /

met with many difficulties because the whole blood spoiled within days, and

the matching of blood types was time-consuming. Nevertheless, Dr. Drew

pa/sma

found there were fewer problems if ~~plasma~~, instead of whole blood, was used /

pa/sma

in transfusion. ~~Plasma~~, the liquid part of the blood without the cells, could be /

stored much longer and made the matching of blood types unnecessary.

pa/sma

Anybody could be given ~~plasma~~, and this was important on the battlefields of Ⅹ O *

World War II.

In 1940 the Blood Transfusion Association set up a program for war- ←

pa/sma

torn France. Dr. Drew asked them to send ~~plasma~~ rather than whole blood. Ⅹ O

But, it was started too late since France had fallen into the hands of the

enemy.

Later, when Great Britain suffered heavy losses from air raids, Dr. Drew

pa/sma

was asked to run a program called "~~Plasma~~ for Britain." He organized the Ⅹ O

entire project, and thousands of Americans gave blood to help the British.

* *Miscues occurring more than twice were not counted.*

$$Errors: \frac{5}{192} = 3\%$$

$$Comp: \frac{8}{8} = 100\%$$

$$Rate: \quad 96 \ sec = 1.6 \ min$$

$$192 \ words / 1.6 \ min = 120 \ w/m$$

COMPREHENSION QUESTIONS AND POSSIBLE ANSWERS

✓ 1. What was the area of Dr. Drew's major work?
(blood transfusion) *blood – transfusions*

✓ 2. What is meant by the word *difficulties?*
(problems) *problems*

✓ 3. Why did Dr. Drew decide to devote his time to solving the problems of blood transfusion?
(Thousands were dying on the battlefields of World War II.)
because of men dying- World War II

✓ 4. What is *plasma?*
(the liquid portion of the blood without cells)
part of blood – not cells

✓ 5. In 1940 what program was organized to aid war-torn France?
(Blood Transfusion Association)
Blood Transfusion Program — No, Association

✓ 6. What is meant by the phrase "fallen into the hands of the enemy"?
(France had lost battles to the enemy.)
You lose a battle to the enemy.

✓ 7. Why did Americans give blood to help their British neighbors?
(Britain had suffered heavy losses from air raids.)
Because air raids killed lots of them

✓ 8. What is said in this story that makes you think more people survived injuries on the battlefield because of Dr. Drew's work in blood transfusion?
(Stated: Plasma could be stored longer; with plasma, blood typing was unnecessary; anybody could be given plasma.)

*There were fewer problems with plasma —
it didn't spoil as easy as blood.*

Retelling: This doctor, Drew was his name, discovered plasma. Because it didn't spoil as easy as blood, it was better for transfusions — and blood types didn't have to match. It was used during World War II, not in France because it was too late, but in Britain for air raid victims

Scoring Guide	
Word Rec.	Comp.
IND 2	IND 0-1
INST 10	INST 2
FRUST 20+	FRUST 4+

Analytical Reading Inventory, Form A
Level 7 (262 words   14 sent.)

EXAMINER'S INTRODUCTION

S. E. Hinton wrote a very sensitive book called *The Outsiders,* showing the loyalties teen-agers in gangs have toward one another. In this passage, Johnny is in serious trouble, and his friends, Ponyboy and Dally, prefer to stick by him until he can decide how best to solve his problem. Please read a retelling of one of the incidents from this memorable book.

13

While he had been hiding out for the past five days, Johnny had given

serious thought to the whole mess. He had decided to return home, turn   *2*

himself in to the police, and take the consequences of his crime. Being only

sixteen, he was too young to have to run away for the rest of his life. He knew /

the fight had been in self-defense, but the fact still remained that he had

killed another person, and the thought of that miserable night in the city /

park sent Johnny into a terrifying panic.   /

He told Dally and Ponyboy of his decision, and now Dally reluctantly

began the long drive home. Dally had gone to jail before, and this was one

wretched experience he did not want his friend to have to endure.   *3*

As they reached the top of Jay Mountain, Dally slammed on the brakes! /

The old church where Johnny and Ponyboy had been hiding was in flames!

Ponyboy and Johnny bolted from the car to question a bystander who ex- /

plained that they were having a school picnic when the church began to burn. *2*

Suddenly, the crowd was shocked to hear desperate cries from inside!

Ponyboy and Johnny ran into the burning church, and the boys lifted the

children one by one through a window to safety. Chunks of the old roof were

already beginning to fall as the last child was taken out. Ponyboy leaped

through the window, vaguely hearing the sound of falling timber. Then, as he /

lay coughing and exhausted on the ground, he heard Johnny's terrifying

scream!

Errors: $^{13}/_{262}$ = 5%
Comp: $^7/_8$ = 88%
Rate: 150 sec = 2.5 min
    262 words/2.5min = 105 w/m

COMPREHENSION QUESTIONS AND POSSIBLE ANSWERS

✓ 1. What difficult conflict did Johnny have to solve?
(He had committed a crime, and he had decided to turn himself in to the police or to run away.) *whether to go home and turn himself in or stay out.*

✓ 2. What is meant by the phrase, "take the consequences"?
(take the punishment for his crime) *he would take whatever punishment they gave him.*

✓ 3. Where did the crime take place?
(in the city park) *in New York. (James was familiar with the book.)*

✓ 4. Why were Dally and the boys returning home?
(Johnny had decided to return home and turn himself in.) *So Johnny could turn himself in.*

✓ 5. Why did Dally slam on the brakes?
(He saw the burning church.) *because the church was burning.*

✓ 6. How did the boys get the children out of the burning church?
(lifted them through the window) *They ran in and the roof was caving in — the boy jumped out the window with the children.*

✗ 7. What is meant by the word *vaguely*?
(not clearly defined, unclear) *D. K.*

✓ 8. What is said in the story that makes you think Johnny thought he should turn himself in?
(Stated: He said that he was too young to run and hide for the rest of his life; the fact still remained that he had killed another person, and this was apparently something he felt he couldn't live with.)
He was running and hiding and things and he just didn't want to stay away from people and be afraid of everyone.

Scoring Guide	
Word Rec.	Comp.
IND 2–3	IND 0–1
INST 13	INST 2
FRUST 26+	FRUST 4+

Analytical Reading Inventory, Form A
Level 8 (286 words   15 sent.)

EXAMINER'S INTRODUCTION

Witch-hunts took place in England back in the 1600s. The following information was derived from an article entitled, "East Anglican and Essex Witches," from *Man, Myth, and Magic: An Illustrated Encyclopedia of the Supernatural.*

Witch-hunts were common in ^the^ seventeenth-century England. The mere ←

presence of a witch-hunter in a village caused such fear among the people

that children would even denounce their parents.

ⓒ Belee
~~Belief~~ in magic was common in those days. Perhaps some of the victims ←

of these hunts did think themselves guilty of witchery, but history has proven

that the majority of men and women accused and tortured by witch-hunters
ⓒ put←   ←
were ~~but~~ poor, defenseless victims of the times.
←

One of the best-known methods ~~for~~ the detection of ⓐ witch was the   o f

ⓒorderly
"swimming test." In this ~~ordeal~~ the suspect was dragged into a pool or stream
←   suspect '
after he was already tired from torture and fear. If the ~~suspect~~ floated to the

top ⓗⓔ was found guilty, and long pins were plunged into his body in search of
devil
the ~~devil's~~ marks. If he sank to the bottom, he was presumed innocent.

1945
In ~~1645~~ a man who titled himself, Witchfinder General Matthew Hop-
ⓒof   ragging   ←
kins, led a severe and cruel hunt. Because a civil war was ~~raging~~ in England at
←   ←—∧
ⓒ tense
the time, ~~tensions~~ and fears were common among the people. The time was
prosecution
ripe for ~~persecution~~.

At
~~In~~ that same year Hopkins imprisoned as many as 200 persons, all
←
and
charged with witchcraft. Among eighteen of those who died by hanging ~~was~~
ⓒ and
one John Lowes, a seventy-year-old clergyman who had been accused of
the   ←   ⓒ inter
witchcraft by ~~his~~ congregation. After undergoing ~~intolerable~~ torture, the old
a leggled
man admitted ownership of an evil spirit which he ~~allegedly~~ ordered to sink a
←
ship. No one bothered to check out the existence of such a vessel or to ask

about ~~any~~ reported sinkings on that day, and he was hanged ~~after~~ reading his

own burial service.

Errors: 22/286 = 8%

Comp: 5/8 = 62.5%

Rate: 188 sec = 3.13 min

286 words / 3.13 min = 91 w/m

COMPREHENSION QUESTIONS AND POSSIBLE ANSWERS

✓1. What commonly happened in seventeenth-century England?
(witch-hunts) *they had trials of bewitched*

✓2. According to this passage, what has history proven about witch-hunts?
(Most of the men and women accused and tortured for being witches
were but poor and defenseless people.) *that there really is no such
thing as witchcraft.*

✗ 3. Why would children even denounce their parents as witches?
(The mere presence of a witch-finder caused such fear among the people
and children.) *if their parents got mad at them and accused
them and told.*

✓ 4. What is meant by the phrase, "method of detection"?
(way of finding something out) *it's a test to see if a person's
a witch or evil*

✓ 5. In seventeenth-century England, why was the time ripe for persecution?
(A civil war was raging, causing tension and fear.) *a civil war*

✗ 6. What is meant by the word *allegedly?* *he said he would sink a ship*
(asserted to be true or exist but not proven) *and the people thought
he was a witch because they got no report.*

✗ 7. What did John Lowes allegedly do?
(owned an evil spirit which sank a ship) *he was the guy who committed
people to death was in the witch hunts.*

✓ 8. What is said in the story that makes you think the swimming test was
unjust?
(Stated: If the accused person sank, thus being proven innocent, he or
she was probably dead from drowning.) *If they weren't a witch, they
would die anyway. If they were innocent, they would die anyway.*

Scoring Guide	
Word Rec.	Comp.
IND 3	IND 0–1
INST 15	INST 2
FRUST 30+	FRUST 4+

Analytical Reading Inventory, Form A
Level 9 (339 words   18 sent.)

EXAMINER'S INTRODUCTION

This selection, based upon information from two articles appearing in a 1973 issue of *Plain Truth,* entitled, "Who's That Polluting My World?" and "How One Town Solves Pollution and Saves Water," describes some interesting facts concerning pollution and its control.

"This lake is all treated sewer water," the old gentleman murmured in admiration. The old man sat on a bench as close to the bank as possible with

his elbows resting on his knees while gazing at the rippling water. The breeze sweeping across the lake caused the sailboats to glide about with amazing

ease.

"We are making great ecological strides," he thought to himself. He knew well the story of this remarkable lake nestled in the foothills of southern California. He swelled with pride to recall the wise choice the Santee citizens had made when they elected not to join the metropolitan sewage

system where the waste would have been discharged into the Pacific with

only inadequate primary treatment. Rather, the residents constructed their own sewage facility, reclaiming the sewer water, thus extending their own

supply to provide basic needs and clean recreational extras.

"This is probably the only city park in the world which is built just yards

downstream from a sewer plant," the gentleman thought. He leaned forward

scooping up a handful of water. "This lake is more sanitary than most natu-

ral streams."

It has taken ingenious foresight to make this unprecedented plan viable. Its resourcefulness lay in the fact that clean water provided not only lucra-

tive recreational facilities, but the sewage waste solids furnished marketable

soil conditioners and plant fertilizers.

As the old gentleman arose he caught sight of paper trash carelessly
←   content   © charged

tossed beside the shore. His ~~contented~~ expression ~~changed~~ to one of concern.   2
                        ← discharged

He already knew that twenty million tons of paper are ~~discarded~~ each year in   1
                         © thirty

the United States representing a net loss of ~~340~~ million trees to the envi-   1
                              © needle

ronment. The gentleman shook his head to think of this ~~needless~~ waste. He   1
                            ←

knew the United States comprises only 6 percent of the world's population,
  the ←

yet ~~its~~ citizens consume 30 percent of the world's total energy output, only to   1

waste half of it. The old gentleman shuddered at these thoughts as he picked

up the discarded paper and placed it into the trash container.

Errors: 24/339 = 7%

Comp: 2/8 = 25%

Rate: 234 sec = 3.90 min

     339 words / 3.9 min = 87 w/m

COMPREHENSION QUESTIONS AND POSSIBLE ANSWERS

X   1. What is the main idea of this passage?
(We are making progress in pollution control, but still there is needless waste.) *how many people think bad thoughts about pollution.*

X   2. What is meant by the phrase *inadequate primary treatment?*
(insufficient water treatment) *does not give good treatment to the water*

✓   3. Where is this remarkable lake?
(in Santee in southern California) *in a city park — in California*

X   4. What happened when the Santee citizens constructed their own sewage facility?
(It provided basic needs and clean recreational extras.)
to stop pollution and sewage from going into the lake

X   5. What is meant by the phrase *an unprecedented plan?*
(one not done before)
it wasn't given to them — it wasn't stated to them

X   6. How much of the world's total energy does the United States use?
(30 percent)   *350%*

✓ 7. Why did the old gentleman's expression change when he got up from the bench?

(He caught sight of paper trash carelessly tossed beside the shore.)

He saw a piece of paper and it kills the beauty and the trees around the lake

✗ 8. What is said in the story that makes you think the Santee plan to reclaim sewage water was an ingenious and well thought-out ecological one?

(Stated: The clean water provided not only lucrative recreational facilities, but the waste solids furnished marketable soil conditioners and plant fertilizers.)

He would stop pollution going into the lake

Scoring Guide			
Word Rec.		Comp.	
IND	3 – 4	IND	0 – 1
INST	18	INST	2
FRUST	36+	FRUST	4+

Analytical Reading Inventory, Form B
Level 7 (234 words   15 sent.)

EXAMINER'S INTRODUCTION

Dave's Song, a book by Robert McKay, is a very sensitive story about a young girl who finds out that she can learn to appreciate and care for someone quite different from other young adults in her class. Please read a retelling of some of the information from this memorable book.

Kate sat in her senior biology class, but she wasn't hearing a single word the teacher was saying since her mind was thoroughly preoccupied. She could only think about Dave and her date with him last Friday night.

The entire thing was so confusing and distracting that she kept glancing sideways to where he was sitting near the windows. He was by far the most handsome boy at Tylerton High. He was tall, strong, with shaggy hair, and brilliant blue eyes, but there was something very different about Dave Burdick which she found difficult to accept. She knew that he was independent, and at times he seemed actually defiant. She found this disturbing. He always neglected his appearance as if he didn't care what others thought. He was an excellent football player, probably the best in the entire school, but he quit the team. He was stubborn and belligerent, and he would argue with anyone over anything. He never hung around the other kids, so it seemed to her that he was a loner. He drove an old Ford pickup, which had chicken feathers and farm tools scattered all over the floor. Kate felt that he was more interested in raising chickens than in having friends. Yet, even knowing all of these things, there was something crazy going on in her mind. To her surprise she found Dave Burdick fascinating and quite to her liking.

Comp: 4½/8 = 56%
Rate: 126 sec = 2.1 min
     234 words/2.1 min = 111 w/m

COMPREHENSION QUESTIONS AND POSSIBLE ANSWERS

√1. Why was Kate confused and distracted?
(Dave was very different from her other friends but she still found that she liked him.) *cause she kept thinking about the last date she had with Dave*

√2. Why didn't Kate hear anything the biology teacher was saying?
(She was preoccupied.) *cause she was too interested in dreaming about Dave*

✗3. What is meant by the word *independent*?
(not dependent upon others) *he's dedicated to work*

✓4. What did Kate find disturbing about Dave?
(his defiant attitude) *he didn't care for other people.*

✗5. What is meant by the word *belligerent*?
(hostile, waging war) *D.K.*

✓6. What did Dave's truck have in it?
(chicken feathers and old farm tools) *chicken feathers and farm equipment*

✗7. Why did Kate think Dave was a loner?
(because he never hung around other kids) *because he wouldn't talk at all – just sit around and think to himself.*

½8. What is said in the story that makes you think Dave had a negative attitude?
(Stated: He seemed defiant, stubborn, belligerent.) *The one date he had with the girl – she said he was too much to himself. If anyone said something about him, he didn't care what they said about h..*

Retelling : *It's about this one girl saying about she was in class– she was sittin there dreaming about that one last dream that she had with Dave and felt that he was the cutest boy in school – she saw how strong he was and she said he has furry hair and he was skinny and had shaggy ha.. and all – he was on the football team – he was the best one on th.. football team and he quit the team and he drove a pick-up truc.. that had feathers in the back of it. She knew that he was mor.. interested in farming than he was in school.*

Scoring Guide		
Word Rec.		Comp.
IND	2–3	IND	0–1
INST	13	INST	2
FRUST	26+	FRUST	4+

Analytical Reading Inventory, Form B
Level 6 (186 words   12 sent.)

EXAMINER'S INTRODUCTION

Garrett A. Morgan, a black American inventor, was born in 1877. He not only invented the first electric traffic signal but also other important inventions. The following information was derived from a book entitled, *Black Pioneers of Science and Invention,* by Louis Haber.

The explosion was horrible that tragic day in Cleveland, Ohio, in 1916.

Thirty-two men were trapped in a tunnel 250 feet below Lake Erie. No one

could enter the smoke-filled tunnel to rescue the survivors.

"Someone get Garrett Morgan to help those men down there," shouted a

man from the crowd. "Morgan and his breathing device are the only chance

those men have!"

Garrett Morgan and his brother quickly came to the aid of the men

trapped in the tunnel. Morgan had invented what he called a "Breathing

Device," later to be known as the *gas mask.* Two years before, Morgan's

invention had been tested by filling an enclosed tent with the foulest, thick-

est smoke possible. Placing the device over his head, a man entered this

suffocating atmosphere, stayed twenty minutes, and emerged unharmed!

Later, using a poisonous gas in a closed room, another test also provided the

same successful results.

Although not all lived, every man was brought to the surface by the

brothers. It was Morgan's concern for safer working conditions that saved

lives that day and in the years to come.

$Comp: 6 \frac{1}{2}/8 = 81 \%$

$Rate: 115 \ sec = 1.92 \ min$

$186 \ words / 1.92 \ min = 97 \ w/m$

COMPREHENSION QUESTIONS AND POSSIBLE ANSWERS

✓ 1. What did Garrett Morgan invent?
(gas mask — breathing device) *a gas mask*

✓ 2. Where was the tunnel located in which the men were trapped?
(250 feet below Lake Erie) *Cleveland, Ohio - 250 feet down*

½ 3. What happened as a result of the terrible explosion in Cleveland?
(thirty-two men were trapped) *gas filled the tunnel*

✓ 4. What is meant by the phrase, "this suffocating atmosphere"?
(the air in the tent was without oxygen)
run out of air - can't breathe - you'll die

✓ 5. What is meant by the word *device*?
(something intricate in design; a machine)
Something used to help someone — like a camera is a device.

✓ 6. What happened to the man who stayed in the tent for twenty minutes?
(He emerged unharmed.) *he survived — he got out of it*
— he could breathe

✗ 7. What was used to test the gas mask the second time?
(a poisonous gas) *smoke — I don't know*

✓ 8. What is said in the story that makes you think Morgan cared for the safety of others?
(Stated: It was Morgan's concern for safer working conditions which saved lives that day.)

He came as fast as he could with the breathing thing —
and he invented it to save lives.

Scoring Guide	
Word Rec.	Comp.
IND 2	IND 0-1
INST 10	(INST 2)
FRUST 20+	FRUST 4+

Analytical Reading Inventory, Form B
Level 5 (197 words   12 sent.)

EXAMINER'S INTRODUCTION

This is a story about Robyn Smith who left a career as a movie star to become one of the first female jockeys. The following information was derived from an article appearing in *The Lincoln Library of Sports Champions.*

"I know that I was last in the race," announced Robyn Smith, "but I am determined to be the best woman jockey! I want to ride race horses!"

It was a rainy morning in 1969, and as Robyn stood outside talking to the trainer, Frank Wright, she was so dripping wet that water came running out of the top of her boots. Many people had doubts about Robyn's riding ability, but Wright was sure she could be a successful rider. He decided to give her a first big chance.

By December of that same year she had proven herself by placing fourth in a race. Robyn not only had skill as a jockey, but she also had a way with horses which made them run fast for her.

Soon, she became accepted by others as an excellent rider. She went on to highlight her career with a surprising victory riding a horse named North Star. This horse was known for being wild on the track, but Robyn was able to handle him. Together they outran a horse named Onion. This was a special victory for Robyn because later, in another race, Onion defeated the famous horse, Secretariat!

Comp: 8/8 = 100%

Rate: 108 sec = 1.8 min

197 words / 1.8 min = 109 w/m

COMPREHENSION QUESTIONS AND POSSIBLE ANSWERS

1. What was Robyn Smith determined to be?
   (the best woman jockey) *the best woman jockey*

2. Why did water run out of the top of Robyn's boots?
   (because she was standing outside in the rain)
   She was in the rain

3. What did Frank Wright do for Robyn?
   (gave her a first big chance) *Gave her a chance to ride*

4. What is meant by the phrase, "proven herself"?
   (She showed that she could ride well.) *to show she could do it*

5. What did others think of Robyn when she proved her riding skill?
   (She was accepted as a good jockey.)
   thought she was a good jockey

6. What was North Star known for?
   (being wild on the track) *being wild and hard to handle*

7. Why was this a special victory for Robyn?
   (North Star defeated Onion; Onion defeated the famous horse Secretariat.) *because she beat the horse who later beat Secretariat*

8. What is said in the story that makes you think Robyn's trainer had confidence in her riding?
   (Stated: Wright was sure she could be a successful rider; she had a way with horses which made them run fast for her; she had skill as a rider.)
   Because he gave her a chance

Scoring Guide		
Word Rec.	Comp.	
IND	2	IND	0-1
INST	9	INST	2
FRUST	18+	FRUST	4+

Analytical Reading Inventory, Form C
Level 8 (257 words   15 sent.)

EXAMINER'S INTRODUCTION

The next selection you are to read is about vampires. At one time in our history vampires and other supernatural beings were believed to exist. The following information was derived from an article entitled, "Vampires," from *Man, Myth, and Magic: An Illustrated Encyclopedia of the Supernatural.*

"I am . . . Dracula," murmured a black-caped, fanged-toothed, pointed-eared monster. "I never drink . . . wine," he declared as movie-goers sat petrified in their seats.

In 1931, a novel by Irish author Bram Stoker became vividly alive on the movie screen as thousands flocked to see this re-creation of the vampire superstition which dates back to the sixteenth century.

According to the novel, a vampire looks pale, lean, and has a death-like icy touch. His eyes gleam or flash red, his ears are pointed like those of a werewolf, and his fingernails are curled and sharp. Some tales describe him as skeletal and often dressed in a black costume. His limited diet of blood gives him a foul-smelling breath. Old legends depict him with only one nostril and a barbed tongue. These creatures have the power to change their form into a cloud of mist or a bizarre nocturnal animal.

Despite modern disbelief in vampires, during the seventeenth century many thought they existed. It was believed that once a person died he could possibly return as a vampire. A corpse was often fastened in its grave with pegs or iron skewers to prevent a potential vampire from escaping.

Since the vampire was dormant during the day, graves were examined for small holes through which the monster could escape. If a grave was discovered with such holes, vampire hunters would remove the body and destroy it. This procedure took place during the daytime hours and all the

hunters returned to their homes before sunset.

Comp : $\frac{7}{8}$ = 88 %

COMPREHENSION QUESTIONS AND POSSIBLE ANSWERS

  ✓ **1.** What is the main idea of this article?
      (Belief in vampires existed in the 16th and 17th centuries.)
      they used to believe in vampires

  ✓ **2.** What are a vampire's eyes supposed to look like?
      (gleaming or flashing red) flash red

  ✓ **3.** What is meant by the phrase, "bizarre animal"?
      (unique or strange) strange

  ✓ **4.** How did old legends describe a vampire?
      (one nostril and a barbed tongue) one nostril [Anything else?]
                   a funny tongue - a barb tongue
  ✗ **5.** What is meant by the phrase, "barbed tongue"?
      (a forked or pointed tongue) D.K.

  ✓ **6.** Why were iron skewers used to fasten a corpse to its grave?
      (to prevent it from escaping) to stop it from getting away

  ✓ **7.** Why were the graves examined during the day?
      (There was less danger as vampires slept during the day.)
      the vampires slept then
  ✓ **8.** What is said in this story that makes you think people in the 16th and
      17th centuries believed in and feared vampires?
      (Stated: They fastened corpses in their graves with iron skewers; they
      searched graves for perforations and if holes were found they destroyed
      the corpse.) they went hunting for them

Scoring Guide	
Word Rec.	Comp.
IND 3	IND 0–1
INST 15	INST 2
FRUST 30+	FRUST 4+

Analytical Reading Inventory, Form C
Level 9 (315 words   17 sent.)

EXAMINER'S INTRODUCTION

Jean-Pierre Haller, a Belgian explorer and author, was born and raised in the Belgian Congo. Since his childhood playmates had been members of the Efé Pygmy society, he returned in 1957 to become an adopted member and assist them in their dramatic struggle for survival. The following information was derived from an article entitled, "To Save a People," appearing in a 1975 issue of *The Plain Truth.*

A young Pygmy stood in the parching equatorial African sun. He stood but five feet tall and his stature was bent from hard labor. His skin was golden brown and his hair was short and curled tightly to his head. His feet were bare and his clothes tattered. His eyes had the dull stare of a man once proud and free, but now deprived of the will to maintain his own gentle life-style.

The Pygmies are central Africa's oldest known surviving people and in the 1930's about 35,000 proudly lived in the Itiru Forest of the eastern Congo, now called Zaire. By 1957 their population had fallen to 25,000.

During the fifties, the Pygmies' ancestral forest was wastefully chopped down by lumber industrialists, robbing them of the vegetation and game they depended upon for survival. Consequently, the people were forced into the blistering sun to which they were unaccustomed. Large plantations closed in on their environment. National parks and game reserves were established, but no land was set aside to aid the Pygmy societies in their struggle for survival. Tourists brought contagious diseases to which the Pygmies had no immunity, and as a result their population continued to decline.

In 1960 the Belgian Congo received political independence, becoming the nation of Zaire. This political change brought civil war for which the nonaggressive Pygmies were the first to suffer and their number rapidly dwindled to 15,000. They became victims of new burdens such as paying income taxes, being drafted into the Zaire army, further loss of cultural identity, and by 1975 their size numbered some 3,800.

The Pygmies have a warm and gentle life-style with a dignified moral code which forbids killing, lying, theft, devil worship, sorcery, disrespect for elders, and blasphemy. They do not engage in cannibalism, mutilation, ritual murder, intertribal war, initiation ordeals, or other cruel customs sometimes associated with equatorial Africa.

Comp: 6½/8 = 81%

COMPREHENSION QUESTIONS AND POSSIBLE ANSWERS

✓ 1. What is the main idea of this passage?
(This Pygmy tribe is facing near extinction.) about how Pygmies were forced to become like our society

✓ 2. Where is the Itiru Forest?
(eastern Congo, now called Zaire) in Africa

½ 3. What happened to the Pygmy society when their forests were chopped down?
(They were robbed of the vegetation and game they depended upon for survival.) they weren't used to the sun beating down on them

✓ 4. What is meant by the word *immunity*?
(condition of being able to resist a particular disease) if a person isn't immune to a sickness, they'll probably get it

✓ 5. What did tourists bring to the Pygmies?
(contagious diseases) diseases

✗ 6. What is meant by the phrase, "nonaggressive Pygmies"?
(nonhostile, nonwarlike) you're not selfish, like someone who is crazy and always wanting something, they're nonaggressive

✓ 7. In 1960, what happened when the Belgian Congo received political independence?
(civil war and new suffering for the Pygmies) they had to pay taxes and were drafted into the army.

8. What is said in this story that makes you think no one cared enough to protect the Pygmies' rights?
    (Stated: Lumber industrialists wastefully chopped down the Pygmies' forests; parks and game reserves were set aside but no land was saved for the Pygmies.) they had to move to the cities and countryside with people

Scoring Guide	
Word Rec.	Comp.
IND 3-4	IND 0-1
INST 18	INST 2
FRUST 36+	FRUST 4+

References

Ames, W. S. 1966. The development of a classification scheme of contextual aids. *Reading Research Quarterly 2,* 57–82.

Anderson, R. C. 1972. How to construct achievement tests to assess comprehension. *Review of Educational Research 42,* 145–170.

Anderson, R. C., & Freebody, P. 1981. Vocabulary knowledge. In J. Guthrie (Ed.), *Comprehension and teaching: Research reviews.* Newark, Del.: International Reading Association.

André, M. E., & Anderson, T. H. 1978–1979. The development and evaluation of a self-questioning study technique. *Reading Research Quarterly 14,* 605–623.

Anglin, J. M. 1977. *Word, object, and conceptual development.* New York: Norton.

Asch, S. E., & Nerlove, H. 1960. The development of double-function terms in children: An exploratory investigation. In B. Kaplan & S. Wapner (Eds.), *Perspectives in psychological theory: Essays in honor of Heinz Werner.* New York: International Universities Press. Cited in Gardner, H., Winner, E., Bechhofer, R., & Wolf, D. 1978. The development of figurative language. In K. E. Nelson (Ed.), *Children's language* (Vol. 1). New York: Gardner.

Baer, J. A. 1926. Case studies in reading. *Educational Research Bulletin* (Ohio State University) *5,* 319–321.

Baldwin, R. S., Luce, T. S., & Readence, J. E. 1982. The impact of subschemata on metaphorical processing. *Reading Research Quarterly 17,* 528–543.

Barr, R. 1972. The influence of instructional conditions on word recognition errors. *Reading Research Quarterly 7,* 509–579.

Barr, R. 1974. Influence of instruction on early reading. *Interchange 5,* 13–22.

Barr, R. 1974–1975. The effect of instruction on pupil reading strategies. *Reading Research Quarterly 10,* 555–582.

Barr, R., & Dreeben, R. 1983. *How schools work.* Chicago: University of Chicago Press.

Barrett, T. C. 1976. Taxonomy of reading comprehension. In R. Smith & T. C. Barrett, *Teaching reading in the middle grades.* Reading, Mass.: Addison-Wesley.

Barron, R. 1969. The use of vocabulary as an advance organizer. In H. L. Herber & P. L. Sanders (Eds.), *Research in reading in the content areas: First year report.* Syracuse, N.Y.: Syracuse University Reading and Language Arts Center.

Bartlett, B. J. 1978. *Top-level structure as an organizational strategy for recall of classroom text.* Unpublished doctoral dissertation, Arizona State University. Cited in Meyer, B. J. F., Brandt, D. M., & Bluth, G. J. 1980. Use of top-level structure in text: Key for reading comprehension of ninth-grade students. *Reading Research Quarterly 16,* 72–103.

Bean, T. W., & Pardi, R. 1979. A field test of a guided reading strategy. *Journal of Reading 23,* 144–146.

Beck, I. L., & McCaslin, E. S. 1978. *An analysis of the dimensions that affect the development of code-breaking ability in eight beginning reading programs.* (LRDC Publication 1978/6) Pittsburgh: University of Pittsburgh, Learning Research and Development Center.

Beck, I. L., McKeown, M. G., McCaslin, E. S., & Burkes, A. M. 1979. *Instructional dimensions that may affect reading comprehension: Examples from two commercial reading programs.* (LRDC Publication 1979/20). Pittsburgh: University of Pittsburgh, Learning Research and Development Center.

Beck, I. L., Omanson, R. C., & McKeown, M. G. 1982. An instructional redesign of reading lessons: Effects on comprehension. *Reading Research Quarterly 17,* 462–481.

Beck, I. L., Perfetti, C. A., & McKeown, M. G. 1982. The effects of long-term vocabulary instruction on lexical access and reading comprehension. *Journal of Educational Psychology 74,* 506–521.

Bennett, A. 1942. An analysis of errors in word recognition made by retarded readers. *Journal of Educational Psychology 33,* 25–34.

Betts, E. A. 1934. A physiological approach to the analysis of reading disabilities. *Educational Research Bulletin 8,* 135–140, 163–164.

Betts, E. A. 1954. *Foundations of reading instruction* (Rev. ed.). New York: American Book.

Biemiller, A. 1970. The development of the use of graphic and contextual information as children learn to read. *Reading Research Quarterly 6,* 75–96.

Biemiller, A. 1979. Changes in the use of graphic and contextual information as functions of passage difficulty and reading achievement level. *Journal of Reading Behavior 11,* 307–318.

Blachowicz, C. 1977. Cloze activities for primary readers. *Reading Teacher 31,* 300–302.

Bloom, B. S., Engelhardt, M. D., Furst, E. J., Hill, W. H., & Krathwohl, D. R. 1956. *Taxonomy of educational objectives. The classification of educational goals. Handbook I: Cognitive domain.* New York: David McKay.

Bolinger, D. 1968. *Aspects of language.* New York: Harcourt, Brace, & World.

Bond, G. L. 1935. *The auditory and speech characteristics of poor readers.* Teachers College Contributions to Education, No. 657, Columbia University.

Bortnick, R., & Lopardo, G. 1973. An instructional application of the cloze procedure. *Journal of Reading 16,* 296–300.

Bridge, C. A., & Tierney, R. J. 1981. The inferential operations of children across text with narrative and expository tendencies. *Journal of Reading Behavior 13,* 201–214.

Bronowski, J., & Bellugi, U. 1970. Language, name, and concept. *Science 168,* 669–673.

Bruce, D. 1964. Analysis of word sounds by young children. *British Journal of Educational Psychology 34,* 148–169.

Carpenter, P. A., & Just, M. A. 1977. Reading comprehension as eyes see it. In M. A. Just & P. A. Carpenter (Eds.), *Cognitive processes in comprehension.* Hillsdale, N.J.: Lawrence Erlbaum.

Chall, J. S. 1967. *Learning to read: The great debate.* New York: McGraw-Hill.

Chall, J. S. 1979. The great debate: Ten years later, with a modest proposal for reading stages. In L. B. Resnick & P. A. Weaver (Eds.), *Theory and practice of early reading* (Vol. 1). Hillsdale, N.J.: Lawrence Erlbaum.

Chall, J. S. 1983. *Stages of reading development.* New York: McGraw-Hill.

Chomsky, C. 1969. *The acquisition of syntax in children from 5 to 10.* Cambridge, Mass.: MIT Press.

Clark, E. V. 1973. What's in a word? On the child's acquisition of semantics in his first language. In T. E. Moore (Ed.), *Cognitive development and the acquisition of language.* New York: Academic Press.

Clay, M. M. 1967. The reading behavior of five year old children: A research project. *New Zealand Journal of Educational Studies 2,* 11–31.

Clay, M. M. 1972. *Sand: Test booklet.* Auckland: Heinemann.

Clay, M. M. 1979a. *Reading: The patterning of complex behavior.* Auckland: Heinemann.

Clay, M. M. 1979b. *Stones: Test Booklet.* Auckland: Heinemann.

Clay, M. M. 1982. *Observing young readers.* Auckland: Heinemann.

Clay, M. M., & Imlach, R. H. 1971. Juncture, pitch and stress as reading behavior variables. *Journal of Verbal Learning and Verbal Behavior 10,* 133–139.

Cleland, C. J. 1981. Highlighting issues in children's literature through semantic webbing. *Reading Teacher 34,* 642–646.

Clowes, H. C. 1930. A reading clinic. *Educational Research Bulletin* (Ohio State University) *9,* 261–268.

Cocks, P. 1974. *Verification of answer categories for a definition task: A study of linguistic and cognitive processes.* Unpublished doctoral dissertation, University of Chicago.

Cohen, A. S. 1974–1975. Oral reading errors of first grade children taught by a code emphasis approach. *Reading Research Quarterly 10,* 616–650.

Cohen, R. 1983. Self-generated questions as an aid to reading comprehension. *Reading Teacher 36,* 770–775.

Crist, B. I. 1975. One capsule a week—A painless remedy for vocabulary ills. *Journal of Reading 19,* 147–149.

Crothers, E. J. 1978. Inference and coherence. *Discourse Processes 1,* 51–71.

Cunningham, J. W., Cunningham, P. M., & Arthur, S. V. 1981. *Middle and secondary school reading.* New York: Longman.

Cunningham, P. M. 1975–1976. Investigating a synthesized theory of mediated word identification. *Reading Research Quarterly 11,* 127–143.

Cunningham, P. M. 1978. Decoding polysyllabic words: An alternative strategy. *Journal of Reading 21,* 608–614.

Cunningham, P. M. 1979. A compare/contrast theory of mediated word identification. *Reading Teacher 32,* 774–778.

Dale, E., & Chall, J. S. 1948. A formula for predicting readability. *Educational Research Bulletin* (Ohio State University) *27*, 11–20, 28, 37–54.

Dank, M. E. 1976. *A study of the relationship of miscues to the mode of formal reading instruction received by selected second graders.* Unpublished doctoral dissertation, University of Massachusetts. (ERIC Document Reproduction Service No. ED 126 431)

Daskal, J. 1983. *Basic strategies for improving comprehension of written materials.* Unpublished manuscript, Chicago.

Davis, F. B. 1944. Fundamental factors of comprehension in reading. *Psychometrika 9*, 185–197.

Davis, F. B. 1968. Research in comprehension in reading. *Reading Research Quarterly 3*, 499–544.

Dearborn, W. F. 1906. The psychology of reading. *Archives of Philosophy, Psychology and Scientific Methods 1*, 71–132.

Dearborn, W. F. 1933. Structural factors which condition special disability in reading. *Proceedings of the 57th Annual Session of the American Association of Mental Deficiency 38*, 268–283.

DeLawter, J. A. 1975. Three miscue patterns: The relationship of beginning reading instruction and miscue patterns. In W. D. Page (Ed.), *Help for the reading teacher: New directions in research.* Urbana, Ill.: National Conference on Research in English, ERIC Clearinghouse on Reading and Communication Skills, National Institute of Education.

Dodge, R. 1905. The illusion of clear vision during eye-movement. *Psychological Bulletin 12*, 193–199.

Dodge, R. 1907. An experimental study of visual fixation. *Psychological Review Monograph Supplements 8*, 1–96.

Dolch, E. W. 1936. Basic sight vocabulary. *Elementary School Journal 36*, 456–460.

Dougherty, M. L. 1929. Reading difficulty. *Johns Hopkins University Studies in Education 11*.

Draper, A. G., & Moeller, G. H. 1971. We think with words (therefore, to improve thinking, teach vocabulary). *Phi Delta Kappan 52*, 482–484.

Drum, P. A. 1983. Vocabulary knowledge. In J. A. Niles & L. A. Harris (Eds.), *Searches for meaning in reading/language processing and instruction* (Thirty-second Yearbook of the National Reading Conference). Rochester, N.Y.: National Reading Conference.

Durkin, D. 1978–1979. What classroom observations reveal about reading comprehension instruction. *Reading Research Quarterly 14*, 481–533.

Durkin, D. 1981. Reading comprehension in five basal reader series. *Reading Research Quarterly 16*, 515–544.

Durrell, D. D. (Chairman). 1936. *Research problems in reading in the elementary school* (Fourth Annual Research Bulletin of the National Conference on Research in Elementary School English). Philadelphia: J. Conrad Seegers, Temple University.

Ehri, L. C. 1975. Word consciousness in readers and prereaders. *Journal of Educational Psychology 67*, 204–212.

Ehri, L. C. 1983. How orthography alters spoken language competencies in children learning to read and spell. In J. Downing & R. Valtin (Eds.), *Language awareness and learning to read.* New York: Springer Verlag.

Ekwall, E. E. 1976. *Diagnosis and remediation of the disabled reader.* Boston: Allyn & Bacon.

Elder, R. D. 1971. Oral reading achievement of Scottish and American children. *Elementary School Journal 71,* 216–230.

Elkonin, D. B. 1963. The psychology of mastering elements of reading. In B. Simon (Ed.), *Educational psychology in the U.S.S.R.* London: Routledge & Kegan Paul.

Feifel, H., & Lorge, I. 1950. Qualitative differences in the vocabulary responses of children. *Journal of Educational Psychology 41,* 1–18.

Fernald, G. M., & Keller, H. 1926. The effect of kinesthetic factors in the development of word recognition in nonreaders. *Journal of Educational Research 4,* 355–377.

Fisher, J. H. 1905. A case of congenital word blindness. *Ophthalmic Review 24,* 315–318.

Ford, C. A. 1928. A case of congenital word blindness showing its social implications. *Psychological Clinic 17,* 73–84.

Freebody, P., & Anderson, R. C. 1983a. Effects of differing proportions and locations of difficult vocabulary on text comprehension. *Journal of Reading Behavior 15,* 19–39.

Freebody, P., & Anderson, R. C. 1983b. Effects of vocabulary difficulty, text cohesion, and schema availability on reading comprehension. *Reading Research Quarterly 18,* 277–294.

Froese, V., & Kurushima, S. 1979. The effects of sentence expansion practice on the reading comprehension and writing ability of third graders. In M. L. Kamil & A. J. Moe (Eds.), *Reading research: Studies and applications* (Twenty-eighth Yearbook of the National Reading Conference). Clemson, S.C.: National Reading Conference.

Fry, E. B. 1968. A readability formula that saves time. *Journal of Reading 11,* 513–516.

Fry, E. B. 1972. *Reading instruction for classroom and clinic.* New York: McGraw-Hill.

Fuchs, L. S., Fuchs, D., & Deno, S. L. 1982. Reliability and validity of curriculum-based informal reading inventories. *Reading Research Quarterly 18,* 6–26.

Gardner, H., Winner, E., Bechhofer, R., & Wolf, D. 1978. The development of figurative language. In K. E. Nelson (Ed.), *Children's language* (Vol. 1). New York: Gardner.

Garner, R., & Reis, R. 1981. Monitoring and resolving comprehension obstacles: An investigation of spontaneous lookbacks among upper-grade good and poor comprehenders. *Reading Research Quarterly 16,* 569–582.

Gates, A. I. 1926. A series of tests for the measurement of diagnosis of reading ability in grades 3 to 8. *Teachers College Record 28,* 1–23.

Gates, A. I. 1927. Methods of constructing and validating the Gates reading tests. *Teachers College Record 29,* 148–159.

Gates, A. I. 1935. *Improvement of reading* (Rev. ed.). New York: Macmillan.

Geva, E. 1983. Facilitating reading comprehension through flowcharting. *Reading Research Quarterly 18,* 384–405.

Gilbert, D. W. 1959. *Breaking the reading barrier.* Englewood Cliffs, N.J.: Prentice-Hall.

Gillet, J. W., & Temple, C. 1982. *Understanding reading problems: Assessment and instruction.* Boston: Little, Brown.

Goodman, K. S. 1965. A linguistic study of cues and miscues in reading. *Elementary English 42,* 639–643.

Goodman, K. S. 1967. Reading: A psycholinguistic guessing game. *Journal of the Reading Specialist 6,* 126–135.

Goodman, K. S. 1969. Analysis of reading miscues: Applied psycholinguistics. *Reading Research Quarterly 5,* 9–30.

Goodman, Y. M. 1970. Using children's miscues for new teaching strategies. *Reading Teacher 23,* 455–459.

Gourley, J. W. 1978. This basal is easy to read—or is it? *Reading Teacher 32,* 174–182.

Gourley, J. W., & Catlin, J. 1978. Children's comprehension of grammatical structures in context. *Journal of Psycholinguistic Research 7,* 419–434.

Gray, C. T. 1922. *Deficiencies in reading ability: Their diagnosis and remedies.* Boston: D. C. Heath.

Gray, W. S., & Holmes, E. 1938. *The development of meaning vocabularies in reading* (Publications of the Laboratory Schools, No. 6). Chicago: University of Chicago.

Gray, W. S., with Kibbe, D., Lucas, L., & Miller, L. W. 1922. *Remedial cases in reading: Their diagnosis and treatment* (Supplemental Educational Monograph). Chicago: University of Chicago Press.

Guszak, F. J. 1967. Teacher questioning and reading. *Reading Teacher 21,* 227–234.

Hafner, L. E. 1977. *Developmental reading in middle and secondary schools: Foundations, strategies, and skills for teaching.* New York: Macmillan.

Hansen, J. 1981a. An inferential comprehension strategy for use with primary grade children. *Reading Teacher 34,* 665–669.

Hansen, J. 1981b. The effects of inference training and practice on young children's reading comprehension. *Reading Research Quarterly 16,* 391–417.

Hansen, J., & Ahlfors, G. 1982. Instruction in inferential comprehension: An extension and a summary. In J. A. Niles & L. A. Harris (Eds.), *New inquiries in reading research and instruction* (Thirty-first Yearbook of the National Reading Conference). Rochester, N.Y.: National Reading Conference.

Hansen, J., & Pearson, P. D. 1983. An instructional study: Improving the inferential comprehension of good and poor fourth-grade readers. *Journal of Educational Psychology 75,* 821–829.

Harris, A. J., & Sipay, E. R. 1980. *How to increase reading ability* (7th ed.). New York: Longman.

Hincks, E. M. 1926. *Disability in reading and its relation to personality* (Harvard Monographs in Education, No. 7). Cambridge, Mass.: Harvard University Press.

Holden, M., & MacGinitie, W. 1972. Children's conceptions of word boundaries in speech and print. *Journal of Educational Psychology 63,* 551–557.

Hood, J. 1975–1976. Qualitative analysis of oral reading errors: The inter-judge reliability of scores. *Reading Research Quarterly 11,* 577–598.

Huey, E. B. 1898. Preliminary experiments in the physiology and psychology of reading. *American Journal of Psychology 9,* 575–586.

Huey, E. B. 1900. On the psychology and physiology of reading, I. *American Journal of Psychology 11*, 283–302.

Huey, E. B. 1968. *The psychology and pedagogy of reading.* Cambridge, Mass.: MIT Press. (Originally published, 1908.)

Hughes, A., Bernier, S. A., & Gurren, L. (Eds.). 1979. The eagle and the baker. In *The Gold Book, The Headway Program.* LaSalle, Ill.: Open Court Publishing Co.

Huttenlocher, J. 1964. Children's language: Word–phrase relationship. *Science 143*, 264–265.

Ilg, F. L., & Ames, L. B. 1950. Developmental trends in reading behavior. *Journal of Genetic Psychology 76*, 291–312.

Irwin, J. W. 1980. The effects of explicitness and clause order on the comprehension of reversible causal relationships. *Reading Research Quarterly 15*, 477–488.

Jackson, E. 1906. Developmental alexia (congenital word blindness). *American Journal of Medical Sciences 81*, 843–849.

Jastak, J. 1934. Interferences in reading. *Psychological Bulletin 21*, 244–272.

Jenkins, J. R., Pany, D., & Schreck, J. 1978. *Vocabulary and reading comprehension: Instructional effects* (Technical Report No. 100). Urbana, Ill.: University of Illinois, Center for the Study of Reading. (ERIC Document Reproduction Service No. ED 160 999)

Kameenui, E. J., & Carnine, D. W. 1982. An investigation of fourth-graders' comprehension of pronoun constructions in ecologically valid texts. *Reading Research Quarterly 17*, 556–580.

Kameenui, E. J., Carnine, D. W., & Freschi, R. 1982. Effects of text construction and instructional procedures for teaching word meanings on comprehension and recall. *Reading Research Quarterly 17*, 367–388.

Karpova, S. N. 1955. Osoznanie slovesnogo sostava rechi rebenkom doshkol'nogo vozrasta (The preschooler's realization of the lexical structure of speech). *Voprosy Psikhol.,* No. 4, 43–55.

Katz, E. S., & Brent, S. B. 1968. Understanding connectives. *Journal of Verbal Learning and Verbal Behavior 7*, 501–509.

Kibby, M. W. 1979. Passage readability affects the oral reading strategies of disabled readers. *Reading Teacher 32*, 390–396.

LaBerge, D., & Samuels, S. M. 1974. Toward a theory of automatic information processing in reading. *Cognitive Psychology 6*, 293–323.

Lake, M. L. 1971. Improve the dictionary's image. *Elementary English 48*, 363–365.

Langacker, P. W. 1973. *Language and its structure: Some fundamental linguistic concepts* (2nd ed.). New York: Harcourt Brace Jovanovich.

Lesgold, A. M. 1972a. *Effects of pronouns on children's memory for sentences.* (LRDC Publication 1972/17). Pittsburgh: University of Pittsburgh, Learning Research and Development Center. (ERIC Document Reproduction Service No. ED 068 974)

Lesgold, A. M. 1972b. Pronominalization: A device for unifying sentences in memory. *Journal of Verbal Learning and Verbal Behavior 11*, 316–323.

Lesgold, A. M. 1974. Variability in children's comprehension of syntactic structures. *Journal of Educational Psychology 66*, 333–338.

Lesgold, A. M., & Resnick, L. B. 1982. How reading difficulties develop: Perspectives from a longitudinal study. In J. P. Das, R. F. Mulcahy, & A. E. Wall (Eds.), *Theory and research in learning disabilities.* New York: Plenum.

Liberman, I., Shankweiler, D., Fischer, F., & Carter, B. 1974. Explicit syllable and phoneme segmentation in the young child. *Journal of Experimental Child Psychology 18,* 201–212.

Lopardo, G., & Sadow, M. W. 1982. Criteria and procedures for the method of repeated readings. *Journal of Reading 26,* 156–160.

MacGinitie, W. H. 1983. A critique of what classroom observations reveal about reading comprehension instruction and reading comprehension instruction in five basal reader series: Durkin's contribution to our understanding of current practice. In L. M. Gentile, M. L. Kamil, & J. S. Blanchard (Eds.), *Reading research revisited.* Columbus, Ohio: Charles E. Merrill.

Mandler, J. M., & Johnson, N. S. 1977. Remembrance of things parsed: Story structure and recall. *Cognitive Psychology 9,* 111–151.

Manzo, A. V. 1969. The ReQuest procedure. *Journal of Reading 11,* 123–126.

Manzo, A. V. 1975. Guided reading procedure. *Journal of Reading 18,* 287–291.

Maratsos, M. P. 1976. *The use of definite and indefinite references in young children.* New York: Cambridge University Press.

Marshall, N., & Glock, M. 1978–1979. Comprehension of connected discourse: A study into the relationships between the structure of text and information recalled. *Reading Research Quarterly 16,* 10–56.

Mason, J. M. & The Staff of The Center for the Study of Reading, University of Illinois. 1984. A schema-theoretic view of the reading process as a basis for comprehension instruction. In G. G. Duffy, L. R. Roehler, and J. Mason (Eds.), *Comprehension instruction: Perspectives and suggestions.* New York: Longman.

McDonald, G. E. 1978. *The effects of instruction in the use of an abstract structural schema as an aid to comprehension and recall of written discourse.* Unpublished doctoral dissertation, Virginia Polytechnic Institute and State University. Cited in Meyer, B. J. F., Brandt, D. M., & Bluth, G. J. 1980. Use of top-level structure in text: Key for reading comprehension of ninth-grade students. *Reading Research Quarterly 16,* 72–103.

McGee, L. M. 1982. The influence of metacognitive knowledge of expository text structure on discourse recall. In J. A. Niles & L. A. Harris (Eds.), *New inquiries in reading research and instruction* (Thirty-first Yearbook of the National Reading Conference). Rochester, N.Y.: National Reading Conference.

Metropolitan Achievement Tests, Form B, Elementary Reading Test. 1959. New York: Harcourt, Brace & World.

Meyer, B. J. F. 1977. The structure of prose: Effects on learning and memory and implications for educational practice. In R. C. Anderson, R. J. Spiro, & W. F. Montague (Eds.), *Schooling and the acquisition of knowledge.* Hillsdale, N.J.: Lawrence Erlbaum.

Meyer, B. J. F., Brandt, D. M., & Bluth, G. J. 1980. Use of top-level structure in text: Key for reading comprehension of ninth-grade students. *Reading Research Quarterly 16,* 72–103.

Mezynski, K. 1983. Issues concerning the acquisition of knowledge: Effects of vocabulary training on reading comprehension. *Review of Educational Research 53*, 253–279.

Miller, G. A. 1977. *Spontaneous apprentices*. New York: Seabury Press.

Monroe, M. 1928. Methods for diagnosis and treatment of cases of reading disability. *Genetic Psychology Monographs 4*, 335–456.

Monroe, M. 1932. *Children who cannot read*. Chicago: University of Chicago Press.

Morgan, W. P. 1896. A case of congenital word blindness. *British Medical Journal 2*, 1378.

Morris, D. 1980. Beginning readers' concept of word. In E. H. Henderson & J. W. Beers, *Developmental and cognitive aspects of learning to spell: A reflection of word knowledge*. Newark, Del.: International Reading Association.

Nelson, K. 1974. Concept, word, and sentence: Interrelations in acquisition and development. *Psychological Review 81*, 267–285.

Orton, S. T. 1928. A physiological theory of reading disability and stuttering in children. *New England Journal of Medicine 99*, 1046–1052.

Page, W. D., & Barr, R. C. 1975. Use of informal reading inventories. In W. D. Page (Ed.), *Help for the reading teacher: New directions in research*. Urbana, Ill.: National Conference on Research in English, ERIC Clearinghouse on Reading and Communications Skills, National Institute of Education.

Palincsar, A. S., & Brown, A. L. 1983. *Reciprocal teaching of comprehension-monitoring activities* (Technical Report No. 269). Champaign, Ill.: University of Illinois, Center for the Study of Reading.

Pearson, P. D. 1974–1975. The effects of grammatical complexity on children's comprehension, recall, and conception of certain semantic relations. *Reading Research Quarterly 10*, 155–192.

Pearson, P. D., Hansen, J., & Gordon, C. 1979. The effect of background knowledge on young children's comprehension of explicit and implicit information. *Journal of Reading Behavior 11*, 201–210.

Pearson, P. D., & Johnson, D. D. 1978. *Teaching reading comprehension*. New York: Holt, Rinehart and Winston.

Pelosi, P. L. 1977. *The origin and development of reading diagnosis in the United States: 1896–1946*. Unpublished doctoral dissertation, State University of New York at Buffalo.

Petty, W. T., Herold, C. P., & Stoll, E. 1968. *The state of the knowledge about the teaching of vocabulary*. Champaign, Ill.: National Council of Teachers of English.

Pikulski, J. A. 1974. A critical review: Informal reading inventories. *Reading Teacher 28*, 141–153.

Powell, W. R. 1970. Reappraising the criteria for interpreting informal reading inventories. In D. L. DeBoer (Ed.), *Reading diagnosis and evaluation*. Newark Del.: International Reading Association.

Powell, W. R., & Dunkeld, C. G. 1971. Validity of the IRI reading levels. *Elementary English 48*, 637–642.

Pressley, M., Levin, J. R., & Miller, G. E. 1981. How does the keyword method affect vocabulary comprehension and usage? *Reading Research Quarterly 16*, 213–226.

Quantz, J. O. 1897. Problems in the psychology of reading. *Psychological Review Monograph Supplements 2*, 52.

Readence, J. E., Baldwin, R. S., & Rickelman, R. J. 1983. Instructional insights into metaphor and similes. *Journal of Reading 27*, 109–112.

Richek, M. A., List, L. K., & Lerner, J. W. 1983. *Reading problems: Diagnosis and remediation*. Englewood Cliffs, N.J.: Prentice-Hall.

Robinson, H. M. 1937. The study of disabilities in reading. *Elementary School Journal 38*, 15–38.

Robinson, H. M. 1946. *Why children fail in reading*. Chicago: University of Chicago Press.

Rosch, E. H. 1973. On the internal structure of perceptual and semantic categories. In T. E. Moore (Ed.), *Cognitive development and the acquisition of language*. New York: Academic Press.

Roser, N., & Juel, C. 1982. Effects of vocabulary instruction on reading comprehension. In J. A. Niles & L. A. Harris (Eds.), *New inquiries in reading research and instruction* (Thirty-first Yearbook of the National Reading Conference). Rochester, N.Y.: National Reading Conference.

Rosner, J., & Simon, D. 1971. The auditory analysis test: An initial report. *Journal of Learning Disabilities 4*, 384–392.

Rumelhart, D. E. 1975. Notes on a schema for stories. In D. G. Bobrow & A. Collins (Eds.), *Representation and understanding: Studies in cognitive science*. New York: Academic Press.

Sadow, M. W. 1982. The use of story grammar in the design of questions. *Reading Teacher 35*, 518–522.

Sanders, N. M. 1966. *Classroom questions: What kinds?* New York: Harper & Row.

Schlein, M. 1966. The big cheese. In B. Martin, Jr. (Ed.), *Sounds of the storyteller*. New York: Holt, Rinehart and Winston.

Singer, H. 1978. Active comprehension: From answering to asking questions. *Reading Teacher 31*, 901–908.

Singer, H., & Donlan, D. 1982. Active comprehension: Problem-solving schema with question generation for comprehension of complex short stories. *Reading Research Quarterly 17*, 166–186.

Slobin, D. 1966. English abstract of Soviet studies of child language. In F. Smith & G. Miller (Eds.), *The genesis of language*. Cambridge, Mass.: MIT Press.

Söderbergh, R. 1971. *A linguistic study of a Swedish preschool child's gradual acquisition of reading ability*. Stockholm: Almquist and Wiksell.

Spache, G. D. 1953. A new readability for primary-grade materials. *Elementary School Journal 53*, 410–413.

Spache, G. D. 1972. *Diagnostic Reading Scales* (Rev. ed.). Monterey, Calif.: CTB/McGraw-Hill.

Spache, G. D. 1976. *Diagnosing and correcting reading disabilities*. Boston: Allyn and Bacon.

Stahl, S. 1983. Differential word knowledge and reading comprehension. *Journal of Reading Behavior 15*, 33–50.

Stauffer, R. G. 1970. *The language experience approach to the teaching of reading*. New York: Harper & Row.

Stein, N. L., & Glenn, C. G. 1979. An analysis of story comprehension in elementary school children. In R. O. Freedle (Ed.), *Advances in discourse processes, Vol. 2: New directions in discourse processing*. Norwood, N.J.: Ablex.

Straw, S. B., & Schreiner, R. 1982. The effect of sentence manipulation on subsequent measures of reading and listening comprehension. *Reading Research Quarterly 17,* 339–352.

Taylor, B. M., & Beach, R. W. 1984. The effects of text structure instruction on middle-grade students' comprehension and production of expository text. *Reading Research Quarterly 19,* 134–146.

Thomas, C. J. 1905. Congenital word blindness and its treatment. *Ophthalmoloscope 3,* 380–385.

Thorndike, E. L. 1917. Reading as reasoning: A study of mistakes in paragraph reading. *Journal of Educational Psychology 8,* 323–332.

Thorndike, R. L. 1973. *Reading comprehension education in fifteen countries.* New York: Wiley.

Thorndike, R. L. 1973–1974. Reading as reasoning. *Reading Research Quarterly 9,* 135–147.

Thurstone, L. L. 1946. Note on a reanalysis of Davis's reading tests. *Psychometrika 11,* 185–188.

Tinker, M. A. 1934. The role of eye-movements in diagnostic and remedial reading. *School and Society 39,* 147–148.

Tuinman, J. J., & Brady, M. E. 1974. How does vocabulary account for variance on reading comprehension tests? A preliminary instructional analysis. In P. L. Nacke (Ed.), *Interaction: Research and practice in college–adult reading* (Twenty-third Yearbook of the National Reading Conference). Clemson, S.C.: National Reading Conference.

Uhl, W. L. 1916. The use of the results of reading tests as a basis for planning remedial work. *Elementary School Journal 17,* 266–275.

Vacca, R. T. 1981. *Content area reading.* Boston: Little, Brown.

Vaughan, J. L., Castle, G., Gilbert, K., & Love, M. 1982. Varied approaches to preteaching vocabulary. In J. A. Niles & L. A. Harris (Eds.), *New inquiries in reading research and instruction.* (Thirty-first Yearbook of the National Reading Conference). Rochester, N.Y.: National Reading Conference.

Venezky, R. 1970. *The structure of English orthography.* The Hague: Mouton, 1970.

Weaver, P. A. 1979. Improving reading compehension: Effects of sentence organization instruction. *Reading Research Quarterly 15,* 129–146.

Weber, R. 1968. The study of oral reading errors: A review of the literature. *Reading Research Quarterly 4,* 96–119.

Whaley, J., & Kibby, M. W. 1981. The relative importance of reliance on intraword characteristics and interword constraints for beginning reading achievement. *Journal of Educational Research 74,* 315–320.

White, E. B. 1952. *Charlotte's Web.* New York: Harper and Brothers.

Wittrock, M. C., Marks, C. B., & Doctorow, M. J. 1975. Reading as a generative process. *Journal of Educational Psychology 67,* 484–489.

Wixson, K. L. 1979. Miscue analysis: A critical review. *Journal of Reading Behavior 11,* 163–175.

Wolman, R. N., & Barker, E. N. 1965. A developmental study of word definitions. *Journal of Genetic Psychology 107,* 159–166.

Zirbes, L. 1918. Diagnostic measurement as a basis for procedure. *Elementary School Journal 18,* 507–523.

Index

Administration, test
  comprehension and, 141, 179,
    186–187, 193
  instructional passages and, 179,
    186–187
  IRI-standardized, 219–226, 228–
    229, 230, 234
  IRI-teacher constructed, 203,
    208–209, 210, 212–213
  print skills and, 42
  questions and, 141
  word knowledge and, 90, 91, 95, 101
Affixes (see Word identification)
Ahlfors, G., 171
Ames, L. B., 24
Ames, W. S., 88
Analysis
  comprehension performance,
    139–141, 179–180, 187, 193
  instructional passages and, 179–
    180, 187, 193
  IRI-standardized, 234–237
  oral reading, 53–57, 60–63, 64–68
  print skills and, 42–52, 53–57,
    60–63, 64–68
  word knowledge and, 90, 91–92,
    97–98, 105–108
Anaphoric relations, 149, 162
Anderson, T. H., 164
André, M. E., 164
Antonyms, 81

Arthur, S. V., 88
Asch, S. E., 78
Assessment
  comprehension, 114–128, 139–141
  IRI-teacher constructed
    performance, 202–203
  reading rate, 19–20
  (See also Diagnosis)
Auditory acuity, 39
Automaticity (see Integration; Fluency)

Baer, J. A., 2
Baldwin, R. S., 78, 79
Barker, E. N., 73
Barr, R., 17, 22, 24, 32, 36
Barrett, T. C., 115
Barron, R., 86
Bartlett, B. J., 148, 168
Bean, T. W., 167
Bechhofer, R., 78, 80
Bellugi, U., 70
Bennett, A., 23
Bernier, S. A., 90
Biemiller, A., 19, 22–23
Blachowicz, C., 37
Blachowicz Informal Phonics Survey,
    33, 245–248
Blending, 18, 21, 33, 49
Bloom, B. S., 115
Bluth, G. J., 147–148, 168

Bond, G. L., 2
Borderline reading level, 43, 177, 178
Bortnick, R., 37
Brady, M. E., 69
Brainstorming, 87
Brandt, D. M., 147–148, 168
Brent, S. B., 159
Bronowski, J., 70
Bruce, D., 18
Burkes, A. M., 169–172

Capsule words, 86
Carnine, D. W., 83, 85, 159
Carpenter, P. A., 120–121, 122
Case studies
    Ann, 59–64
    Chuck, 222
    comprehension, 151–157, 183–198
    Eva, 53–59
    instructional passages, 183–189
    IRI-standardized, 222, 228–240
    IRI-teacher constructed, 204–218
    Jacob, 207–210
    James, 234–240
    John, 212–218
    John (diagnostic model), 6
    Larry (diagnostic model), 7
    Marie, 210–212
    Mary (diagnostic model), 6–7
    Patricia, 193–198
    Paul, 151–157
    Peter, 204–206
    print skills, 53–68
    Raymond, 91, 92–101
    reading diagnosis model, 6–8
    Sara, 230–233
    Sharon, 184–192
    Stan, 64–68
    Tanya, 101–109
    Tom (diagnostic model), 7–8
    word identification, 56–68
    word knowledge, 92–109, 184–198,
        207–218, 228–240
    word learning, 54–64
Castle, G., 86
Categories: words and, 70, 71–73,
    74–76, 87
Catlin, J., 158
Chomsky, C., 159
Clark, E. V., 81
Cleland, C. J., 166

Clowes, H. C., 1
Cloze, 37
Cocks, P., 74
Code programs, 21, 22–24
Cohen, A. S., 23–24
Cohen, R., 164
Comprehension, 11, 111–141, 143–173
    administration of tests and, 141,
        179, 186–187, 193
    analysis of tests and, 139–141,
        179–180, 187, 193
    anaphoric relations and, 149
    assessment of, 114–128, 139–141
    cases about, 151–157, 183–198
    diagnosis of, 4–5, 143–150, 175–198
    inference and, 118–124, 147
    instruction and, 113–114, 144–146,
        157–172, 183, 192, 197–198
    instructional passage diagnosis of,
        183, 191–192, 197
    integration and, 118–124, 147–148,
        183, 192, 197
    interactive strategies and, 162–165
    interpretation of tests and, 141,
        180–183, 191–192, 193, 197
    IRI-standardized, 228, 239
    IRI-teacher constructed, 202,
        202–203, 207, 208–209, 210,
        211, 214, 216
    nature of, 111–114
    organizing information and, 166–172
    preparation of tests and, 178–179,
        185–186, 193
    print skills and, 180–182, 191, 193,
        197
    probe techniques and, 149, 150,
        151–157, 180, 187, 191, 193
    processes of, 118–124
    questions and, 114–118, 125–139,
        147, 148, 176–177
    sentences and, 158–162
    word knowledge and, 69–109, 182,
        191, 197
    (See also Diagnostic patterns;
        Meanings; Word knowledge)
Concepts: meanings and, 74–76, 82
Connective inferences, 123–124
Connective terms, 122–123, 161–162
Consonants, 48, 49 (See also Word
    identification)
Content words (see Word

identification; Word knowledge)
Context clues, 29–32 (see Errors, reading; Word learning)
Cunningham, J. W., 88

Dale, E., 200
Dale-Chall formula, 200
Daskal, J., 162
Davis, F. B., 69, 147
Dearborn, W. F., 1, 2
Definite articles, 122
Definitions (see Meanings; Synonyms; Word knowledge)
Deno, S. L., 200
Diagnosis
  based on an instructional passage, 175–198
  case studies of model, 6–8
  history of, 1–2
  major decisions of 3–5
  model of reading, 1–12
  with a series of passages, 199–218
  with a standardized informal reading inventory, 219–242
  (See also specific areas of difficulty: e.g., Comprehension; Fluency; Integration; Print skills; Word identification; Word knowledge; Word learning; Writing conventions)
Diagnostic model: developmental flexibility of, 10–12
Diagnostic patterns, 8–10
Doctorow, M. J., 69
Dodge, R., 1
Dolch, E. W., 2, 29
Dougherty, M. L., 1
Dreeben, R., 24
Drum, P. A., 81
Dunkeld, C. G., 43
Durrell, D. D., 2
Dolch Word List, 29, 243–244
Eclectic programs, 17, 21, 22–24, 34–35
Ehri, L. C., 14, 15
Ekwall, E. E., 43
Engelhardt, M. D., 115
Errors, reading, 22–38, 43–52 (See also Case studies; Fluency; Integration; Probe techniques; Word identification; Word learning)

Extended word meanings, 77–80

Figurative language (see Meanings; Metaphors)
Fischer, J. H., 1
Fluency: integration and, 19, 38, 46 (See also Integration)
Ford, C. A., 2
Freschi, R., 83, 85
Froese, V., 160
Frustration reading level, 176, 177, 178, 233
Fry Readability Chart, 200–201
Fry, E. B., 200–201
Fuchs, D., 200
Fuchs, L. S., 200
Function words (see Word learning)
Furst, E. J., 115

Gardner, H., 78, 80
Garner, R., 148, 165
Gates, A. I., 2
Gilbert, D. W., 121
Gilbert, K., 86
Gillet, J. W., 31
Gilmore Oral Reading Test, 19–20
Goodman, Y. M., 24
Gordon, C., 170
Gourley, J. W., 122, 158
Graphemes, 18
Guided reading procedure, 166–167
Gurren, L., 90

Herold, C. P., 88
Hill, W. H., 115
Hincks, E. M., 2
Holden, M., 15
Homework, 176–177
Hood, J., 27
Huey, E. B., 1, 111
Hughes, A., 90
Huttenlocher, J., 15

Ilg, F. L., 24
Imlach, R. H., 24
Independent reading level, 43, 144, 176–177, 206, 227, 233
Inference, 118–124, 147 (See also Comprehension)
Informal reading inventories (IRI) (see IRI-standardized; IRI-teacher constructed)

Instruction
  comprehension and, 113–114,
    144–146, 157–172, 183, 192,
    197–198
  error patterns and, 22–25
  fluency/integration and, 37–38
  instructional passages and, 183, 192,
    197–198
  IRI-standarized, 239–240
  IRI-teacher constructed, 209–210,
    211–212, 217–218
  learning programs and, 22–24
  phonics and, 20–21
  print skills and, 52, 58–59, 63–64,
    68, 144–146
  reading development and, 20–25
  word identification and, 33–36
  word knowledge and, 82–89, 90, 92,
    99–101, 108–109
  word learning and, 29–32, 144–146
    (See also Passages,
    instructional; Writing
    conventions)
Instructional passages (see Passages,
    instructional)
Instructional reading level, 144–146,
    176, 177, 227
Integration, 19
  comprehension and, 118–124,
    147–148, 183, 192, 197
  instruction and, 37–38
  instructional passages and, 183, 192,
    197
  IRI-standarized and, 239
  print skills and, 36–37, 46, 56–57,
    59, 63, 67–68
  probe techniques and, 37, 38
  response characteristics and, 36–39
Interactive strategies, 162–163
Interpretation
  comprehension and, 141, 180–183,
    191–192, 193, 197
  IRI-standarized and, 226–228,
    230–233, 237–239
  IRI-teacher constructed and,
    204–207, 209, 211, 216–217
  instructional passages and, 180–
    183, 191–192, 193–197
  print skills and, 52, 57–59, 60–63,
    64–68
  response characteristics and, 27–38

  word knowledge and, 90, 92, 99,
    108–109
IRI (Informal Reading Inventories)
    standardized, 219–242
  administration of, 219–226,
    228–229, 230, 234
  analysis and, 234–237
  cases about, 222, 228–240
  comprehension and, 228, 239
  instruction and, 239–240
  integration and, 239
  interpretation of, results of,
    226–228, 230–233, 237–239
  list of inventories of, 220
  listening task of, 225–226, 230
  oral reading task of, 224–225, 229,
    232
  print skills and, 227, 237
  probe techniques and, 234–237
  silent reading task and, 225, 232
  word knowledge and, 227–228, 239
  word lists of, 224
IRI (Informal Reading Inventories)
    teacher constructed, 199–218
  administration of, 203, 208–209,
    210, 212–213
  cases about, 204–218
  comprehension and, 202–203, 207,
    208–209, 210, 211, 214, 216
  construction of, 200–203
  criteria for assessing performance
    of, 202–203
  instruction and, 209–210, 211–212,
    217–218
  interpretation of results of, 204–
    207, 209, 211, 216–217
  organization of information and, 209
  passage selection and, 200–202
  print skills and, 207, 208, 209, 211,
    216–217
  questions and, 202
  word identification and, 218
  word knowledge and, 202, 207, 208,
    211–212, 217
  word meanings and, 209, 214
Irwin, J. W., 159

Jackson, E., 1
Jastak, J., 2
Jenkins, J. R., 69
Johnson, D. D., 127

Johnson, N. S., 129
Just, M. A., 120–121, 122

Katz, E. S., 159
Keller, H., 1
Kibbe, D., 2
Kibby, M. W., 29
Krathwohl, D. R., 115
Kurushima, S., 160

Lake, M. L., 87
Langacker, P. W., 70, 77
Language: reading and, 112–113
Learning: word knowledge and, 80–82
Lerner, J. W., 219
Lesgold, A. M., 22, 121, 159
Letter sounds, 48–49 (*See also* Word identification)
Levin, J. R., 89
Lieberman study, 84
List, L. K., 219
Listening task, 225–226, 230 (*See also* IRI-standardized)
Lookback strategies, 148, 165
Lopardo, G., 37, 38
Lorge, I., 73
Love, M., 86
Luce, T. S., 79
Lukas, L., 2

MacGinitie, W. H., 15, 172
Mandler, J. M., 129
Maratsos, M. P., 158–159
Markers, 34, 50 (*See also* Word identification)
Marks, C. B., 69
Mason, J. M., 112
Materials, instructional (*see* IRI-standardized; IRI-teacher constructed; Passages, instructional; Passages, series of; Reading level)
McDonald, G. E., 148, 168
McGee, L. M., 137
Meanings
  concepts and, 74–76, 82
  contextual material and learning, 88–89
  extended, 77–80
  metaphors and, 77–80
  multiple, 76–77

word knowledge and, 70–82
words and, 71–74, 88–89
  (*See also* Word knowledge)
Metaphors, 77–80
Meyer, B. J. F., 147–148, 168
Miller, G. E., 89
Miller, L. W., 2
Miscues (*see* Errors, reading)
Mnemonic devices, 89
Model for reading diagnosis, 1–12
Monroe, M., 1, 2
Morgan, W. P., 1
Multiple meanings of words, 76–77

Nerlove, H., 78

Omanson, R. C., 42
Orton, S. T., 2
Oral reading
  analysis of, 53–57, 60–63, 64–68
  assessing errors in, 25–27, 27–38, 43–46
  fluency and, 19
  influence of passage difficulty on, 42–46
  reconceptualization of, 25–27
  response characteristics and, 25–27
  symbols for recording responses, 26–27
Oral reading *(continued)*
  (*See also* Errors, reading; Instruction; Interpretation of tests; IRI-standardized; IRI-teacher constructed; Reading levels)
Oral reading task, 224–225, 229, 232
  (*See also* IRI-standardized)
Organization of information, 124–125, 147–148, 166–172, 209
Overgeneralization, 81, 82

Page, W. D., 36
Pany, D., 69
Pardi, R., 167
Passages, instructional, 175–198
  administration of, 179, 186–187
  analysis of results of, 179–180, 187, 193

case studies based on diagnosis of,
183–189
comprehension and, 183, 191–192,
197
difficulty, 24–25, 42–44, 175–198,
199–218
error patterns and, 24–25
instruction and, 183, 192, 197–198
integration and, 183, 192, 197
interpretation of results of, 180–
183, 191–192, 193–197
preparation of, 178–179, 185–186
print skills and, 42–44, 180–182,
191, 193–197
probe techniques and, 180, 187–191,
193
reading levels and, 176–177
word knowledge and, 182, 191, 197
Passages, series of
diagnosis with a, 199–218
selection for IRI-teacher
constructed, 200–202
(*See also* IRI-standardized)
Pearson, P. D., 127, 159, 170, 171
Petty, W. T., 88
Phonemes, 14, 17–18, 21, 24, 33–34
(*See also* Phonics)
Phonics, 17–18, 20–21, 32–37,
245–248
Physical condition: reading and, 39
Pikulski, J. A., 43
Preparation, 41–42, 53, 60, 64
comprehension and, 178–179,
185–186, 193
instructional passages and, 178–
179, 185–186
print skills and, 41–42, 53–64
word knowledge and, 90, 91, 92–94,
101
Pressley, M., 89
Print skills, 13–40, 41–68
administration of tests and, 42
analysis of, 42–52, 53–57, 60–63,
64–68
cases about, 53–68
comprehension and, 180–182, 191,
193, 197
developing strategies for, 13–40
diagnosing strategies for, 41–68

instruction and, 52, 58–59, 63–64,
68, 144–146
instructional passages and, 42–44,
180–182, 191, 193–197
integration and fluency and, 36–37,
46, 56–57, 59, 63, 67–68
interpretation of tests and, 52,
57–59, 60–63, 64–68
IRI-standardized and, 227, 237
IRI-teacher constructed and, 207,
208, 209, 211, 216–217
knowledge about, 14–19
model for reading diagnosis and,
3–4, 5, 11
preparation of tests and, 41–42, 53,
64
probe techniques and, 46–52,
57–59, 60–63, 64–68
sight words and, 44, 57, 58
word identification and, 32–35,
44–46, 56, 57, 58–59, 63, 67
word knowledge, 58, 68, 97, 105
word learning and, 29–32, 35–36,
44, 54–56, 57, 58, 60–63, 65–67
(*See also* Diagnostic patterns;
Writing conventions)
Probe techniques
advanced, 47–52
basic, 46–47
comprehension, 149, 150, 151–157,
180, 187, 191, 193
fluency/integration, 37, 38
instructional passages and, 180,
187–191, 193
IRI-standardized and, 234–237
print skills and, 46–52, 57–59, 60–
63, 64–68
word identification, 32–33
word knowledge, 90, 92, 98–99, 108
word learning, 29
writing conventions and, 27–28
Pronouns, 121

Quantz, J. O., 1
Questions
administration of tests and, 141
beyond-text, 116–118, 125–128
comprehension and, 114–118,
125–139, 147, 148, 176–177

construction of, in expository
materials, 135–138
construction of, in story materials,
128–135
evaluating responses to, 139–141
interpreting performance on, 141
IRI-teacher constructed, 202
recall and, 114, 116, 138–139, 148
scoring performance on, 141
self, 163, 164–165
text-related, 116–118, 125–128

Rate of reading (*see* Reading rate)
Readence, J. E., 78–79
Reading
comprehension (*see* Comprehension)
diagnosis (*see* Diagnosis)
difficulty: areas of, 206–207
instructional programs, 20–25
language and, 112–113
levels
Betts' criteria, 144, 176
borderline, 43, 177, 178
frustration, 43, 176, 177, 178
independent, 43, 144, 176–177, 206
instructional, 43, 144–146, 176,
177, 204–206
rate
chart for assessing, 19–20
fluency and, 19
Reciprocal teaching/modeling,
160–161
Reis, R., 148, 165
ReQuest procedure, 163–164
Resnick, L. B., 22
Response characteristics
integration and fluency and, 36–39
interpretation of, 27–38
oral reading and, 25–27
word identification and, 32–36
word learning and, 29–32
writing conventions and, 27–29
Richek, M. A., 219
Rickelman, R. J., 78, 79
Robinson, H. M., 2
Rosch, E. H., 75
Rosner, J., 18
Rumelhart, D. E., 129

Sadow, M. W., 38, 114
Schreck, J., 69
Schreiner, R., 160
Self-questioning, 163, 164–165
Self-monitoring, 148
Semantic feature hypothesis, 81
Semantic webbing, 166
Sentence
comprehension, 158–162
method, 16
topic, 120–121
word awareness and a, 15–16
Sight vocabulary (*see* Word learning)
Sight word recognition (*see* Word
learning)
Silent reading (*see* independent
reading level; IRI-standardized)
Similes (*see* Metaphor)
Simon, D., 18
Slobin, D., 15
Söderbergh, R., 24
Spache, G. D., 147, 200
Stahl, S., 90
Stauffer, R. G., 30
Stoll, E., 88
Story grammar, 128–135
Straw, S. B., 160
Structural analysis (*see* Word
identification)
Syllabication, 33, 34, 35, 44–46,
47–49, 51–52 (*See also* Word
identification)
Synonyms, 121–122 (*See also*
Meanings)
Syntactic knowledge, 122

Temple, C., 31
Thomas, C. J., 1
Thorndike, E. L., 111
Thorndike, R. L., 69, 147
Thurstone, L. L., 147
Tinker, M. A., 2
Tuinman, J. J., 69

Undergeneralization, 82

Vacca, R. T., 87
Vaughan, J. L., 86

Venezky, R., 34
Verbal knowledge (see Word
    knowledge)
Visual acuity, 19, 39
Vocabulary (see Word knowledge)
Vowels, 21, 33, 49–50 (See also Word
    identification)

Weaver, P. A., 160
Weber, R., 25
Whaley, J., 24
White, E. B., 117–118
Winner, E., 78, 80
Wittrock, M. C., 69
Wixson, K. L., 27
Wolf, D., 78, 80
Wolman, R. N., 73
Word awareness, 15–16
Word banks, 30–31
Word discrimination, 17
Word identification, 17–18, 21–22,
    32–36
    blending, 18, 21, 33, 49
    cases about, 53–68
    consonants, 48, 49
    diagnosis of difficulty in, 32–33
    instructional techniques and, 33–36
    IRI-teacher constructed, 218
    markers, 34, 50
    phoneme awareness, 14, 17–18, 21,
        24, 33–34
    phonics and, 17–18, 20–21, 32–37,
        245–248
    print skills and, 32–36, 44–46, 56,
        57, 58–59, 63, 67
    syllables, 33, 34, 35, 44–46
    vowels, 21, 33, 49–50
    (See also Word knowledge; Word
        learning)
Word knowledge, 69–109
    administration of tests of, 90, 91,
        95, 101
    analysis of tests of, 90, 91–92,
        97–98, 105–108
    cases about, 92–109, 184–198,
        207–218, 228–240
    comprehension and, 69–109, 182,
        191, 197

diagnosis of difficulty in, 89–92
    instruction and, 82–89, 90, 92, 99–
        101, 108–109
    instructional passages and, 182, 191,
        197
    IRI-standardized, 227–228, 239
    IRI-teacher constructed, 202, 207,
        208, 211–212, 217
    learning and, 80–82
    meanings and, 70–82
    model for reading diagnosis and, 4,
        5, 11
    preparation of tests of, 90, 91,
        92–94, 101
    print skills and, 58, 68, 97, 105
    probe techniques and, 90, 92,
        98–99, 108
    interpretation of tests of, 90, 92, 99,
        108–109
    (See also Diagnostic patterns; Word
        identification; Word learning)
Word learning, 15–17, 80–82
    cases about, 53–64
    diagnosis of difficulty in, 29
    instruction and, 29–32, 144–146
    print skills and, 29–32, 35–36, 44,
        54–56, 57, 58, 60–63, 65–67
    word awareness, 15–16
    word discrimination, 17
    (See also Word identification; Word
        knowledge)
Word lists, 224
Word meaning, 70–74, 88–89
    antonyms, 81
    extensive, 72
    intensive, 72
    IRI-teacher constructed and, 209,
        214
    learning of, 80–82
    overgeneralization, 81, 82
    synonyms, 121–122
    undergeneralization, 82
Word recognition (See Word learning)
Writing conventions, 14–15, 27–29

Zirbes, L., 1